Robert J. Sternberg and Richard K. Wagner have produced *Mind in context* to serve as a bridge between the work of radical constructivists, who propose that all cognition depends upon interaction with the outside world, and traditional cognitive scientists, who feel that all cognition resides in the mind. The concepts of distributed cognition and situated learning are here translated into constructs and methodologies that are more accessible to researchers and students.

Mind in context

Mind in context
Interactionist perspectives on human intelligence

Edited by

ROBERT J. STERNBERG
Yale University

RICHARD K. WAGNER
Florida State University

CAMBRIDGE
UNIVERSITY PRESS

Published by the Press Syndicate of the University of Cambridge
The Pitt Building, Trumpington Street, Cambridge CB2 1RP
40 West 20th Street, New York, NY 10011-4211, USA
10 Stamford Road, Oakleigh, Melbourne 3166, Australia

First published 1994

Printed in the United States of America

Library of Congress Cataloging-in-Publication Data

Mind in context : interactionist perspectives on human intelligence /
edited by Robert J. Sternberg, Richard K. Wagner.
p.   cm.
Includes bibliographical references and index.
ISBN 0-521-41114-9. – ISBN 0-521-42287-6 (pbk.)
1. Intellect.   2. Context effects (Psychology)   I. Sternberg,
Robert J.   II. Wagner, Richard K.
BF431.M524   1994
153–dc20   93-21756
                                                         CIP

A catalog record for this book is available from the British Library

ISBN 0-521-41114-9 hardback
ISBN 0-521-42287-6 paperback

Contents

Contributors

Cynthia A. Berg
Department of Psychology
University of Utah
Salt Lake City, Utah

Katerina S. Calderone
Department of Psychology
University of Utah
Salt Lake City, Utah

Steven Ceci
Department of Human Development and
   Family Studies
Cornell University
Ithaca, New York

Fred Fiedler
Department of Psychology
University of Washington
Seattle, Washington

Howard Gardner
Graduate School of Education
Harvard University
Cambridge, Massachusetts

Michael K. Gardner
Department of Education Psychology
University of Utah
Salt Lake City, Utah 84112

Nira Granott
The Media Laboratory
Massachusetts Institute of Technology
Cambridge, Massachusetts

Man-Chi Leung
Department of Psychology
University of North Carolina
Chapel Hill, North Carolina

Thomas Link
Department of Psychology
University of Washington
Seattle, Washington

Antonio Roazzi
Department of Psychology
Federal University of Pernambuco
Brazil

Richard E. Snow
School of Education
Stanford University
Stanford, California

Robert J. Sternberg
Department of Psychology
Yale University
New Haven, Connecticut

Jaan Valsiner
Department of Psychology
University of North Carolina
Chapel Hill, North Carolina

Richard K. Wagner
Department of Psychology
Florida State University
Tallahassee, Florida

Preface

A college student arrives for a math test. At the signal, she and her classmates whip out their calculators and start solving problems. To the student's horror, she discovers that the batteries of her calculator are either dead or on strike. The calculator doesn't work. The result: a low grade on the test. Another student, whose pencil has mysteriously disappeared, loses time trying to corral another, and also performs well below her ability.

A successful businessman decides that the country needs his common-sense approach to management. He runs for political office, determined to show that he can run any business, including that of the country. But he makes big mistakes: The trusted and, he thought, true strategies that always worked for him in business fail in politics. He loses the election ... dismally.

A boy with middling to poor grades in math and science becomes, years later, a great physicist. His professional success, he tells people, is in spite of, not because of, his academic preparation. He also credits his various assistants, most of whom were "straight-A" students in school.

What these stories have in common is the theme of this book: mind in context. Although traditional views of abilities have tended to view them as inherent and internal properties of the organism, the views propounded in this book have in common their ascription of abilities to the interaction between minds and the contexts in which they are to be found. The bright student without her pencil or calculator can no longer demonstrate the same competence as she could with them. But, you may say, she still has the competence; she's just unable to show it. Before calculators or computers were even invented, many may have "had" the competence to use them well; whether they would have or not is clearly a moot point. Indeed, one could even argue that the nature of what it means to be competent in mathematics has changed with the invention of these devices. The computational abilities which were once so important in school mathematics are quickly diminishing in importance, much as has the ability to ride a horse in order to transport oneself quickly. Even politicians, who scarcely rate as the most sophisticated theorists of abilities that the world has produced, have come to recognize how technology has changed and upgraded the skills needed for survival. For example, in a rapidly changing world, flexibility and the ability to cope with novelty are more important to survival than in a world that is relatively more stable and static.

The interactionist perspective is not, of course, a new one. Both Piaget (1972) and Vygotsky (1978) were interactionists. Vygotsky, especially, recognized the extent to which the development of abilities depends on context. Even fervent hereditarians have recognized that when genotypes are expressed phenotypically, there is a reaction range that potentially limits the extent to which a genotype is able to be expressed in the environment. Thus, the work reported here is a culmination of a long tradition. At the same time, it is a departure from psychometric and cognitive approaches to intelligence that view abilities as "in the head," and it is a departure from radical–contextualist approaches that view abilities as wholly in the contexts in which people live (see Sternberg, 1982, 1990). The views expressed in the chapters of this book differ, but they have in common the world view of abilities at the intersection between mind and context.

The book is divided into three main parts, each representing a somewhat different emphasis. The chapters of Part I deal primarily, although not exclusively, with performances in academic and test-like tasks. The chapters of Part II focus primarily on tasks encountered outside the academy – in everyday settings. And the chapters in Part III present overviews and general frameworks within which the earlier chapters can be placed. The final chapter specifically refers back to the earlier chapters in an attempt to place them within a unifying framework.

In Chapter 1, which opens Part I, Richard Snow explicitly applies the interactionist perspective to academic tasks. He considers a number of different frameworks for expressing the interactionist perspective, and ends up proposing a framework that is process-based. One of the most interesting aspects of his framework is his use of Gibson's (1979) concept of situational affordances in the domain of abilities and not just of visual perception.

In Chapter 2, Michael Gardner considers the role of novelty, primarily of tasks, in the interactionist perspective on intelligence. In this view, the abilities one manifests depend largely upon the tasks life presents. A person who is constantly faced with tasks that are far outside his or her zone of comfort with respect to task familiarity may appear less able than someone who is constantly faced with familiar tasks. The latter person, however, lacking challenges, may have less of an opportunity to develop his or her abilities than the former.

Whereas Gardner concentrates primarily on task novelty in his chapter, Stephen Ceci and Antonio Roazzi concentrate primarily on situational novelty in Chapter 3. They show that tasks that are structurally isomorphic may be performed very differently as a function of the situational context in which they are performed. For example, the very same person who may perform mathematical operations well in a "street context" may perform them only poorly in an abstract context.

In Chapter 4, the opening chapter of Part II, Cynthia Berg and Katerina Calderone look at the abilities of people of different ages to solve everyday problems; for example, youngsters who want to go to a movie but will potentially have problems arriving home in time for a curfew. The investigators studied problem solving across age levels, and turned up some interesting findings. One of the most interesting was that what appears to be the same problem for two different people may not actually be the same problem. Whereas much of the developmental literature has recently emphasized the role of knowledge in cognitive development (e.g., Carey, 1985; Chi, 1978; Keil, 1984), Berg and Calderone emphasize the importance of interpretation. People at different ages may interpret what appears to be the same problem differently, leading to differences in their solutions.

Whereas Berg and Calderone focus primarily on children of different ages, Richard Wagner focuses on adults in Chapter 5. In particular, he argues that the analyses of fairly academic tests used for job selection tend to overestimate the validity of these tests for job performance. From his interactionist perspective, tests of academic abilities should not predict particularly well to most occupational domains. Available data indicate a modest level of prediction, and Wagner argues that even this modest appearance overestimates their true validity.

In Chapter 6, Fred Fiedler and Thomas Link look at a specific kind of job performance: leadership. Moreover, they relate this performance to standard measures of intelligence under varying levels of stress. What they find is that fluid intelligence predicts success in leadership under conditions of low but not of high stress. Leaders with high fluid intelligence show a marked decrement in performance when under stress. Those results suggest that at least in one domain, that of leadership, the correlation between abilities and performance is moderated by an important contextual variable – stress.

Part III of the book opens with Chapter 7, by Nira Granott and Howard Gardner. In this chapter, the authors apply Gardner's (1983) theory of multiple intelligences to the problem of person–context interaction. In their chapter, they distinguish between first-order and second-order multiple intelligences. First-order ones are those with which we are born, whereas second-order ones are those that are selectively promoted or retarded by the environment. For example, a person with high innate musical potential may never show this potential if he or she grows up in a family in which music plays no significant role in their lives whatsoever. The same child, growing up in a household where music plays a central part, will be at a considerable advantage in developing his or her talent.

In Chapter 8, Jaan Valsiner and Man-Chi Leung present what they refer to as a sociogenetic approach to abilities and their interaction with context. Among the key features of this approach is its constructivist view of human nature. People are not merely passive recipients of information, nor are they even just active processors of information. Rather, they are active constructors of information. They do not just receive the world, but in fact, make it what it is for them.

Finally, in Chapter 9, Robert Sternberg presents a framework called "PRSVL" for understanding person–context interactions. This framework takes into account the respective roles of the person, the roles the person fills, the situations in which the person finds himself or herself, the values the person brings to these situations, and the luck he or she experiences. The earlier chapters are discussed in terms of this framework.

We as editors, and the authors as well, hope you find our framework of abilities as interactions between persons and contexts compelling, and that you both enjoy and learn from the chapters in this book.

RJS
RKW

References

Carey, S. (1985). *Conceptual change in childhood.* Cambridge, MA: MIT Press.

Chi, M. T. H. (1978). Knowledge structure and memory development. In R. S. Siegler (Ed.), *Children's thinking: What develops?* (pp. 73–96). Hillsdale, NJ: Erlbaum.

Gardner, H. (1983). *Frames of mind: The theory of multiple intelligences.* New York: Basic Books.

Gibson, J. J. (1979). *The ecological approach to visual perception.* Boston: Houghton Mifflin.

Keil, F. C. (1984). Transition mechanisms in cognitive development and the structure of knowledge. In R. J. Sternberg (Ed.), *Mechanisms of cognitive development* (pp. 81–99). New York: Freeman.

Piaget, J. (1972). *The psychology of intelligence.* Totowa, NJ: Littlefield Adams.

Sternberg, R. J. (Ed.). (1982). *Handbook of human intelligence.* New York: Cambridge University Press.

Sternberg, R. J. (1990). *Metaphors of mind: Conceptions of the nature of intelligence.* New York: Cambridge University Press.

Vygotsky, L. (1978). *Mind in society: The development of higher psychological processes.* Cambridge, MA: Harvard University Press.

Part I

Academic tasks

1 Abilities in academic tasks

Richard E. Snow

According to the editors, this book takes the perspective that intelligence resides in the interaction between the organism, the task the organism confronts, and the situation in which the task is confronted. The present chapter examines this perspective in research on human cognitive abilities in relation to the kinds of learning tasks typically found in academic situations. In particular, it interprets abilities as interstitial constructs concerned with explaining what happens in the interface between persons and tasks during performance.

To begin, some history is noted and some expansion of terms and concepts is introduced, since research on abilities in academic tasks needs to be seen in a larger framework. It contrasts four views of interaction. It adopts a hierarchical model of aptitude complexes, ability constructs, and component processes. It also distinguishes between three levels of instructional situation; task, treatment, and context. Next, steps toward a person–situation interaction theory of intelligence in academic learning and transfer are discussed, and some empirical examples of current research are given. The adaptation of persons to variations in instructional tasks and treatments, and of tasks and treatments to variations among persons, is considered in this light. Along the way, theoretical and methodological problems and prospects are noted for those who would pursue this kind of research. In sum, the chapter seeks to contribute to the elaboration of interactional psychology, with particular reference to theories of situated cognition and learning related to the design and analysis of formal instruction.

Terms, concepts, and problems

There are several terminological and conceptual issues that need to be addressed first. Chief among these are the various meanings of the term "interaction" and the various levels at which persons and instructional situations can be described. A further problem is the need for a conceptual language that can connect such descriptions in a common framework.

Historical notes

We need not detail its history here (see Cronbach, 1957; Ekehammer, 1974), but it is important to recognize that interactionism is not singular, new, or unique to psychology. Several forms of interactionist thinking can be traced to ancient philosophy and identified in physical and biological science, both old and new. In psychology, there have been various fits and starts through this century (Kantor, 1924), in learning theory (Tolman, 1951), perception (Allport, 1955; Broadbent, 1973; Gibson, 1979), psychophysics (Helson, 1964), as well as personality and social psychology (Lewin, 1936; Murray, 1938).

The modern program of interactional psychology began in the late 1960's and took clear shape by the mid 1970's. Its center has been in personality theory (Endler & Magnusson, 1976; Magnusson & Endler, 1977; Mischel, 1973, 1984) but there are many new facets and connections to related fields in both European and North American research (see, e.g., Heckhausen, Schmalt & Schneider, 1985; Hettema, 1979, 1989; Hoefert, 1982; Lantermann, 1980; Magnusson & Allen, 1983; Nygaard, 1977; Pervin & Lewis, 1978; Schneider & Weinert, 1990; Wachs & Plomin, 1991). An interactionist approach to instructional psychology has advanced under the label "aptitude-treatment interaction" or ATI for short (Cronbach & Snow, 1977; Snow, 1989a). There is now a similar approach to research in psychotherapy (Dance & Neufeld, 1988; Snow, 1991a).

Generic vs. paradigmatic interactionism. Historically, many schools of psychology have claimed to address the interaction of organism and environment, or of internal and external determinants of behavior. Many theorists today make this claim, in one or another terminology. But I distinguish this loose and often unspecified, generic commitment to interactionism from a paradigmatic interactionist position, in which the relevant aspects of person and situation are specified, their interaction is demonstrated empirically, and some process explanation of how and why this occurs is offered. In other words, in my view a true interactionist position does not merely assume that some vague interactive processes operate; rather it specifies a theoretical form and methodology explicitly designed to study and understand such processes.

General vs. differential psychology. Also, in my view, a true interactionist position acknowledges the importance of individual differences among persons and addresses them explicitly. Historically, general psychology has used situation variations to study persons, but ignored person variations as irrelevant to a psychology of either persons or situations (Cronbach, 1957). Research that takes person differences seriously also has to recognize the importance of relations among cognitive, conative, and affective functions within and across persons and situations. Most past psychology, whether general or differential, has focused on one or another of these three basic functions in isolation (Hilgard, 1980). In particular, cognitive and personality psychology remain mostly noncommunicative. This chapter focuses on an interactionist theory of cognitive abilities and academic tasks, but it occasionally steps back to the larger perspective elsewhere called "aptitude theory" (Snow, 1989a, 1989b, 1991b, 1992).

Interactionism vs. new situationism. As a final historical note, it is interesting in this regard that cognitive and personality psychology have come via oddly different routes over the last three decades to similar present positions. Personality theory developed interactionist perspectives out of the debates about broad stable traits vs. situation-specific conditioning of behavior. The focus moved from the internal determinants of personology to the external determinants of situationism (and behaviorism), to the reconciliation offered by interactionism. Through more recent, social constructivist influences, one extreme form of interactionist theory now interprets personality as existing not within persons or situations but *between* them; that is, it views personality traits, presumably including cognitive abilities, as primarily social constructions (see, e.g., Hampson, 1982, 1984). Over roughly the same time scale, cognitive theory developed out of the rejection of situationist–behaviorist determinants to a personology composed of mental representations, procedures, and models (rather than traits) as internal determinants. Through more recent confluence with the interactionist emphases of cultural anthropology and linguistics, some forms of cognitive theory now interpret cognition as *situated*; that is, rather than being located in persons' heads, the structures and processes of knowing, understanding, reasoning, and learning are activities defined by *relations* between persons and tasks, or between persons. Thus, not only personality traits and abilities but also learning and reasoning processes may be thought of as social constructions (see, e.g., Lave & Wenger, 1991).

In extreme form, some theories of situated personality and situated cognition seem to promote a new situationism. Though more subtly than in old situationism, these theories also leave most of the individuality of the person, and all of individual differences among persons, out of the picture. In any interactionist theory, in my view, a balance must be found wherein person-in-situation includes individual person predisposition and postdisposition, and thus individual difference variation within and across situations. In other words, a concept of aptitude transfer into, through, and out of learning activity in the present situation is needed. These are problems to which the discussion returns at several points below.

Interpretations of interaction

There seem to be four paradigmatic interactionist perspectives, differing mainly in their interpretation of interactive relations between persons and situations. Person–situation interactions may be seen as reflecting *independent, interdependent, reciprocal,* or *transactive* systems. The first view imposes a traditional statistical definition. The second and third accept different degrees of psychological relativity. The fourth adopts a more comprehensive relativism, and approaches the new situationism just mentioned. Unfortunately, different authors use the four terms in different ways (see, e.g., Pervin & Lewis, 1978; Wachs & Plomin, 1991). The four also imply different research methods. If at least the language can be standardized here, then a provisional eclecticism with respect to methodology and interpretation can be recommended as likely to be most productive for research in the near term.

Independent interaction. In statistical terms, two independent variables are said to interact when their joint effect on a third, dependent variable is multiplicative rather than additive. Such interaction is usually evaluated using regression methods or analysis of variance (see Cronbach & Snow, 1977). Thus, for example, if an ability variable and a task variable interact in influencing learning outcome, then the ability-outcome regressions will be nonparallel across the two (or more) task conditions. In other words, the difference in learning outcome between more and less able persons (or experts and novices) is seen to be greater in one task condition than in another; there is differential reactivity of different persons to the task conditions. The regression slope difference may even be reversed from one condition to another.

Though technically correct, this construction can be carelessly used to interpret ability and task variables that are statistically independent as though they were *psychologically* independent and therefore inherent characteristics of persons and situations, respectively. Statistical methods are certainly useful in studying interaction, but statistical and psychological independence should not be confused.

Interdependent interaction. Two or more variables are said to be in interdependent interaction when their effects can only be understood psychologically with respect to one another. Though measured independently and treated statistically as such, the person and situation constructs are thought not to be meaningfully interpretable in isolation. For example, person ability and task difficulty can be independently measured as aspects of persons and tasks when there are applicable norms as external standards. However, ability and task difficulty are also fundamentally interdependent. Tasks can be judged difficult or easy only relative to particular persons' ability to perform them successfully. Similarly, judgments of persons' ability depend on the tasks they can and cannot perform. Clearly, no statistical analysis compels psychological interpretation to choose between independent and interdependent interaction; given the presence of statistical interaction, either interpretation may apply.

Reciprocal interaction. Beyond independent or interdependent interaction, when two or more variables also act to change one another over time, they are said to be in reciprocal interaction. The reciprocity need not be equal among all variables in a system. So for example, a person working on a task learns to change strategy, which affords use of different abilities in the task performance; the task changes as the abilities and strategies brought to bear on it change. Thus, a person who shifts from verbal analysis to spatial visualization midway through a task has changed the task psychologically. A task that affords such learning has changed the person psychologically. Such changes in person and task at one point in time may change the person–task interaction not only later in the present task sequence, but also later in other task sequences. A person who learns to shift strategy in one task may start a new task with the new strategy, but also with the transferable idea that strategy shifting sometimes helps. Thus, learning in the task can change both the types and the levels of abilities that apply to this task performance, and to other task performances, and can do so differently for different individuals.

Transaction. When variables are regarded as in constant reciprocal interaction they are often said to be in transaction. Then they may be granted no relevant history or existence outside of the transactive system in which they are engaged, and there are no cause–effect relations to be isolated. In effect, the focus of scientific inquiry shifts away from the elements to emphasize relations among them in an action system (Dewey & Bentley, 1949). Relationships define phenomena. There are then no independent, interdependent, or reciprocal person and situation influences, but only person–situation systems and their actions; person ability and task difficulty cannot exist as meaningful concepts outside of these unions.

In the extreme version of this view, nothing known about the person or the task outside of the transactional situation is useful in studying it. This is the position referred to as "new situationism" above; there is a person-in-situation, but no personal history. However, in older transactional theories of perception (e.g., Ittelson & Cantril, 1954), cognitive development (e.g., Riegel & Meacham, 1978), and personality (e.g., Lazarus & Launier, 1978), this extreme view was not strictly maintained; each line of research needed some distinction between elements and their relationships, and between antecedent and consequent elements and relationships. As Allport (1955) put it:

" . . . there are *some* things about both organism and environment that can be studied and known about in advance of . . . [as well as after] their interrelationship, even though the fact that in their relationship they contribute something *to each other* is undeniable. What, then, *is* this residual nature or property of the parties to a transaction?" (p. 287, emphasis in original)

Some new transactional theories also acknowledge, at least implicitly, these residual properties as kinds of structure that can exist before and after interaction, in persons or situations or both. Summarizing the Lave and Wenger (1991) theory of learning in apprenticeships, Hanks (1991) noted that preexisting interpersonal or content structures could influence learning; also, outcomes of the transaction could adapt the participative framework in which later learning occurs. In Greeno's (1989; Greeno, Smith & Moore, in press) theory of transfer of situated learning, invariants in the structure of activities across person–situation interactions are the key. Situations provide affordances for activities. Persons learn to engage in these activities but also to perceive the relevant affordances. As two situations afford a person the same activities, as perceived, then the activities can be said to transfer from one to the other, even though the two situations might differ in many other ways. Thus, persons and situations can have transfer-relevant histories with respect to one another. Also, the changes wrought by the present person–situation transactions can have implications for these and other persons and situations in the future.

My own theory of aptitude (Snow, 1991b, 1992, in press) encompasses a reciprocal and transactional view with histories and futures and, like Greeno's, emphasizes transfer. But I focus on individual differences in learning and transfer and thus on the residual properties as much as the transaction. I also urge that interaction research must both use and explain evidence developed from any of the four models.

A provisional eclecticism. At least initially, an eclectic stance should be most productive. Research on a transactive theory of learning abilities can use evidence from research that assumes interactions among independent person and situation variables, and vice versa. Such evidence may help classify residual properties as relatively stable vs. malleable with respect to the person–task transaction of interest (Snow, 1992). Research on interdependencies and reciprocities can help establish and extend this classification. There will likely be person properties that exist and are definable independently of situations, but also person properties that are meaningfully definable only in union with specific kinds of situations. A similar stance is needed in describing situations. There are both stable and malleable properties of academic tasks. Some define situation variables that exist independently of persons, whereas others become meaningful only as they are seen in union with persons.

Finally, a provisional eclecticism allows us to postpone some difficult theoretical choices until a thicker evidential base helps show what kind of theory we are entitled to. Although reciprocal and transactive models of interaction seem to be increasingly popular in today's postpositivist climate, some philosophers of psychological science warn that their uncritical use can lead to conceptual retrogressions (Phillips, 1987).

Levels of interaction

Both persons and situations also need description at several "grain-size" levels. Different levels involve different kinds of aggregation across persons, tasks, and time. Interactions at one level may thus appear to be quite different from those at another.

Components, abilities, and aptitude complexes. Cognitive abilities can be hierarchically organized. The history of factor-analytic research has been reviewed and reanalyzed by Carroll (1989; 1993) to yield a comprehensive and integrated hierarchical model. First-order abilities are incorporated into the second-order ability constructs of fluid reasoning (G_f), crystallized language (G_c), visual perception (G_v), auditory perception (G_a), memory (G_m), speed (G_s), and idea production (G_i) under a third-order general intelligence (G). Horn's (1989) summary is similar. And Gustafsson (1984, 1988, 1989) has demonstrated that G_f can be equated with G and also with Thurstone's (1938) first-order induction (I) factor, that residualizing G_c and G_v for G reproduces Vernon's (1950) hierarchical model, and finally that both higher-order and first-order abilities are needed to understand individual differences in learning from instruction; different ability levels can relate differently to achievement, within or between instructional treatments, and each level is needed to clarify the influence of the other.

Some theorists argue that this model reflects only a narrow, psychometrically defined, academic intelligence, which should be sharply distinguished from a broader concept of practical, everyday, real-world intelligence (see, e.g., Sternberg & Wagner, 1986). Although it is true that much psychometric and factor-analytic research on abilities has been motivated by educational problems, it is a mistake in my view to assume that academic tests and tasks represent only an artificial world disconnected from reality. In any case, the issue need not be argued here; the hierarchical model at least represents academic intelligence, the focus of this chapter.

Figure 1.1 shows an abstract version of the ability hierarchy that also includes, for the G, G_f, I column, a further breakdown into the performance tasks (i.e., tests) often used as markers for this factor, and then into the information-processing components identified by experimental analysis as constituents of performance on these tests. The best markers for this general ability factor are matrices, classification, series completion, and analogical reasoning tests. However, as suggested by the figure, tests associated with "nearby" factors, such as Necessary Arithmetic Operations, for quantitative reasoning (QR), may be described using essentially the same components plus some crystallized knowledge. The Paper Folding test represents spatial visualization (VZ) ability, but fluid analytic reasoning is one nonspatial solution strategy that can be effective, so it too may be described using the same components, at least in part, or for some people. As shown, the componential analysis is only schematic of Sternberg's (1977, 1985) theory; it merely lists the performance components, suggests some of the further component processes involved in knowledge acquisition, retrieval, and transfer, and interposes without detail the metacomponent processes that decide what the task is, choose appropriate components, organize them into a strategy, and monitor the performance. Left out also are the related interpretations of other investigators (e.g., Carpenter, Just & Shell, 1990; Embretson, 1985; Pellegrino & Glaser, 1982; Snow & Lohman, 1984). One could expand the figure by showing all the first-order abilities and their marker tests, not just those identified in it as ideational fluency (IF), verbal comprehension (VC), spatial relations (SR), sound discrimination (SD), memory span (MS), and perceptual speed (PS), along with QR, I, and VZ. Componential analyses of VC, VZ, and SR could be added (see Lohman, 1988, 1989; Sternberg, 1987), but comparable analyses are not yet available for the task markers of most other ability factors.

Also shown schematically in Figure 1.1, above the ability hierarchy, is the possibility of constructs elsewhere called "aptitude complexes" (Snow, 1987). These represent hypothesized combinations of aptitude variables that jointly influence learning in some particular situation. They reflect the view that persons are not adequately characterized by lists of independent ability variables studied in isolation. Rather, there are likely to be patterns, profiles, or compounds (i.e., complexes) of person and situation characteristics that identify qualitatively different types. There may be mixtures of several abilities, or of abilities with specialized prior knowledge, or abilities with conative or affective aptitudes (or inaptitudes), and each may have important situational aspects to their definition.

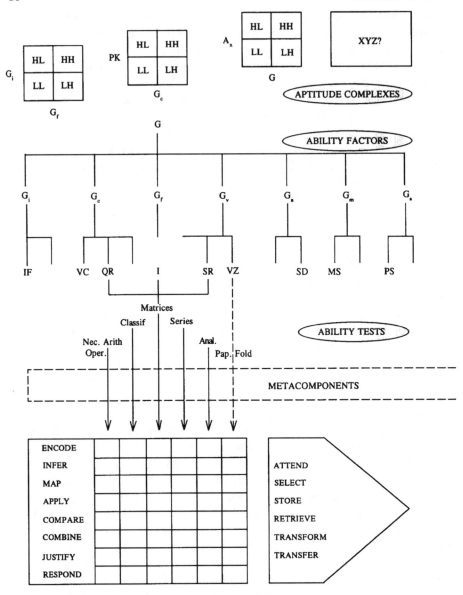

Figure 1.1. Hierarchical model of cognitive abilities showing three levels of ability factors, ability tests used as markers for the central ability G = G_f = I, and component processes involved in these tests. Aptitude complexes at the top are intended to suggest combinations of abilities and other characteristics of particular importance.

Three simple examples are given to suggest these possibilities. In the first, G_f and G_i are combined to identify four kinds of learners. Persons in each quadrant will differ in various ways, but only some high–high persons are likely to be described as creative, and this will be in conjunction with particular kinds of situations. Of course, many person and situation characteristics go into the making of creative perform-ances (Sternberg & Lubart, 1991) and the pattern analysis is not simple (Cronbach, 1968); the point is that creative thinking is an aptitude complex, defined in part by situation characteristics, not a single ability. The second example shows a G_cx special prior knowledge (PK) mix, to reflect current controversies about the relative impor-tance of general vs. situation- or domain-specific skills. Here also, what constitutes an optimum mix depends on the situation, but it is clear that high G_c–low PK learners and low G_c–high PK learners are very different persons for the purposes of instruc-tional treatment (see, e.g., Hall & Edmondson, 1992; Schneider & Weinert, 1990; Snow & Swanson, 1992). The third example combines G and test anxiety (A_x), because there is much evidence that anxiety effects are relative to ability x task-difficulty interactions; some instructional research has also shown that high–high and low–low learners might need one kind of task structure, whereas learners in the middle ranges might need another (see Snow, 1977, 1987). The XYZ box in Figure 1.1 simply signifies that many potentially important aptitude complexes have yet to be investigated. In particular, ability–personality mixes beyond G and A_x need to be brought into instructional research (see Snow, 1989b). Interactionist approaches to personality, as noted earlier, are forming many such constructs based on complexes of person and situation variables (Mischel, 1984).

Although the ability hierarchy provides an initial taxonomy from which to choose constructs for further research, it is by no means complete. Many other kinds of person characteristics would need to be added to reach a comprehensive list of potential aptitudes for academic tasks (see, e.g., Gardner, 1983, this volume; Snow, 1990, 1992; Snow & Swanson, 1992). Furthermore, there is no "best" level from which to choose. Gustafsson (1989) showed that both broad and narrow ability constructs are needed each to help interpret the effects on learning of the other. The same can be said for components and complexes. The role of abilities is clarified when prior knowledge and personality reference variables are present, and vice versa. The nature of component processes in learning is better understood when ability reference variables are included, and vice versa. It is not clear that components, ability factors, or aptitude complexes should be regarded as more or less basic in any given instance (Carroll, 1980; Sternberg, 1980).

Finally, the ability hierarchy should not be regarded as some kind of fixed trait structure. It is rather the complex result of human development, produced by the accumulation of person–situation interactions, reciprocal and transactive, over each person's history (see Brown & Campione, this volume). There is growing evidence that differentiated learning histories influence ability profile development (Balke-Aurell, 1982; Demetriou, Efklides & Platsidou, in press; Gustafsson, Demetriou & Efklides, 1989). A theory to that effect, though vague in detail, has long been in hand

(Ferguson, 1954, 1956). Thus the situations in which particular abilities develop and are specialized become part of the definitions of those abilities as aptitudes for future use in similar situations (Snow & Lohman, 1984; Snow, 1992). Particular ability–situation complexes, with conative and affective constituents as well, may be among the "acquired contextual modules" Bereiter (1990) believes to be the proper units for educational theory.

Tasks, treatments, and contexts. On the situation side, one can think of instructional treatments as composed of particular sequences of learning tasks and embedded in particular classroom or school contexts. Situation variables might then be defined within or across these three levels. But so far there are no models, hierarchical or otherwise, of such situation variables. In some limited domains, distinct situation dimensions might be identified using a factor-analytic approach that parallels that used for abilities (Frederiksen, 1972); variations among instructional films (Snow, 1963), teacher characteristics (Gage, 1963), classroom climates (Moos, 1979), and college campus cultures (Pace & Stern, 1958) have been studied this way. However, in most past research, situation variables have been measured using fairly molar indicators or manipulated experimentally, one or two at a time; distinctions between levels of these situation variables have not been emphasized. In ATI research, T has usually stood for complex combinations of task, teacher, subject matter, and instructional method. The physical and social contexts of classroom, school, and community have often been ignored. When task, treatment, and context variables are separated and explicitly studied, complicated higher-order interactions are often found (Cronbach, 1975, 1982). Natural correlations among situation variables within and between levels often cannot be disentangled (Brunswik, 1956; Snow, 1974). And it is impossible to study all relevant layers and kinds of situation variation simultaneously, just as it is impossible to study all relevant person variables simultaneously.

Thus, building a useful taxonomy of task, treatment, and context variables is a major problem not yet solved, or even fully faced. Some propose that academic tasks must be the first and central focus in the analysis of instructional person–situation interactions (Rhetts, 1972, 1974; Tobias, 1969), but treatments, contexts, and relations between levels cannot be ignored.

Doyle (1983) defined academic tasks by the products students must formulate, the operations used to produce them, and the external resources available for student use in the process. Four types of academic tasks result: memory tasks, requiring recognition or reproduction of previously exposed information; procedural or routine tasks, requiring application of standard formulae or algorithms; comprehension or understanding tasks, requiring recognition of transformations of previously exposed information or procedures, inferences from them, or applications in new circumstances; and opinion tasks in which preferences are stated.

Doyle's four types are listed in Table 1.1. Connected with each are various types of learning thought to be distinguishable at a process level. Although the problem of taxonomy for learning tasks and processes has a long history in both research on

Table 1.1. *Some types of academic tasks and associated learning activities*

Types of tasks (Doyle, 1983)	Types of learning (Ryan, 1981)	Types of learning and teaching strategies (Kyllonen & Shute, 1989)
Memory	Memorization Recognition Recollection	Rote learning Learning from being told Storing frequently used knowledge to avoid relearning effort
Procedural–routine	Learning perceptual skills Learning motor skills Learning localized habits	Compiling declarative knowledge into procedural form Composing micro- to macro-procedures Drill and practice
Comprehension–understanding	Learning to understand Conceptual accumulation and organization Language learning	Chunking lower- to higher-level descriptions Induction by analogy Induction by examples Induction by observation and discovery
Opinion	Learning specific interests Learning general attitudes and values	Modeling

learning (Melton, 1964) and instructional design (Gagne, Briggs & Wager, 1988), two recent contributions identified in Table 1.1 are useful in new ways. Kyllonen and Shute (1989) focus explicitly on cognitive learning and teaching strategies used in instruction, and Ryan's (1981) listing goes beyond cognitive distinctions. Each of their types is listed only once in the table, but clearly there is a network of multiple relations across columns. Also, I have modified their language slightly and added modeling as a particular type of observation learning relevant especially to opinion tasks.

Kyllonen and Shute (1989) also distinguish eight types of knowledge resulting from learning (proposition, schema, rule, general rule, skill, general skill, automatic skill, and mental model) and envision a multidimensional, subject-matter space wherein courses, topics, or jobs could be arrayed. Each academic task, then, is designed to promote learning of particular subject matter (e.g., Newton's Second Law) by particular means (e.g., analogy) with particular outcome (e.g., schema induction). The space is characterized by dimensions such as degree of quantitative technical emphasis in a course. These are not merely content dimensions, since different academic subject matters may call for and help develop specialized styles of learning and thinking adapted to their own particular characteristics. Different domains may also promote, or somehow be naturally correlated with, particular styles or methods of teaching. For example, hands-on experiments in science, text analysis in history, role playing in social studies, and one-on-one tutoring in art, all seem "natural" as combinations of instructional method and content domain.

Thinking of styles of learning and teaching that characterize whole fields of study, however, goes beyond task dimensions to a more molar level of situation description. And, as Doyle (1983) noted, there are important molar dimensions of academic work that arise because the tasks are typically organized by teachers in classrooms. One of these dimensions is ambiguity – the degree to which correct performance is clearly definable for or by learners in advance. Another is risk – the degree to which rigorous evaluative criteria are used by the teacher and the likelihood of their being met by learners. Doyle would classify his memory and procedural tasks as low in ambiguity and either low or high in risk depending on whether the information burden on the learner is light (e.g., a short spelling list) or heavy (e.g., a long poetry recitation), respectively. Opinion tasks are high in ambiguity and low in risk; although there are many answers, many can be correct. Comprehension tasks are high in both ambiguity and risk. Since these tasks typically represent the more difficult higher-order objectives, it is not surprising that students routinely invent strategies for reducing the ambiguity and risk associated with them. Doyle reviewed evidence showing that students attempt to increase teacher explicitness and structure, reduce emphasis on understanding, and restrict and monitor their own output to minimize risk of error; some also adopt strategies aimed more at meeting the teacher's evaluation practices than at learning the material (d'Ydewalle, 1984; Marton, Hounsell & Entwistle, 1984). These practices transcend the task level to influence instructional treatment over the course of weeks and months. They also emphasize that learner intentions help define both task and treatment characteristics.

Other dimensions of tasks and treatments are defined in part by learner characteristics. In reviewing research on problem solving, Greeno and Simon (1988) contrasted well versus ill-structured problems that do versus do not involve domain-specific knowledge and are novel versus familiar for novices versus experts. Novices attempting novel, knowledge-lean tasks rely on general abilities and strategies. As knowledge relevance and expertise increase, there are shifts to domain-specialized mental representations and strategies, and then to automatic processing, at least for well-structured tasks. With difficult, ill-structured, or novel tasks, experts revert to the general methods of novices. When shifts to transfer tasks are required, general abilities reenter the picture (Ackerman, 1989). There are probably also thresholds of task difficulty and learner ability within task types, where shifts between heuristic and algorithmic processing occur (Elshout, 1987). If many tasks in a situation are characterized as novel, unstructured, and difficult, relative to the prior knowledge and ability status of relevant learners, then it is a whole instructional treatment that is so characterized, not just a task. And person characteristics that might not be important at the task level can come into play at the treatment level. An able learner might maintain confidence when a few novel, unstructured tasks appear but turn anxious when the treatment is made primarily novel and unstructured, for example.

Similarly, two identical treatments may show different effects in different classrooms or schools. A discovery treatment, for example, will be a novelty in a school traditionally committed to direct, didactic, reception learning; it will be routine in a context where indirect, discovery experiences have been broadly emphasized.

Problems of aggregation. These are figure–ground problems that can also be thought of as problems of aggregation. Instructional tasks aggregate to form instructional treatments. The character of a treatment depends on the mix of tasks that comprise it. But the character of each task also depends on the treatment in which it is embedded. Memorizing a poem in a diversified treatment on poetry appreciation is not the same task in a treatment composed entirely of memorizing poems. In turn, treatments add up to define contexts, but the contexts also work down to characterize treatments. Discovery learning in a traditional school was the example given above. Many other dimensions define school context. Also, context can differ for different students in the same school. Aggregation causes person characteristics to become part of the situation definition, just as situation characteristics become part of the person definition.

Most research interprets ability–learning relations assuming each individual is independent of every other. In schools, however, many learning tasks are addressed in groups. Often small groups of students are organized for academic work by the teacher. Such groups may be purposely formed to be homogenous or heterogeneous in ability. Often academic work is conducted in whole classes. Because of school-level tracking policies, classes may represent high, middle, low, or heterogeneous ability groups. Beyond this, school communities differ in ability distribution just as they do in socioeconomic distribution; this can influence school practices at treatment and task levels. Thus, individual students have "absolute" ability levels but also several "relative" ability levels, defined by their positions in each relevant group ability distribution. Many aspects of academic tasks take on different meanings for individuals depending on their standing relative to other group members. The meaning of teacher feedback for individuals standing in different positions in ability distributions is one obvious example. There might also be differential ability effects; consider the student who is rewarded for contributing spatial visualization to group problem solving but criticized for the inability to write good prose about it. In cooperative learning groups, differential effects of ability on learning can depend on the social role adopted by each learner, which in turn depends on the mix of ability in the group (Webb, 1982, 1989). Also, extraverted, moderately anxious learners seem to benefit most in cooperative learning groups, so again ability is not the only issue (Hall, Dansereau & Skagus, 1990). In short, person aggregations become situation variables.

Some summary implications

Figure 1.2 provides a list of the instructional context, treatment, and task variables touched upon explicitly or implicitly in the foregoing discussion. The categories and

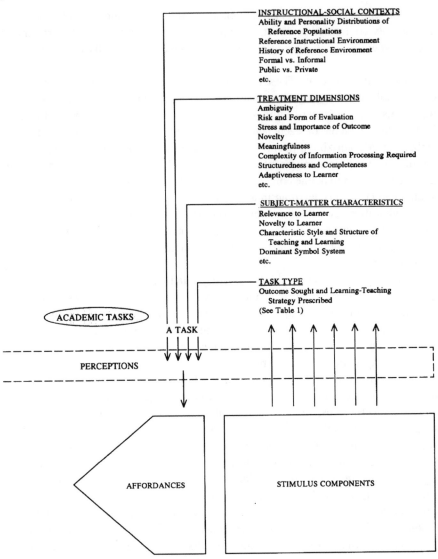

Figure 1.2. Instructional context, treatment, and task variables manifested in the affordances of academic tasks.

variables are neither exhaustive nor mutually exclusive, yet the list is already full enough to suggest how complexly determined and relative is the meaning of any particular academic task. Some situation variables depend more on interaction with person variables for their definitions than do others. Some may be understood more in relation to person ability (e.g., meaningfulness, novelty), some more in relation to anxiety (e.g., risk, ambiguity), and some both (e.g., stress). Despite this clear interdependency of person and situation variables, interactional approaches have not been prominent in research on these dimensions until recently, at least not in instructional psychology. Now, meaningfulness, novelty, and stress are seen as dimensions to which whole chapters can be devoted (as seen elsewhere in this volume). Ambiguity and risk are also important but can be addressed only with personality and motivation theory included. Accordingly, the rest of the present chapter concentrates on examples of complexity, structuredness, and adaptiveness.

Three features of the task box in Figure 1.2 should be noted. First, just as metacomponential processing intervenes between ability tests and hypothesized component processes in Figure 1.1, it also does so in Figure 1.2. Here, however, it is called "perception" to emphasize that task, treatment, and context characteristics influence persons only as they are perceived. Second, the perceptions are not only of task demands or requirements but also of opportunities. The concept of affordances is chosen from Gibson's (1979) theory of perception to cover both demands and opportunities; it is here interpreted also to include supports and prosthetic devices designed into a situation for instructional purposes. Third, the task box is drawn to coincide with the component-process box of Figure 1.1, if the two figures are brought together.

This suggests that academic task analysis and ability test analysis are not fundamentally different. The componential process approach to ability (and achievement) tests can be applied to academic tasks. The componential knowledge (and structure) approach to academic tasks can be applied to ability tests. Many of the same components and metacomponents can be identified in both kinds of tasks; these will encompass knowledge structures as well as the bits and pieces of knowledge and process skills brought to bear in task performances. Of course, each test and task will have specifics. And, as the academic tasks studied involve larger systems of knowledge organization, richer descriptions in terms of schemata, scripts, networks, and mental models will be needed. Such analyses are accumulating, especially with tasks representing abstract, verbal, and spatial reasoning abilities and mathematics and science achievement (Greeno & Simon, 1988; Snow, 1992; Snow & Lohman, 1989). Unfortunately, many of these analyses take no account of individual differences or interactions; there has been little systematic cross-task, within-construct analysis and modeling of multiple performances. There is as yet no theory of the person–situation interface represented in the confluence of Figures 1.1 and 1.2.

Examples, hypotheses, and prospects

There are, however, important examples, hypotheses, and accumulations of evidence available from previous studies of ability–learning task correlations, componential analyses, and ATI. A substantial portion of these concern complexity and structure as task or treatment characteristics and the adaptation of instruction in this regard. Although for the most part, past work has interpreted person and situation variables as in independent or interdependent interaction, the results help consider reciprocal and transactive models. There are also reconceptualizations of the ability–task interface that move in this direction. The second half of this chapter suggests briefly how these ideas might work in future theory, and gives examples toward that end, but there is no attempt at comprehensive literature review.

Past evidence

Ability–learning task correlations. The correlational evidence on ability test intercorrelations summarized in the hierarchical factor model of Figure 1.1 can also be represented as an inverse Guttman Radex model (using nonmetric multidimensional scaling; see, e.g., Snow, Kyllonen & Marshalek, 1984). The two models are conformable, but the radex has the advantage that it provides a map-like structure into which arrays of ability tests and factors, and also learning tasks, can be placed according to their intercorrelations. Componential analyses of the tests and tasks can also be entered.

   What evidence there is using this approach suggests the schematic summary shown in Figure 1.3. The radex structure provides a crude but useful map of cognitive abilities and learning tasks. It distinguishes the more complex and general ability constructs in the center of the radex from the simpler, more specialized and domain-specific abilities distributed around the periphery, and suggests that the arrays of the radex represent continua of increasing information-processing complexity as one moves from periphery to center. The central ability constructs show much stronger correlations with academic learning tasks than do the peripheral abilities. Although particular special abilities may correlate highly with learning in particular tasks, such as perceptual-speed abilities with air-traffic control learning for example (Ackerman, 1989), initial learning and transfer stages of performance on such tasks also correlate highly with general abilities. It seems that learning tasks correlate more centrally as they require meaningful learning in complex tasks. Information-processing analyses also suggest that the more central tests and tasks involve more variance due to adaptive, inferential, and strategic assembly and control processes. In other words, cognitive ability and learning differences in the center of the radex seem to represent in significant part person differences in within-task flexible adaptation of processing.

Ability–treatment interactions. The central abilities of Figure 1.3 not only show higher correlations with learning tasks, they also show more potent and reliable ATI. The ATI literature displays many such results (Cronbach & Snow, 1977; Snow, 1977, 1989a). Most are best interpreted as reflecting the functioning of the broad general ability factor G. Consistent with the correlational evidence, G seems to relate to achievement increasingly as the instructional tasks require students to assume more of the information processing burden of learning. When academic tasks are complex or poorly structured, or unstructured, incomplete, or otherwise imperfect, G will relate more highly with learning; when tasks are not so described the relations will be lower (Snow, 1982). Indeed, academic intelligence has been defined as the ability

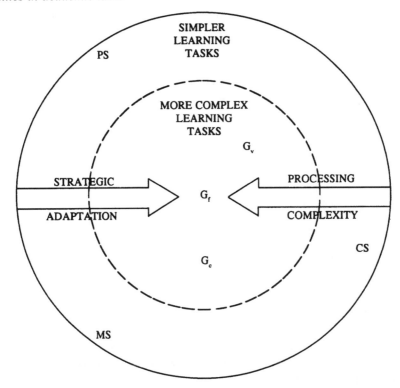

Figure 1.3. A schematic radex structure showing more complex learning tasks and general abilities (G_f, G_c, G_v) in the center and simpler learning tasks and abilities (MS, PS, CS) in the periphery. Processing complexity and the need for strategic adaptation in task performance increase as one moves from periphery to center.

to learn from incomplete instruction (Resnick & Glaser, 1976). The interpretation again points to adaptive, inferential, strategic assembly and control processes; more complex, incomplete tasks require more of such processing, whereas less complex, more complete tasks require less of such processing. G distinguishes between learners who can and cannot produce and sustain this sort of processing.

Some ATI studies have sought to distinguish G_f and G_c, or to distinguish this complex from G_v. G_f seems to relate more to learning in novel situations where analysis of significant task features is required or where inductive reasoning is needed to infer essential but missing knowledge elements. G_c relates more to learning in familiar situations where connections between new and old learning are important and verbal elaborations of their meaning are needed. G_v abilities seem to pop in and out of relevance as learning tasks require difficult figural–spatial cognition. With G_c interpreted as generalized prior knowledge, an occasional study has also sought to separate specific prior knowledge as a distinct aptitude from G_c or G. So far, however, the methodology for this kind of study of expertise has not been well worked out. All expert–novice comparisons that manipulate task characteristics are ATI studies of prior knowledge and its correlates as aptitude, incidentally.

The accumulation of ATI results makes a motley collection. Replication has been difficult because the molar aptitude and treatment variables studied are not well understood, the complexities of instructional treatments and school contexts are confounded in higher-order interactions, as noted earlier, and the learning criteria reflect multiple, conflicting, and often unstable sources of influence. Nonetheless, conventional ATI evidence provides many important starting points. Each major ATI hypothesis is a focus for analyses aimed at understanding the reciprocal and trans-active processes of the person–situation interface.

The ability × structure hypothesis

One of the strongest G × task correlations, as noted earlier, is that between ability tests and complex learning tasks involving lack of structure and completeness – the so-called information-processing burden hypothesis (Snow, 1982). One of the strongest G × T interactions also involves treatments that differ in the structure, directness, and completeness of instruction. For simplicity, I label this contrast high structure (HS) vs. low structure (LS).

In HS treatments, the teachers or instructional conditions maintain a high level of external control of student learning activities, attention, pacing, feedback, and reinforcement; the instructional tasks are broken down into small units in clear sequence; and the contents and procedures of learning are made explicit and concrete. Such treatments help low G learners but seem to thwart high G learners. In LS treatments where learners must act more independently and rely more on their own structuring to fill in gaps, high G learners tend to do well while low G learners do poorly. Treatments typically described as direct instruction, mastery-oriented, or teacher-controlled, would be considered high-structure treatments, whereas those described as indirect, inductive, discovery-oriented, or learner-controlled would be considered low-structure treatments. So-called conventional teaching would fall between these extremes; depending on particular teacher style, it might be closer to LS or to HS.

This ATI pattern does not always occur, since many other personal and situational factors may moderate it. But it occurs often enough, and in widely different contexts, that it is one major candidate for more detailed analysis and it is a good example for discussion here. Indeed, it is essentially the same contrast Glaser and Bassok (1989) used to summarize a large amount of research on the two major kinds of computerized instructional designs being developed today. The two design theories are called "mastery" and "guided discovery" for short. Mastery (or HS) imposes specific transition paths through progressive curriculum units that represent sequenced subgoals. It provides relatively structured, explicit, and complete tutoring, with substantial system control over feedback and correction. Discovery (or LS) provides a microworld environment to explore with guidance and assistance as needed, and places responsibility on learners for structuring and controlling instruction; it is thus less structured and complete, relative to mastery instruction. If these two major kinds of instructional treatment fit different kinds of learners, as the ATI evidence suggests, then it is foolish to argue about which approach is best. Both are needed, but each needs to be tuned to a different type of learner, or perhaps to a different stage of learner development in a knowledge domain; rather different achievement theories seem required for each person–situation combination.

An ATI example with context effects. A study by Tsai (1992) provides one example of the G × treatment structure hypothesis in contemporary research. It shows the importance of learner experience with instructional treatments and also exemplifies the moderating effects of school context.

Tsai developed a schema-induction (HS) treatment for use in high school computer programming courses. Such courses typically rely on individual practice with piece-meal exercises and examples to represent the variety of useful programming features – a kind of unstructured, discovery approach (LS). In contrast, schema structures can be imposed to serve as generic plans for action sequences that accomplish particular tasks the way experts might perform them. Schema-based expert models are now used in several computerized tutoring systems for programming. These are regarded as rather strictly structured in contrast to the open exploratory discovery learning environments of some other kinds of computerized systems. There is prior evidence that the G × structure hypothesis works in programming instruction as it does elsewhere (Mayer, 1988).

Tsai used measures of G_f, prior programming knowledge, and two conative con-structs (mindfulness and self-efficacy) as aptitudes. Separate measures of surface vs. deep problem representation and programming competence were obtained as post-tests. Think-aloud protocols were also obtained on a subset of students. The treat-ments were run independently in two schools for three weeks. To simplify, only the regression results for G and mindfulness are shown in Figure 1.4. G here is the sum of G_f and prior-knowledge measures. The mindfulness measure reflects degree of self-reported metacognitive awareness and effort investment.

The regressions on G are distinctly different for HS and LS and support the hypothesis in one school, but not the other; the same ATI pattern occurs for mind-fulness. Small sample size precluded multiple-regression analysis.

The two schools represent different contexts. In comparison to School A, School B (where ATI was clear) serves a population with lower socioeconomic status (and far fewer personal computers at home), fewer native English speakers, and more discipline and absence problems, on average. However, School B students also had more prior computer-programming experience and more example elaboration though less emphasis on problem solving in regular computer teaching, than students in School A. The resulting aptitude complex hypothesis, in brief, goes as follows: in contexts providing relatively few external supports and resources for relevant learn-ing and problem solving, able, mindful, students with prior successful experience with unstructured discovery learning of programming will continue to be better off

School A   School B

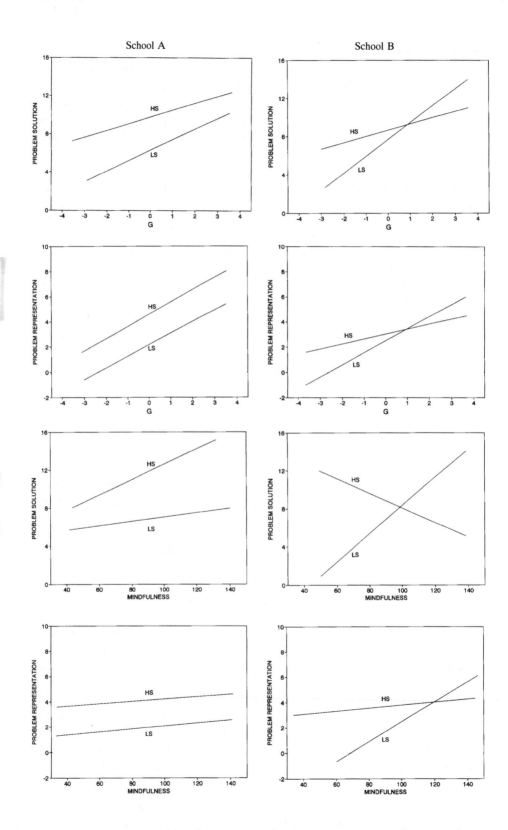

with such treatment than with structure imposed, whereas students who are relatively less able, mindful, and successful with unstructured learning will benefit especially from new treatments imposing structure. Students in advantaged contexts with external supports and resources, but without experience in unstructured discovery learning of programming, benefit from imposed structure rather than discovery. In this context, more able students do better than less able students in both treatments. The implication is that local context and student history as well as the details of past and present learner experience with particular instructional tasks will condition continuing learner improvement with respect to such tasks.

An ATI example with task adaptation. A study by Swanson (1990) shows how an instructional treatment called "contingent tutoring" might provide for adaptive shifting between HS and LS to optimize instruction for each kind of student. The concept of contingent tutoring derives from Wood's (1980) studies of mothers teaching children, Bruner's (1978) notion of scaffolding, and Vygotsky's (1978) ideas about proximal development and the internalization of social interaction. It relates in turn to analyses of instruction in apprenticeships. Briefly, it assumes that learning depends on one already understanding something of the nature of what is to be learned, so an important function of teaching is to create links between the goal and context of a novel task and more familiar tasks, allowing the learner to apply skills and knowledge previously acquired. The tutor also controls those aspects of the task that are initially too difficult for learners, thereby permitting them to concentrate upon and complete those aspects that each is able to perform. By adapting the task demands, keeping them within each learner's zone of proximal development, the tutor not only helps the learner complete the task at hand, but also gradually promotes the additional skill and strategy development that will enable eventual performance of similar tasks independently. Tutor effectiveness depends on this scaffolding being contingent upon the interaction of task demands and student performance; tutorial interventions are inversely related to the student's level of competence. The more difficulty a student has with a task, the more directive the tutor. The more success the student experiences, the more the tutor encourages the student to work independently. To make tutoring interventions contingent, the tutor must understand what the student is attempting to achieve, and be able to diagnose degrees and kinds of success and failure.

Swanson (1990) compared contingent tutoring with HS and LS strategies in teaching optics to college undergraduates who varied in G (as represented by combined SAT score). A "lecture" (HS) condition put tutors in full control of the transaction and a "discovery" (LS) condition gave students full control; in the contingent condition, tutor control varied to adapt to individual student needs and progress as described above. There were two tutors and 48 students. Pretests indicated

Figure 1.4. Regression slopes showing aptitude–treatment interaction results for two schools comparing high (HS) and low (LS) structure treatments, using general ability (G) and mindfullness as aptitude and problem solution and representation as separate learning outcome measures. Data from Tsai (1992).

minimal prior knowledge. Posttests included knowledge and problem-solving tasks. All sessions were videotaped.

Results are shown in Figure 1.5. Panel a, which gives the aggregated results, shows that LS was good for the most able students, but it was particularly ineffective with lower G students, who benefitted most from contingent tutoring. HS produced intermediate results. In Panel b, the tutor who was best at contingent control produced the highest learning outcomes across the G range with this treatment. For the tutor in Panel c, this strategy proved difficult to use, so HS was more effective for less able students.

In effect, this result is a macro-level ATI used to evaluate a microadaptation of instruction. Tutoring that is contingent on learner performance should provide more scaffolding for less able learners and less scaffolding for more able learners. In the extreme, the tutor ranges between mastery-style direct instruction (HS) and guided discovery (LS), the major treatment contrast emphasized by Glaser & Bassok (1989). Furthermore, the tutors seem to be adapting not only to the student's specific responses but to behavioral correlates of more general aptitude differences. Thus, human tutors may integrate domain-general and domain-specific learner communications in their adaptations. Further research is needed to understand how this is done. Meanwhile, however, the macro- and micro-ATI results of both the Swanson and Tsai research taken together underscore the need for a more detailed, transactive process model of adaptive person–situation interaction.

A process model of person–situation interaction

The above examples hardly represent adequately the wealth of prior research evidence regarding cognitive abilities and academic tasks and treatments. But they do make the structure hypothesis concrete and suggest how context, treatment, and task variables can moderate one another's effects to produce different local accounts of optimal instruction. They also show how traditional ATI research, although focussed on statistical interactions among independent variables, provides a shell within which interdependent, reciprocal, and transactive interpretations can be considered.

Over the past decade or so, my colleagues and I have sought to bring together the process-analytic research on A and T variables, including our own studies, within this ATI shell. The aim has been to reinterpret the concept of aptitude, including ability, as a property of the person–task interface and to build a process model of person–situation interaction that would account for all the evidence in hand. The model would need to be general enough to cover conative and affective as well as cognitive aptitude. It would have to account for individual differences in person adaptation to task conditions and show how changes in treatment could change this process interaction. The development of this view can be traced through a series of earlier publications (Snow, 1978, 1981, 1989a, 1992, in press; Snow & Lohman, 1984; see also Kyllonen, Lohman & Woltz, 1984, and Snow, Kyllonen & Marshalek, 1984). Only a brief version can be given here.

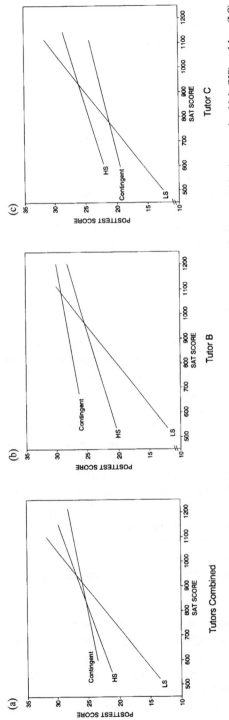

Figure 1.5. Regression slopes showing aptitude–treatment interaction results for two tutors, separately and combined, comparing high (HS) and low (LS) structure treatments with contingent tutoring, using SAT score as aptitude and optics posttest as learning outcome. Data from Swanson (1990).

Starting hypotheses. We first hypothesized that important individual differences in cognitive task performance in relation to learning would appear as within-person as well as between-person variations in information processing. Although individual differences in performance components could be identified as in Figure 1.1, persons would also differ in the sequence in which they executed these component steps and in the kinds of component steps they included; these sequence and route differences would shift during learning. Most important would be the person's facility in assembling component sequences and routes into a strategy for task performance and in reassembling or adapting this assembly as task performance proceeded, or as tasks changed. Intraindividual differences in these functions should show adaptations within cognitive performance tasks (e.g., ability tests) that would account for similar differences in academic-learning tasks. These adaptive functions are called *assembly* and *control* processes; they clearly overlap with much of what Sternberg (1985) calls *metacomponents* (though I prefer to avoid the "executive" connotation).

When complex ability tests and academic-learning tasks are highly correlated, the traditional interpretation has been that the kind of inductive reasoning, or verbal comprehension, or spatial visualization (or whatever ability) required in the test is also required in the learning task. Then, ATI occurs when one instructional treatment requires some ability, or some degree of ability, that another does not. This interpretation is substantially elaborated if through more analytic research the component and metacomponent processes involved in the ability test and learning task variance can be specified and arranged in a performance program that works for both test and task. However, in all but the simplest and shortest of situations, variance also seems to arise from the person's continuing need to adapt the performance program to the fine structure of task and treatment characteristics as they unfold. Tests and tasks that are novel to a person will require the creation and control of new performance programs. Even highly familiar tests and tasks will require some adaptation of performance programs retrieved from memory as units, because complex academic learning situations are dynamic. Thus, ability differences in learning appear in the person–task interface as differences in within-person adaptation to the stream of continuing changes in task and treatment demands and opportunities. Learners construct their performances in academic tasks by drawing on their resources and assembling, reassembling, and controlling them to adapt to perceived needs and opportunities in the situation. Individual differences in learning occur because of qualitative and quantitative differences in this adaptation function across person–situation unions.

The sampling–assembly–control process. The result is a way of describing both intraindividual adaptation and interindividual differences, within and across situations, that seems flexible enough to capture the dynamics of transactive processing in person–situation interactions. For short, I call it a sampling–assembly–control model of the person–task interface.

The basic event at the interface is a sampling, of person by situation and situation by person, governed by associative networks of stimulus and response components residing in the inner environment of the person and the outer environment of the situation. These associative networks are the residual properties to which Allport (1955) referred. They reflect the history of person and situation and provide the stuff from which a variety of reciprocal structures and representations can be assembled as needed in a particular ongoing person–situation match. The neutral term *component* is used to cover many kinds of hypothesized units or connections, including Sternberg's (1985) information-processing components and Guttman's (1970) response components, but also S–R bonds, plans, images, learning sets, schemata, nodes in semantic networks, productions in production systems, and the like. The model is thus not restricted to any one mental representational construct, and accommodates the nonrepresentational constructs of connectionism as well. Furthermore, although components are described here as bits and pieces of ability (and knowledge), the term applies as well to key aspects of conative and affective aptitude constructs. It also applies to aspects of the stimulus situation that "call for" corresponding response components. Academic tasks as performance situations are composed of networks of situation components that demand or invite particular kinds of performance in response.

Each person's inner environment contains many response components probabilistically interconnected in multiple associative networks. Many sorts of assemblies of these components can be constructed in different ways in response to different situations. They are also decomposable, so parts can be used in other assemblies as needed. The products of past learning are component assemblies available as units to be triggered anew by situations similar to those previously faced. The products of continuing learning are additional components, new assemblies of both new and old components, and strengthened connections between them. But learning also exercises and thus strengthens the assembly and control functions themselves. In short, the human mental system is designed to be loosely coupled and flexible in assembling and reassembling components into performance programs to meet varying situational needs. Since it reflects personal learning history in this regard, it is also highly idiosyncratic.

Each performance situation samples from each person, in the sense that the demands and opportunities it presents draw forth whatever relevant response components and assemblies each person can muster. But the person also samples the situation, in the sense that stimulus components are perceived and selected. Some stimulus components may represent a demand for particular response components or assemblies. Some may also provide an opportunity to use particular response components or assemblies. Of course, each person's learning history will influence this perception-selection process. The sampling will be designed partly by the demands and opportunities afforded by the performance situation presented, and partly by the possibilities and constraints afforded by the assembly and control history of the performing person.

Considering the person's learning history suggests some further distinctions between several kinds of situational demands and opportunities. There are those requir-ing the retrieval and application of old familiar component assemblies versus those requiring the construction and application of novel component assemblies. Here is the contrast between G_c and G_f again. Also, however, there are those that support the use of certain performance assemblies by the learner versus those that supplant the need for such performance assemblies – that provide stimulus components as prostheses that can substitute for response components. It is in this sense that some theorists refer to "distributed" intelligence (see, e.g., Pea, 1990; Perkins, 1990; Salomon, 1990). The person and the situation each contribute components to be integrated in successful performance. Academic tasks and treatments will typically involve some of each kind of component, and will further require the flexible reassembly of interconnections within and between them as learning proceeds. But all these situational components are there to be perceived and used as such, at least for persons who are tuned to do so.

Thus, situations can be described as consisting of networks of stimulus components that represent either demands for or opportunities to use particular response compo-nents or assemblies, but that may also supplant the need for particular response components or assemblies, and that may be either familiar or novel with respect to the person's learning history. Note that these essential aspects of situations are defined by their connections with aspects of person performance, just as the essential features of person performance were defined earlier by their connections to situations. We can now simplify the language, and bring out some other implications, by recognizing that all these person–situation connections are *affordances* in Gibson's (1966, 1979) sense of that term, and also *artifacts* in Simon's (1969) sense of that term.

Affordances, artifacts, and ability differences. Gibson's concept of affordances ad-dresses the mutuality of person and situation components in the control of percep-tion–action sequences. To paraphrase Gibson (1979, pp. 127–9, pp. 138–9), the affordances of a situation are what it offers the person – what it provides or furnishes, for good or ill. The term implies a complementarity of person and situation, as in an ecological niche. A niche is a place or setting that is appropriate for a person – a pattern of situational components into which the person "fits" by virtue of a congruent pattern of person components. So a situation is an assembly of affordances with respect to some particular person or kind of person. Affordances reflect the invitation, demand, or opportunity structure of a situation for those persons who are tuned or prepared to perceive them. Particular affordances invite particular actions. The po-tential actions of which a person is capable are called effectivities.

Research on abilities in academic tasks thus requires a detailed analysis of the affordance–effectivity pattern matches of different learners and different instructional tasks and treatments. This analysis would emphasize the opportunities offered by a particular treatment to be detected and capitalized upon by a particular person to achieve a goal. The analysis also would have to remain at a level that identifies the unique person–situation synergy in local contextual terms, rather than abstracting to generalized principles. Since contextual information is likely to be unique to particular person–situation systems, there is probably no detached or abstracted list of qualities of instructional tasks that will be equally important for all persons, or of persons that will be equally important for all tasks. Abilities are thus unique coalitions of affordances and effectivities in particular person-treatment systems.

This analysis of abilities as affordances emphasizes the important ways in which person and situation are tuned to one another – to be in harmony for successful performance. But an equally important question is the analysis of inabilities – the disharmonies in the person–situation interface that result in failure. Some aspects of these disharmonies can be described as failures in perceiving affordances. But other aspects seem better described in Simon's language of artifacts in interface redesign. This language seems particularly useful for considering task and treatment contrasts in instruction.

To paraphrase Simon (1969, pp. 7–13), artifacts are interfaces between inner and outer environments. If these inner and outer environments are appropriate to one another – that is, if they are adapted or designed to fit one another optimally – then the artifact serves its purpose unnoticed. When interface design is only approximate, however, then the limiting properties of the inner system appear in its failure to match the demands of the taxing outer environment. The empirical evidence of interaction arises from the inabilities of some persons to adapt perfectly to some treatments, and vice versa. For a person who is perfectly suited to a treatment or a treatment that is perfectly suited to a person, the goal is reached successfully; the presence of ability is inferred from this fact, but it is attributable not to either person or treatment alone, but rather to their benign interface. For a person who is not perfectly adapted to a treatment or a treatment that is not perfectly adapted to a person, the goal is not successfully reached; this fact shows that inability of some kind is present. But again, inability is attributable to the interface; either the inner system or the outer system, or both, need redesign to bring them into adaptive harmony. Research aimed at system redesign thus needs to find the key inabilities in the interface that constitute mismatches, and correct them. This redesign process can proceed by reshaping the treatment to eliminate or circumvent demands, or by adding opportunities, or both. But it must not add or subtract component assemblies that create one kind of mismatch while eliminating another. Each person brings a unique pattern of residual components to the learning task. The affordance profiles of different person–task interfaces differ. Ability differences "show through" at the interface in different ways in different treatments, and different contexts. The same component that is mathemagenic (i.e., that gives birth to learning) for one person can be mathemathanic (i.e., can bring death to learning) for another (see, e.g., Lohman, 1986). Two tasks or treatments can have opposite affordance patterns with respect to different persons. In short, whenever there is mismatch of this sort, ATI happens.

Adaptive instructional design. Instructional tasks and treatments can be made adaptive to individual differences. To continue the earlier examples, LS treatment samples just the kinds of component assemblies that persons described as able, mindful, and experienced with lack of situational structure are tuned to produce. Moreover, it demands such assemblies, so that persons not sufficiently able, mindful, or experienced to produce them will probably fail. HS treatment does not demand such assemblies; rather, its situational structure and completeness provides some of the component assemblies that less able, mindful, or experienced persons cannot provide for themselves, and it does not demand what such learners cannot produce. Unfortunately, by imposing certain kinds of structure and completeness, HS deprives persons who are able to produce the needed component assemblies of the opportunity to do so on their own. Also, by forcing a structure on such persons that is not their own, HS may produce for them cognitive interference or motivational turnoff, or both.

Tsai's (1992) example fits this classic ATI hypothesis well, at least in part. Although her two schools differed in many ways, it is particularly noteworthy that students in the ATI school had had previous LS style instruction. Some of them – the able and mindful – may have developed the assemblies that allowed adaptative transfer to further LS situations, while HS helped those who had not profited from that prior experience. In the other school, the HS schemata helped all students because none had the residual learning experience with LS. Note, however, that more able students benefitted more than less able students, and especially, that the performance of more able LS students exceeded the performance of less able HS students, on average; so it seems that able learners had some of the residual assemblies and control experience needed to profit from LS, even though all learners benefitted from imposed HS.

Swanson's (1990) example provides the same ATI pattern for HS and LS; structure helps the less able students and hurts the more able students, on average. But her results yield three further, related hypotheses. One is that continuous adaptive variation that ranges between HS and LS as a function of learner response may reach an optimal mix and match of components for each student; in effect, the adaptation creates a different niche for each. A second hypothesis, however, is that continuous adaptation may not be optimal in all contexts; Swanson's Tutor C got better results by fixing on HS and LS. In either case, a third hypothesis recognizes that the mix of components that defines HS or LS, or some point between, may differ for different students as well as different tasks; an affordance structure may rely on the presence or absence of imposed questions, segmentations, attention directions, and procedural or conceptual schemata, in various combinations with other components.

In short, all academic tasks are demanding in some ways – they carry certain component requirements that must be met to complete the task successfully. But academic tasks and treatments can be designed to remove demands that are unnecessary to reach instructional goals, and then to provide opportunities for persons to capitalize on their strengths and external supports and prosthetic devices to compensate for their weaknesses. Of course, the design can also include auxiliary tasks aimed at removing learner weaknesses directly by training on missing or problematic components. But direct training is difficult to accomplish successfully in the short term; because of individual differences among learners, it also requires adaptive task design itself, and thus a recycling through the same approach recommended above.

Some summary prospects

To sum up, abilities are affordances – properties of the union of person and environment that exhibit the opportunity structure of a situation and the effectivity structure of the person in taking advantage of the opportunities afforded for learning. Particular persons are tuned or prepared to perceive particular affordances in a situation that invite the particular actions they are able to assemble. But inabilities are also artifacts – properties of the interface between an inner personal environment and an outer situational environment. Ability differences are invisible when inner and outer environments are perfectly adapted to one another. When the outer environment is demanding, however, limiting properties of the inner environment show through at the interface, as ability differences. Instructional-treatment redesign seeks to circumvent these inner limiting properties by adapting the outer environment, or by changing the inner environment.

From the view of Simon's artifact design, future research on abilities in academic tasks requires a detailed analysis of the task and treatment-design features that seem mismatched to the person when limiting properties of the person show through in the performance interface. The analysis is geared to detect *inabilities* so as to *remove or circumvent* them in treatment redesign. From the view of Gibson's affordance theory, this future research requires a detailed analysis of the affordance–effectivity matches in different person–task unions. The analysis is geared to detect *abilities* so as to *capitalize* upon them in treatment redesign. *The two views are complementary because the most successful instructional tasks and treatments will be those that both capitalize on strengths and compensate for weaknesses,* for each individual to be treated.

Thus, a new theory of intelligence needs to start with the proposition that abilities are situated. They are reflected in the tuning of particular persons to the particular demands and opportunities of a situation, and thus reside in the union of person in situation, not "in the mind" alone. The union is a two-way sampling of performance components and their assembly between person and situation, so ability is also distributed between person and situation; the situation contains some pieces of what the person needs or can use to accomplish a given task. But persons must be tuned to perceive and use these pieces, and also to supply needed pieces from their own learning histories. Some persons are prepared to perceive these affordances, to use the pieces provided by the situation, and to complement these with pieces they provide, but some are not. Among those who are so tuned, each may use and supply slightly different pieces; there is functional equivalence despite idiosyncracy. The result is that some persons succeed in learning in a given situation; they are in *harmony* with it. Others do not, because they are not tuned to use the opportunities the situation provides or to produce what it demands.

Persons assemble their performances in response to these perceived affordances from residual networks of potential response components. As a function of individual learning history, parts of these networks may be tightly coupled and triggered as units automatically when familiar assemblies are needed, whereas other parts may be loosely coupled and easily disconnected when triggered, when novel combinations are needed. Persons also control and adapt these component assemblies as affordances change in a dynamic situation. In a comparison of any two persons, some components and assemblies will be held in common and some will not. The connections among components will differ in strength. The assembly and control history of these components and assemblies will also differ from person to person, and so will their facility for adaptive assembly and control during performance in a present situation. Thus, except in trivial instances, unitary sources of individual difference variance will not be found; i.e., tests and tasks will not be univocal.

In this view, valid ability measures are situations that evoke some semblance of the sample of components and assemblies and their adaptations that are also evoked by academic tasks to which the ability measures are therefore correlated. The predictor and criterion performance situations involve affordances that are invariant across these situations; that is, the samples drawn by the two situations overlap substantially, so transfer occurs. The size of the correlation suggests how large is the overlap. However, since ability tests and academic learning tasks and treatments do not seem to overlap *primarily* in component networks, it would seem that future research should focus also on their shared assembly and control functions; that is, both applicational and aptitudinal transfer need attention.

There seems to be a performance assembly pathway, from activation in and retrieval from the person's bank of experience, to adaptation in the person–task interface, to action in the task and treatment situation. Performance is assembled and reassembled along this path to meet the characteristic affordance profile of the situation. An analysis of this profile with respect to familiarity–novelty, structure–completeness, and the use of special knowledge and skills will provide a picture of its cognitive ability requirements and opportunities for each person. But each person's residual networks contain not only bits and pieces of knowledge and skill but also wishes, wants, needs, goals, intentions, preferences, interests, attitudes, etc. These are also residual component networks to be triggered in whole or in part by situational affordances. In parallel with the performance assembly pathway, there may be a performance commitment pathway – from activation to action – that accounts for the appearance of conative and affective differences in association with cognitive differences, as well as situations. The operation of such aptitude complexes may also be describable in terms of assembly, control, sampling, and tuning processes in the person–situation interface (see Snow, 1989b). Future theory will have to reach integrated reciprocal and transactive accounts of cognitive, conative, and affective aptitude complexes in the treatment situations with which they have been associated in traditional ATI research.

References

Ackerman, P. (1989). Individual differences and skill acquisition. In P. L. Ackerman, R. J. Sternberg, & R. Glaser (Eds.), *Learning and individual differences* (pp. 164–217). New York: W. H. Freeman.

Allport, F. H. (1955). *Theories of perception and the concept of structure.* New York: Wiley.

Balke-Aurell, G. (1982). *Changes in ability as related to educational and occupational experience.* Goteborg, Sweden: Acta Universitatis Gothoburgensis.

Bereiter, C. (1990). Aspects of an educational learning theory. *Review of Educational Research, 60,* 603–624.

Broadbent, D. E. (1973). *In defense of empirical psychology.* London: Methuen.

Bruner, J. S. (1978). The role of dialogue in language acquisition. In A. Sinclair, R. J. Jarvell, & W. J. M. Levelt (Eds.), *The child's conception of language* (pp. 241–256). New York: Springer.

Brunswik, E. (1956). *Perception and the representative design of psychological experiments.* Berkeley, CA: University of California Press.

Carpenter, P. A., Just, M. A., & Shell, P. (1990). What one intelligence test measures: A theoretical account of the processing in the Raven Progressive Matrices Test. *Psychological Review, 97,* 404–431.

Carroll, J. B. (1980). Remarks on Sternberg's "Factor theories of intelligence are all right almost." *Educational Researcher, 9*(8), 14–18.

Carroll, J. B. (1989). Factor analysis since Spearman: Where do we stand? What do we know? In R. Kanfer, P. L. Ackerman, & R. Cudeck (Eds.), *Abilities, motivation, and methodology* (pp. 43–67). Hillsdale, NJ: Lawrence Erlbaum Associates.

Carroll, J. B. (1993). *Human cognitive abilities.* New York: Cambridge University Press.

Cronbach, L. J. (1957). The two disciplines of scientific psychology. *American Psychologist, 12,* 671–684.

Cronbach, L. J. (1968). Intelligence? Creativity? A parsimonious reinterpretation of the Wallach–Kogan data. *American Educational Research Journal, 5,* 491–511.

Cronbach, L. J. (1975). Beyond the two disciplines of scientific psychology. *American Psychologist, 30,* 116–127.

Cronbach, L. J. (1982). *Designing evaluations of educational and social programs.* San Francisco: Jossey-Bass.

Cronbach, L. J., & Snow, R. E. (1977). *Aptitudes and instructional methods: A handbook for research on interactions.* New York: Irvington.

Dance, K. A., & Neufeld, R. W. J. (1988). Aptitude-treatment interaction research in the clinical setting: A review of attempts to dispel the "patient uniformity" myth. *Psychological Bulletin, 104,* 192–213.

Demetriou, A., Efklides, A., & Platsidou, M. (in press). Experiential structuralism: A frame for unifying cognitive developmental theories. *Monographs of the Society for Research in Child Development.*

Dewey, J., & Bentley, A. F. (1949). *Knowing and the known.* Boston: Beacon.

Doyle, W. (1983). Academic work. *Review of Educational Research, 53,* 159–199.

d'Ydewalle, G. (1984). Motivational and information processing. Unpublished report, University of Leuven, Belgium.

Ekehammer, B. (1974). Interactionism in personality from a historical perspective. *Psychological Bulletin, 81,* 1026–1048.

Elshout, J. J. (1987). Problem solving and education. In DeCorte, E., Lodewijks, H., Parmentier, R., & Span, P. (Eds.), *Learning and instruction: European research in an international context,* Vol. 1 (pp. 259–273). Leuven, Belgium/Oxford, U.K.: Leuven University Press/Pergamon Press.

Embretson, S. E. (1985). Multicomponent latent trait models for test design. In S. E. Embretson (Ed.), *Test design: Developments in psychology and psychometrics* (pp. 195–218). New York: Academic Press.

Endler, N., & Magnusson, D. (Eds.) (1976). *Interactional psychology and personality.* Washington, DC: Hemisphere.

Ferguson, G. A. (1954). On learning and human ability. *Canadian Journal of Psychology, 8,* 95–112.

Ferguson, G. A. (1956). On transfer and the abilities of man. *Canadian Journal of Psychology, 10,* 121–131.

Frederikson, N. (1972). Toward a taxonomy of situations. *American Psychologist, 27,* 114–123.

Gage, N. L. (Ed.) (1963). *Handbook of research on teaching.* Chicago: Rand McNally.

Gagne, R. M., Briggs, L. J., & Wager, W. W. (1988). *Principles of instructional design.* New York: Holt, Rinehart and Winston.

Gardner, H. (1983). *Frames of mind: The theory of multiple intelligences.* New York: Basic Books.

Gibson, J. J. (1966). *The senses considered as perceptual systems.* Boston: Houghton Mifflin.

Gibson, J. J. (1979). *The ecological approach to visual perception.* Boston: Houghton Mifflin.

Glaser, R., & Bassok, M. (1989). Learning theory and the study of instruction. *Annual Review of Psychology, 40,* 631–666.

Greeno, J. G. (1989). Situations, mental models, and generative knowledge. In D. Klahr & K. Kotovsky (Eds.), *Complex information processing: The impact of Herbert A. Simon* (pp. 285–318). Hillsdale, NJ: Lawrence Erlbaum Associates.

Greeno, J. G., & Simon, H. A. (1988). Problem solving and reasoning. In R. C. Atkinson, R. Herrnstein, G. Lindzey, & R. D. Luce (Eds.), *Stevens' handbook of experimental psychology* (rev. ed., pp. 589–672). New York: John Wiley & Sons.

Greeno, J. G., Smith, D. R., & Moore, J. L. (1992). Transfer of situated learning. In Detterman, D., & Sternberg, R. (Eds.), *Transfer on trial.* In press.

Gustafsson, J. E. (1984). A unifying model for the structure of intellectual abilities. *Intelligence, 8,* 179–203.

Gustafsson, J. E. (1988). Hierarchical models of the structure of cognitive abilities. In R. J. Sternberg (Ed.), *Advances in the psychology of human intelligence* (Vol. 4, pp. 35–71). Hillsdale, NJ: Lawrence Erlbaum Associates.

Gustafsson, J. E. (1989). Broad and narrow abilities in research on learning and instruction. In R. Kanfer, P. L. Ackerman, & R. Cudeck (Eds.), *Abilities, motivation, and methodology* (pp. 203–237). Hillsdale, NJ: Lawrence Erlbaum Associates.

Gustafsson, J. E., Demetriou, A., & Efklides, A. (1989). Organization of cognitive abilities: Training effects. Paper presented at the European Association for Research on Learning and Instruction, Madrid, Spain, September 4–7.

Guttman, L. (1970). Integration of test design and analysis. In *Proceedings of the 1969 conference on testing problems.* Princeton, NJ: Educational Testing Service.

Hall, R. H., Dansereau, D. F., & Skaggs, L. P. (1990). The cooperative learner. *Learning and Individual Differences, 2,* 327–36.

Hall, V. C., & Edmondson, B. (1992). Relative importance of aptitude and prior domain knowledge on immediate and delayed post tests. *Journal of Educational Psychology, 84,* 219–223.

Hampson, S. E. (1982). *The construction of personality: An introduction.* London: Routledge & Kegan Paul.

Hampson, S. E. (1984). The social construction of personality. In H. Bonarius, G. Van Heck, & N. Smid (Eds.), *Personality psychology in Europe* (pp. 3–14). Lisse, Netherlands: Swets & Zeitlinger.

Hanks, W. F. (1991), Foreword. In Lave, J., & Wenger, E., *Situated learning,* (pp. 13–24). New York: Cambridge University Press.

Heckhausen, H., Schmalt, H-D., & Schneider, K. (1985). *Achievement motivation in perspective.* Orlando, FL: Academic Press.

Helson, H. (1964). *Adaptation level theory.* New York: Harper and Row.

Hettema, P. J. (1979). *Personality and adaptation.* Amsterdam, Netherlands: North-Holland.

Hettema, P. J. (Ed.) (1989). *Personality and environment.* Chichester, UK: Wiley.

Hilgard, E. R. (1980). The trilogy of mind: Cognition, affection, and conation. *Journal of the History of the Behavioral Sciences, 16,* 107–117.

Hoefert, H-W. (Ed.) (1982). *Person und situation: Interaktionpsychologische untersuchungen.* Gottingen: Verlag für Psychologie-Dr. D. J. Hogrefe.

Horn, J. L. (1989). Cognitive diversity: A framework of learning. In P. L. Ackerman, R. J. Sternberg, & R. Glaser (Eds.), *Learning and individual differences* (pp. 61–116). New York: W. H. Freeman.

Ittelson, W. H., & Cantril, H. (1954). *Perception, a transactional approach.* Garden City, NY: Doubleday.

Kantor, J. R. (1924). *Principles of psychology*, Vols. 1–2. New York: Knopf.

Kyllonen, P. C., Lohman, D. F., & Woltz, D. J. (1984). Componential modeling of alternative strategies for performing spatial tasks. *Journal of Educational Psychology, 76*, 1325–1345.

Kyllonen, P. C., & Shute, V. J. (1989). A taxonomy of learning skills. In P. L. Ackerman, R. J. Sternberg, & R. Glaser (Eds.), *Learning and individual differences* (pp. 117–163). New York: W. H. Freeman.

Lantermann, E. D. (1980). *Interaktionen – person, situation und handlung*. München: Urban und Schwarzenberg.

Lave, J., & Wenger, E. (1991). *Situated learning*. New York: Cambridge University Press.

Lazarus, R. S., & Launier, R. (1978). Stress-related transactions between person and environment. In L. A. Pervin & M. Lewis (Eds.), *Perspectives in interactional psychology* (pp. 287–327). New York: Plenum.

Lewin, K. (1936). *Principles of topological psychology*. New York: McGraw-Hill.

Lohman, D. F. (1986). Predicting mathemathanic effects in the teaching of higher-order thinking skills. *Educational Psychologist, 21*, 191–208.

Lohman, D. F. (1988). Spatial abilities as traits, processes, and knowledge. In R. J. Sternberg (Ed.), *Advances in the psychology of human intelligence* (Vol. 4, pp. 181–248). Hillsdale, NJ: Lawrence Erlbaum Associates.

Lohman, D. F. (1989). Human intelligence: An introduction to advances in theory and research. *Review of Educational Research, 59*, 333–373.

Magnusson, D., & Allen, V. L. (Eds.) (1983). *Human development: An interactional perspective*. New York: Academic Press.

Magnusson, D., & Endler, N. S. (Eds.) (1977). *Personality at the crossroads: Current issues in interactional psychology*. Hillsdale, NJ: Lawrence Erlbaum Associates.

Marton, F., Hounsell, D. S., & Entwistle, N. J. (1984). *The experience of learning*. Edinburgh: Scottish Academic Press.

Mayer, R. E. (Ed.) (1988). *Teaching and learning computer programming*. Hillsdale, NJ: Lawrence Erlbaum Associates.

Melton, A. W. (Ed.) (1964). *Categories of human learning*. New York: Academic Press.

Mischel, W. (1973). Toward a cognitive social learning reconceptualization of personality. *Psychological Review, 80*, 252–283.

Mischel, W. (1984). Convergences and challenges in the search for consistency. *American Psychologist, 39*, 351–364.

Moos, R. H. (1979). *Evaluating educational environments*. San Francisco: Jossey-Bass.

Murray, H. A. (1938). *Explorations in personality*. New York: Oxford University Press.

Nygaard, R. (1977). *Personality, situation, and persistence*. Oslo: Universitetsforlaget.

Pace, C. R., & Stern, G. G. (1958). An approach to the measurement of psychological characteristics of college environments. *Journal of Educational Psychology, 49*, 269–277.

Pea, R. D. (1990). *Distributed intelligence and education*. Paper presented at the meeting of the American Educational Research Association, Boston, MA, April.

Pellegrino, J. W., & Glaser, R. (1982). Analyzing aptitudes for learning: Inductive reasoning. In R. Glaser (Ed.), *Advances in instructional psychology: Vol. 2* (pp. 269–345). Hillsdale, NJ: Lawrence Erlbaum Associates.

Perkins, D. N. (1990). *Person plus: A distributed view of thinking and learning*. Paper presented at the meeting of the American Educational Research Association, Boston, MA, April.

Pervin, L. A., & Lewis, M. (1978). Overview of the internal–external issue. In L. A. Pervin & M. Lewis (Eds.), *Perspectives in interactional psychology* (pp. 1–22). New York: Plenum.

Phillips, D. C. (1987). *Philosophy, science, and social inquiry*. Oxford, U.K.: Pergamon Press.

Resnick, L. B., & Glaser, R. (1976). Problem solving and intelligence. In L. B. Resnick (Ed.), *The nature of intelligence* (pp. 205–230). Hillsdale, NJ: Lawrence Erlbaum Associates.

Rhetts, J. E. (1972). Attribute–treatment interactions and individualized instruction: A conceptual framework and an example from Project PLAN. In L. Sperry (Ed.), *Learning performance and individual differences* (pp. 269–285). Glenview, IL: Scott Foresman.

Rhetts, J. E. (1974). Task, learning, and treatment variables in instructional design. *Journal of Educational Psychology, 66*, 339–347.

Riegel, K. F., & Meacham, J. A. (1978). Dialectics, transaction, and Piaget's theory. In L. A. Pervin & M. Lewis (Eds.), *Perspectives in interactional psychology* (pp. 23–47). New York: Plenum.

Ryan, T. A. (1981). Intention and kinds of learning. In G. d'Ydewalle & W. Lens (Eds.), *Cognition in human motivation and learning* (pp. 59–85). Leuven, Belgium/Hillsdale, N.J.: Leuven University Press/Lawrence Erlbaum Associates.

Salomon, G. (1990). *If intelligence is distributed, what about the cultivation of individuals' abilities?* Paper presented at the meeting of the American Educational Research Association, Boston, MA, April.

Schneider, W., & Weinert, F. E. (Eds.) (1990). *Interactions among aptitudes, strategies, and knowledge in cognitive performance.* New York: Springer-Verlag.

Simon, H. A. (1969). *The sciences of the artificial.* Cambridge, MA: M.I.T. Press.

Snow, R. E. (1963). *The importance of selected audience and film characteristics as determiners of the effectiveness of instructional films.* Lafayette, IN: Audio Visual Center, Purdue University.

Snow, R. E. (1974). Representative and quasi-representative designs for research on teaching. *Review of Educational Research, 44,* 265–292.

Snow, R. E. (1977). Research on aptitudes: A progress report. In L. S. Shulman (Ed.), *Review of research in education,* Vol. 4 (pp. 50–105). Itasca, IL: Peacock.

Snow, R. E. (1978). Theory and method for research on aptitude processes. *Intelligence, 2,* 225–278.

Snow, R. E. (1981). Toward a theory of aptitude for learning: Fluid and crystallized abilities and their correlates. In M. P. Friedman, J. P. Das, & N. O'Connor (Eds.), *Intelligence and learning* (pp. 345–362). New York: Plenum.

Snow, R. E. (1982). Education and intelligence. In R. J. Sternberg (Ed.), *Handbook of human intelligence* (pp. 493–585). Cambridge: Cambridge University Press.

Snow, R. E. (1987). Aptitude complexes. In R. E. Snow & M. J. Farr (Eds.), *Aptitude, learning, and instruction,* Vol. 3: *Conative and affective process analyses* (pp. 13–59). Hillsdale, NJ: Lawrence Erlbaum Associates.

Snow, R. E. (1989a). Aptitude–treatment interaction as a framework of research in individual differences in learning. In P. L. Ackerman, R. J. Sternberg, & R. Glaser (Eds.), *Learning and individual differences* (pp. 11–34). New York: W. H. Freeman.

Snow, R. E. (1989b). Cognitive–conative aptitude interactions in learning. In R. Kanfer, P. L. Ackerman, & R. Cudeck (Eds.), *Abilities, motivation, and methodology* (pp. 435–474). Hillsdale, NJ: Lawrence Erlbaum Associates.

Snow, R. E. (1990). New approaches to cognitive and conative assessment in education. *International Journal of Educational Research, 14,* 455–473.

Snow, R. E. (1991a). Aptitude–treatment interaction as a framework for research on individual differences in psychotherapy. *Journal of Consulting and Clinical Psychology, 59,* 205–216.

Snow, R. E. (1991b). The concept of aptitude. In R. E. Snow & D. F. Wiley (Eds.), *Improving inquiry in social science* (pp. 249–284). Hillsdale, NJ: Lawrence Erlbaum Associates.

Snow, R. E. (1992). Aptitude theory: Yesterday, today, and tomorrow. *Educational Psychologist, 27,* 5–32.

Snow, R. E. (in press). A person–situation interaction theory of intelligence. In A. Demetriou & A. Efklides (Eds.), *Intelligence, mind, and reasoning: Structure and development.* New York: Elsevier.

Snow, R. E., Kyllonen, P. C., & Marshalek, B. (1984). The topography of ability and learning correlations. In R. J. Sternberg (Ed.), *Advances in the psychology of human intelligence* (Vol. 2, pp. 47–104). Hillsdale, NJ: Lawrence Erlbaum Associates.

Snow, R. E., & Lohman, D. F. (1984). Toward a theory of cognitive aptitude for learning from instruction. *Journal of Educational Psychology, 76,* 347–376.

Snow, R. E., & Lohman, D. F. (1989). Implications of cognitive psychology for educational measurement. In R. L. Linn (Ed.), *Educational Measurement* (3rd ed., pp. 263–331). New York: Macmillan.

Snow, R. E., & Swanson, J. (1992). Instructional psychology: Aptitude, adaptation, and assessment. *Annual Review of Psychology, 43,* 583–626.

Sternberg, R. J. (1977). *Intelligence, information processing, and analogical reasoning: The componential analysis of human abilities.* Hillsdale, NJ: Lawrence Erlbaum Associates.

Sternberg, R. J. (1980). Factor theories of intelligence are all right almost. *Educational Researcher, 9*(8), 6–13, 18.

Sternberg, R. J. (1985). *Beyond IQ: A triarchic theory of human intelligence.* Cambridge, U.K.: Cambridge University Press.

Sternberg, R. J. (1987). The psychology of verbal comprehension. In R. Glaser (Ed.), *Advances in instructional psychology* (Vol. 3, pp. 97–151). Hillsdale, NJ: Erlbaum.

Sternberg, R. J., & Lubart, T. I. (1991). An investment theory of creativity and its development. *Human Development, 34,* 1–31.

Sternberg, R. J., & Wagner, R. K. (Eds.) (1986). *Practical intelligence.* New York: Cambridge University Press.

Swanson, J. (1990). One-to-one instruction: An experimental evaluation of effective tutorial strategies. Unpublished doctoral dissertation, Stanford University.

Thurstone, L. L. (1938). Primary mental abilities. *Psychometric Monographs,* No. 1.

Tobias, S. (1969). Research strategy in the effect of individual differences on achievement from programmed instruction. Paper presented to the American Psychological Association. Washington, D.C., April.

Tolman, E. C. (1951). A psychological model. In T. Parsons & E. A. Shils (Eds.), *Toward a general theory of action.* Cambridge, MA: Harvard University Press.

Tsai, Shu-Er (1992). Schema induction and individual differences in introductory programming learning: Program representation and problem solution. Unpublished doctoral dissertation, Stanford University.

Vernon, P. E. (1950). *The structure of human abilities.* London: Methuen.

Vygotsky, L. S. (1978). *Mind in society: The development of higher psychological processes.* Cambridge, MA: Harvard University Press.

Wachs, T. D., & Plomin, R. (Eds.) (1991). *Conceptualizations and measurement of organism-environment interaction.* Washington, D.C.: American Psychological Association.

Webb, N. M. (1982). Student interaction and learning in small groups. *Review of Educational Research, 52,* 421–445.

Webb, N. M. (1989). Peer interaction and learning in small groups. *International Journal of Educational Research, 13,* 21–39.

Wood, D. J. (1980). Teaching the young child: Some relationships between social interaction, language, and thought. In D. R. Olson (Ed.), *The social foundation of language and thought* (pp. 280–296). New York: W. W. Norton.

2   Novelty and intelligence

Michael K. Gardner and Robert J. Sternberg

People are constantly faced with new and different situations. Some of these situations are fairly mundane, such as figuring out where to get your clothes dry cleaned while your regular dry cleaner is on summer vacation. Others are quite dramatic, such as the recent changes in the political and economic institutions of eastern Europe and the former Soviet Union. Individuals who once felt secure in their jobs under Communism now find that this security has evaporated. These people must learn new skills (e.g., entrepreneurship) and adjust to the rapid pace of change if they are to survive. In short, they must deal with novelty.

How can we define novelty for purposes of our discussion? Situations and problems are novel to the degree that they are unfamiliar. This unfamiliarity requires solutions that cannot be simply retrieved from memory, as a response associated with a stimulus is retrieved. Instead, novel problems must be solved either by creating a completely new solution from existing mental resources (i.e., processes and data), or by finding an analogy between the existing novel situation and relevant past experience (e.g., Raaheim, 1974). Novelty requires the individual to make sense out of a situation that is on the face of it not sensible, that is, not explicitly related to information stored within the database of the individual's experience. Novelty is a function of a person–task interaction. What is novel for one person may not be for another. Moreover, even changing the context in which a familiar task is presented may increase its novelty, or vice versa.

The example of changes in eastern Europe and the Soviet Union may seem the exception rather than the rule. Except for novelty of the mundane sort, it may seem that we live in a relatively stable world. We would argue this is not the case. For instance, Alvin Toffler (1971), in his book *Future Shock,* contends that not only is change inevitable, but that the pace of change is accelerating, and that this is forcing people to deal with ever greater amounts of novelty. While dealing with novelty can lead to psychological stress (as Toffler points out), it can also differentiate people along a continuum. Some people function well in novel environments, while others fare less well. Consistent with this notion, we believe that the ability to deal effectively with novelty is directly linked to intellectual ability.

Why is the ability to cope with novelty related to intelligence? There are many potential answers. One possibility (primarily psychometric in nature) is that novel testing environments reduce differences between test takes due to prior learning. This means that test takers enter the testing situation on a more nearly equal footing. This leads to a technically better test of intelligence. Another possibility (from information-processing psychology) is that novel situations place greater demands on strategy selection and planning processes, and that these processes are centrally involved in intelligent behavior. A third possibility (from developmental psychology) is that the ability to adapt to novel situations is related to the ability to create new mental schemes to handle this novelty. The more mental schemes an individual possesses, and the more differentiated and integrated the structure of these schemes, the more intelligent the individual. There are other possible answers as well.

In this chapter, we look at the role of novelty in intelligence and its assessment. We will consider four different approaches to intelligence: the psychometric approach, information-processing approaches, the development perspective, and the contextual approach. As we consider each approach, we will review literature that bears on the relationship between novelty and intelligence. Most approaches agree that novel contexts are good settings for individuals to display intelligence of one sort or another, and all have something to say about the relationship between novelty and intelligence.

Novelty and the psychometric approach to intelligence

Definition of the approach

Psychometrics has attempted to understand intelligence by studying individual differences in human performance. The performance is usually on tests that require intellect (as judged by experts) for their successful completion. Performance on one test can be related to performance on other tests, and it is possible to isolate those dimensions of performance that are common across tasks (through techniques such as factor analysis). These dimensions (or, in many cases, a single dimension known as *g* or general intelligence) are seen either as the underlying causes of intelligence or as convenient yardsticks for measuring intelligence.

Intelligence, psychometric theories, and rule induction items

Despite the fact that we believe that novelty and intelligence are intimately related, we do not believe that all novel situations are equally good as measures of intelligence. Situations that require some intermediate amount of novelty are best (see also Raaheim, 1974). These situations require the individual to forge a link between what is novel or new in the current situation and past experience. They cause the storehouse of knowledge to grow, and they allow the individual to interrelate concepts in new and potentially useful ways.

Some situations contain too much novelty, however. In these cases the individual cannot find any relationship between the current situation and past experience. Such situations are clearly novel, but they are poor measures of intelligence, because the person involved cannot make use of her/his previous knowledge in solving the problem. While such situations are poor measures of intelligence, they may be good measures of creativity, in that they require a completely unique approach for their solution.

Situations involving too little novelty (e.g., recognizing a previously presented item on a memory test) are also poor measures of intelligence. As with situations containing too much novelty, these situations do not allow the individual to exploit his/her knowledge base of information and strategies. Individuals of high and low intellect solve these problems in much the same way, and, therefore, there is little variance in performance to relate to intelligence.

Given our earlier definition of novelty, then, what tasks might be seen as both novel and also related to intelligence? It would be those tasks that require the individual to make sense out of what is initially not sensible – those tasks that require the individual to find relationships to past experience and apply this new knowledge. The prime example of such tasks are induction items. These tasks require reasoning from part to whole or from particular to general (*Webster's New Collegiate Dictionary*, 1976). Pellegrino and Glaser (1980) have noted that a particular class of induction item is commonly found on tests of intelligence. They refer to these as rule-induction items. These include analogies, matrix problems, series-extrapolation problems, and classifications.

Novelty can arise from either or both of two sources: novelty of the component mental operations, and novelty of the content of the problems. These sources correspond to the categories of process and data. Most individuals find rule-induction items novel from the point of view of process. With the exception of the academic elite, few people spend much time analyzing sets of objects for the rules that relate them. The data or content involved in such items can also be novel. For example, analogies composed of abstract geometric figures involve novelty from the point of view of content as well as process.

Rule-induction problems have a long history in psychometrics. Analogy items first appeared simultaneously in Woodworth and Wells' (1911) Mixed Relations test (in the United States) and in Burt's (1911) Completing Analogies test (in England) (Pellegrino, 1985). Raven's (1938) Progressive Matrices is composed entirely of figural matrix problems. Table 2.1 lists a number of currently popular tests and which, if any, rule induction item types they contain. As can be seen from the table, most tests of intelligence or general academic aptitude contain at least one type of rule-induction problem. It can also be seen that group tests of intelligence are more likely to contain these items than individual tests or college entry exams. Individual tests have other items that measure performance in novel environments (e.g., Block Design and Digit Symbol on the Wechsler Adult Intelligence Scale–Revised [WAIS-R]), while college entry exams tend to be more verbally loaded, and thus more similar to achievement tests.

Psychometric theorists have had differing explanations for the centrality of novelty. Spearman (1923, 1927) saw intelligence as deriving from two different types of

Table 2.1. Rule induction items contained on various tests of intelligence and general academic ability

Test	Item types				
	Verbal analogies	Figural analogies	Matrix problems	Series completion	Classifications problems
Individual tests					
Stanford–Binet (4th Ed.)			X	X	
Wechsler Intelligence Scale for Children-III					
Wechsler Adult Intelligence Scale–Revised					
Kaufman Assessment Battery for Children			X		
Differential Ability Scales			X		
Group tests					
Culture Fair Intelligence Test (IPAT)			X	X	X
Henmon–Nelson Tests of Mental Ability		X			
Kuhlman–Anderson Test	X			X	
Lorge–Thorndike Intelligence Tests		X		X	X
Otis–Lennon School Ability Test		X			X
Progressive Matrices			X		
Cognitive Abilities Test	X	X		X	X
Differential Aptitude Tests	X			X	
College entry tests					
Scholastic Aptitude Test	X				
Miller Analogies Test	X				

factors (based on factor analysis): *g,* a general factor pervading all tasks requiring intelligence, and *s*'s or specific factors, each of which explained performance on a single task. Clearly, Spearman's interest was centered on *g,* since it was general across the entire domain of intelligent tasks. Returning to rule-induction items, Spearman felt analogies were particularly good measures of *g* because they tapped the education of relations and the education of correlates, two of his three basic principles of cognition (Gardner and Clark, 1992). His third principle, the apprehension of experience (somewhat similar to the information-processing notion of encoding) is almost certainly also tapped by analogies.

Thurstone (1931, 1938, 1947) disagreed with Spearman about the existence of a single, general factor underlying all intelligence. Instead, Thurstone believed in several co-equal factors that he termed "primary mental abilities." The primary mental abilities (cited in Cronbach, 1970) were as follows: Verbal, Number, Spatial, Memory, Inductive Reasoning, Deductive Reasoning, Word Fluency, and Perceptual Speed. Tests of rule induction, such as block design, loaded on both Inductive Reasoning and Spatial factors. Thus, novelty was related to induction in Thurstone's theory of intelligence, with some smaller degree of relationship to spatial ability (this being due to a confounding of novelty with item-content variance).

Horn and Cattell (1966; Cattell, 1963; 1971) have extended Thurstone's primary mental abilities theory into a hierarchical model with two general intelligences displayed at the second level in the hierarchy. They begin by factor analyzing a very wide range of tests into a set of primary mental abilities. These abilities, which are themselves correlated, are then factor analyzed to produce second-order factors. Two of these factors are labeled fluid ability, which represents the organism's basic biological ability to learn, and crystallized ability, which represents the products of acculturation and education – i.e., acquired knowledge. Novelty plays a role in the measurement of fluid ability, but not crystallized ability. Horn and Cattell (1966) state:

... fluid intelligence will represent processes of reasoning in the immediate situation in tasks requiring abstracting, concept formation, and attainment, and the perception and eduction of relations. It will be measured most purely when task materials are culture fair; that is, the fundaments are either novel for all persons being measured or else extremely common, overlearned elements of a culture ... (p. 255)

The first-order factors that load on fluid ability include those involving figural reasoning (i.e., Cognition of Figural Relation, measured by tests such as figure series and matrices), symbolic reasoning (i.e., Induction, measured by letter classifications and number series; Intellectual Level, measured by series problems; and Intellectual Speed, also measured by series problems), and semantic reasoning tasks (i.e., Cognition of Semantic Relations, measured by verbal analogies; Formal Reasoning, measured by deduction problems; and General Reasoning, measured by problem-solving items). The prominence of novel rule-induction problems is evident from the preceding list.

Consonant with the description of fluid ability given by Horn and Cattell above, Cattell (1973) developed the Culture Fair Intelligence Test, which relies almost exclusively on novel items (see Table 2.1) with novel content (i.e., abstract figural). This test correlates highly with other intelligence tests involving novel items, as one might expect (e.g., Wrightstone [1958] found a correlation of .51 between Scale 2 of the Culture Fair and Raven's Progressive Matrices), but it also correlates substantially with intelligence tests that are more heterogeneous (e.g., Downing, Edgar, Harris, Kornberg, & Storen [1965] found correlations of .72, .62, and .63 between the Culture Fair and Wechsler Intelligence Scale for Children [WISC] full-scale IQ, verbal IQ, and performance IQ, respectively). This mitigates to some degree against the criticism that novel tests are simply measuring spatial ability or visualization, rather than intellect.

Guttman (1954, 1965, 1970) proposed a theory of intelligence termed the "radex" theory. According to Guttman, tests can be classified in two separate ways (Brody, 1992). First, tests can be ordered according to their complexity. Such an ordering is linear, and results in a simple rank ordering. Second, tests can be ordered according to their content. This ordering is more similar to one of family resemblance, and results in a circular ordering, such that similar contents are adjacent to one another on the circumference of a circle. When these two orderings are combined, a radex results. Tests can be embedded in a circular space with highly complex and intellectually taxing tests near the center of the space and less complex tests located near the periphery. Actual placement of tests with respect to position along the circumference of the circular space is dictated by their content (i.e., numeric, figural, or verbal).

Snow, Marshalek, and their colleagues (Marshalek, Lohman, & Snow, 1983; Snow, Kyllonen, & Marshalek, 1984) have been able to empirically verify Guttman's theory by multidimensionally scaling ability test data. Figure 2.1 presents an idealization of the analyses of several psychometric batteries. In their analyses, tests con-

Figure 2.1. An idealization of the analyses of several psychometric batteries using the radex model. Content differences are represented by position around the circumference of the circle. Complexity or *g*-saturation is represented by distance along the radius from the center of the circle, with the center being the most highly *g*-saturated point. Reprinted by permission from R. E. Snow, P. C. Kyllonen, and B. Marshalek, 1984, The topography of ability and learning correlations. In R. J. Sternberg (Ed.), *Advances in the psychology of human intelligence* [p. 92]. Hillsdale, NJ: Lawrence Erlbaum.

taining novel rule-induction items are consistently found near the center of the radex space. That is, rule-induction items are consistently shown as being highly complex and g saturated, almost regardless of content (near the center of the radex content differences have less effect on spatial placement of a test). Interestingly, when Snow, Kyllonen, and Marshalek (1984) superimposed a clustering of Thurstone's primary mental abilities on their multidimensional scaling results, the Induction factor was centrally located in the radex space.

The final psychometric theory we consider is the structure of intellect (SI) model of J. P. Guilford (1967, 1977, 1985; Guilford & Hoepfner, 1971). Guilford proposed that any given ability could be conceived of as the combination of three independent dimensions: mental operations, stimulus content, and form of product being processed. The SI model is usually presented pictorially as a cube, with each of three dimensions forming an edge of the cube. Guilford's theory originally allowed for five mental operations (cognition [denoted C], memory [M], divergent production [D], convergent production [N], and evaluation [E]), four stimulus contents (figural [denoted F], symbolic [S], semantic [M], and behavioral [B]), and six forms of product (units [denoted U], classes [C], relations [R], systems [S], transformations [T], and implications [I]). Because the dimension are independent, they combine to form 120 separate (uncorrelated) abilities.

Much of Guilford's career was spent attempting to find marker tests for each of the many postulated abilities. By the time of his retirement, tests had been found for nearly 100 of the 120 abilities. Not surprisingly, tests consisting of novel rule-induction problems found their way into the structure of intellect model. For instance, Guilford and Hoepfner (1971) note that certain aspects of reasoning should be related to Cognition of Symbolic Systems (CSS), Cognition of Figural Relations (CFR), Cognition of Semantic Relations (CMR), Convergent Production of Figural Transformations (NFT), and Convergent Production of Figural Relations (NFR), among other SI factors. The marker tests were as follows: (a) CSS: Circle Reasoning, which involves inducing a pattern among circles and dashes, and Letter Triangle, which involves completing a letter series arranged in a triangular pattern; (b) CFR: Figure Matrix: a set of nonverbal matrix problems; (c) CMR: Verbal Analogies and Word Matrix; (d) NFT: Hidden Figures: finding a geometric figure hidden within a larger obscuring context; and (e) NFR: Figure Analogies Completion. Thus reasoning, even as Guilford saw it within the SI framework, was still related to novel tests of rule induction.

It should be noted that Guilford's SI model has been criticized on numerous grounds (see Brody, 1992, and Brody and Brody, 1976, for critical reviews). First, his model ignores the well known finding of a positive manifold among intellectual tests (that is, almost all tests requiring intellect positively correlate with one another). Second, he uses procrustean rotation techniques to rotate his factor-analytic solution to maximal congruence with his theory; most researchers prefer the so-called objective-rotation techniques such as varimax. Finally, many of his individual SI factors have little, if any, predictive validity (though this is not true of the reasoning factors mentioned above). Later in his career (Guilford, 1977, 1985) Guilford made several modifications to his SI theory in an attempt to bring it more in line with empirical data. He allowed his individual factors to correlate, and suggested that the more dimensions two factors had in common (e.g., CFU and CFC versus CFU and CMC), the more they should correlate. Further, he subdivided the figural content category into auditory and visual content categories. This increased the number of factors to 150. Still, the completely orthogonal model of 120 separate abilities represented in a cube is what most researchers remember as Guilford's contribution to the psychometric abilities literature.

Summary. In the preceding section we have argued that a novel class of items known as rule-induction problems are found on many tests of intelligence (especially group tests). These items have also had a central place in many psychometric theories of intelligence. We would argue that the fact that rule-induction items are moderately novel (both in type of task and usually in task content) contributes to their ability to measure intelligence. These items require the induction of rules, relationships, and correlates, and this, in turn, allows individuals to use their intelligence by relating what is new to what is known. This is done by making use of existing knowledge structures, and by the efficient allocation of cognitive resources (e.g., working memory and attention) through strategy selection and planning.

Novelty and cognitive styles

Another line of psychometric research has dealt with cognitive styles. Cognitive styles are somewhat difficult to define. Sometimes they are preferred ways of interacting with the environment, as when certain individuals prefer verbal materials over pictorial, while others prefer the reverse. Sometimes the preference is virtually obligatory; that is, the individual cannot choose to override the preferred way of responding. Researchers differ on whether some cognitive styles are actually "styles" or simply abilities (e.g., Cronbach, 1984, p. 266).

One cognitive style that deserves review because of the novel tasks used to assess it is field dependence/independence (Witkin, 1978; Witkin & Goodenough, 1981; Witkin, Goodenough, & Oltman, 1979). One way that it is assessed is through the Rod and Frame Test (RFT) (Witkin et al., 1954). The testee sits in a chair in a room that is dark except for a luminous frame and rod. The frame is positioned at an angle to true upright (say 30 degrees), and the chair the testee is seated in is also oriented at an angle to true upright. The subject must reorient the rod, by means of a remote control, to true upright while ignoring the context provided by the frame and the chair. A variant of this test, called the Body Adjustment Test (BAT), has the subject sit in a off-upright chair within a room that is itself positioned at an angle to true upright. The testee must reorient the chair to true upright.

From the results of these tests individuals can be sorted along a dimension of field dependence/independence (FDI; more recently subsumed under the more general heading of differentiation/nondifferentiation). Field-dependent individuals have trouble separating visual-environment cues from the internal cues they must use to correctly solve the RFT and BAT; therefore, they tend to misorient the rod or themselves. Field-independent individuals are better able to ignore the distracting visual cues and perform better on the RFT and BAT. These results might seem of limited interest (perhaps one would wish to select pilots on the basis of high field independence), except that they correlate with behavior in a number of other domains. Field-dependent individuals tend to use less active, "spectator" approaches to learning (Anastasi, 1988), they tend to have better social skills in dealing with others, and they tend to be worse at "cognitive restructuring" and fluid ability (Cronbach, 1984). Field-independent individuals have the opposite set of preferences and abilities.

Performance on the RFT and BAT correlates substantially with performance on the Embedded Figures Test (EFT) (Witkin, Oltman, Raskin, & Karp, 1971; see Cronbach, 1970, for a summary of the correlations). This test requires individuals to find a figure within a camouflaging background, and thus also requires one to ignore irrelevant visual information. Indeed, the EFT is now used as one of the means of assessing FDI.

Questions have begun to develop concerning the construct validity of FDI. Some researchers believe FDI is nothing more than renaming of the construct of spatial ability. In a careful study using maximum-likelihood analysis of covariance structures (Joreskog, 1970, 1971), MacLeod, Jackson, and Palmer (1986) found no difference between FDI, as indexed by the RFT and the EFT, and spatial ability, as indexed by a paper and pencil test of spatial relations and the Block Design subtest of the WAIS. Other researchers believe that FDI is nothing more than fluid ability (e.g., Vernon, 1973), which we have already indicated is heavily related to novel tasks such as rule induction. Cronbach (1984) makes this point when he points out the EFT is an excellent measure of fluid ability. We would probably agree more with Cronbach than MacLeod et al. concerning FDI. One of MacLeod et al.'s markers for spatial ability was Block Design, and this test clearly involves both novelty (few people engage in reproducing visual patterns with sets of blocks) and fluid ability (e.g., Cronbach (1970) categorizes it as a measure of analytic or "fluid" ability, p. 282). Thus, FDI and its many behavioral correlates may be another instantiation of the novel testing situations indexing intelligence (in the form of fluid ability).

Novelty and the information processing approach to intelligence

Definition of the approach

Information processing has attempted to understand intelligence by illuminating the processes that encode information, mentally transform it, and produce motor responses. This has been referred to as the "cognitive components" approach (Pellegrino and Glaser, 1979), because it attempts to discover which component processes underlie intelligent-task performance, and which of these components contribute to individual differences. Given that rule-induction problems form a class of novel items found to be related to intelligence, we begin by exploring research aimed at elucidating processing in these tasks.

Models of performance on rule induction problems

Analogies. Some of the earliest work on analogical reasoning has come from artificial intelligence. The best example of this work is a computer program by Evans (1968) that solved geometric analogies of the type found on intelligence tests. Evan's program contained three modules (Winston, 1977): (a) figure and transformation description; (b) rule matching; and (c) difference measurement. The first module decomposes the terms of the analogy into subpatterns and determines the transformations that relate the subpatterns in the first two terms, and as well as the transformations that relate the third term to each answer option (Pellegrino and Glaser, 1980). These transformations are then compared by the second module, using the third module to determine degree of difference between rules. The option whose transformation rule maximally matches the A to B transformation rule is chosen as the correct completion for the analogy.

Mulholland, Pellegrino, and Glaser (1980) examined human performance on geometric analogies from a perspective very similar to that of Evans (1968). They believed that the important elements in geometric-analogy solution were: (a) decomposition of complex analogy terms into constituent elements, and (b) identification and ordering of transformations that applied to each element (Pellegrino and Glaser, 1980). They had college students solve analogies that varied both in terms of the number of constituent elements and the number of transformations relating these elements. Their results indicated strong main effects for both number of elements and number of transformations. In addition, they found a significant interaction between number of elements and transformations. Pellegrino and Glaser (1980) explain the interaction in terms of memory-maintenance operations necessary when an analogy contains large numbers of elements and transformations.

Pellegrino and his colleagues (Alderton, Goldman, & Pellegrino, 1985; Ingram, Pellegrino, & Glaser, 1976; Pellegrino & Ingram, 1977) have also pursued work on verbal analogies. As an example of this work, Alderton, Pellegrino, & Glaser (1985) found support for a model requiring five processes: encoding, inference, application, confirmation, and justification. The first three of these processes were associated with the processing of the analogy stem (the A, B, and C terms), while the latter two were associated with the processing of the answer options. Correlations with forced-choice accuracy indicated that those processes concerned with the evaluation of answer options (i.e., confirmation and justification) were more strongly correlated with ability than those concerned with the processing of stem terms.

Sternberg and his associates (Sternberg, 1977a, 1977b, 1985; Sternberg & Gardner, 1983) have conducted a detailed analysis of the processing involved in solving analogies using a methodology called "componential analysis." Sternberg and Gardner (1983), for instance, studied analogical reasoning by the same subjects across three different content domains: schematic pictures, verbal content, and geometric/figural content. Their findings support a model containing five components: encoding, reasoning, comparison, justification (needed only in forced-choice situations), and response. The reasoning component was actually a combination of three components – inference, mapping, and application – verified in earlier experimental studies (e.g., Sternberg, 1977a, 1977b). Several component-speed measures (collapsed over content differences) showed significant correlations with a reasoning-factor score derived from traditional paper-and-pencil tests of reasoning (reasoning component with reasoning factor, $r = -.70$, $p < .01$; comparison component with reasoning factor, $r = -.61$, $p < .05$; and justification component with reasoning factor, $r = -.58$, $p < .05$).

The studies reviewed demonstrate that researchers are converging on a modal model of information processing in the realm of analogical reasoning. For example, the list of components identified by Sternberg and his colleagues shows considerable overlap with the list identified by Pellegrino and his colleagues. What is perhaps more important is that individual differences in intelligence are at least partially attributable to performance differences on these component processes. Thus, response to novelty, in the form of solving analogies, is related to intelligence through the speed and accuracy of the basic information processes that underlie analogical reasoning and, presumably, other measures of intelligence.

Series completions. As with analogies, early work on series completions came from the field of artificial intelligence. Simon and Kotovsky (1963; Kotovsky & Simon, 1973) developed a program that could solve letter-series items similar to those used by Thurstone and Thurstone (1941). Their program involved two basic steps: discovering the pattern and extrapolating the pattern (Simon, 1976). The first step could be further subdivided into: detecting interletter relations, discovering the periodicity, and completing the pattern description. The knowledge and memory requirements for Simon and Kotovsky's program were quite limited. The program assumed a knowledge of the alphabet, the reversed alphabet, the concepts of same (or equal) and next in a series, and the ability to produce a cyclical pattern. The memory requirement was the ability to keep track of two symbols simultaneously. The most able version of Simon and Kotovsky's (1963) program (variant D) performed quite well. It was able to solve 13 of the 15 series problems presented to it.

Kotovsky and Simon (1973) compared the performance of their program to the performance of college students on letter-series completions. They found substantial agreement between the program's performance and human data.

Holzman, Glaser, and Pellegrino (1976) used Kotovsky and Simon's work as the starting point for a training study involving first-through-sixth-grade children. Children were split into experimental and control groups, matched on the basis of a series-completion pretest by grade level. The experimental group received two hours of training on detecting interletter relations and discovering pattern periodicity. The control group received no such training. On a posttest, the experimental group showed a significant reduction in errors relative to the control group (32% versus 13%

reduction), although both groups showed improvement on posttest relative to pretest. In a second experiment, Holzman et al. showed that practice alone was sufficient to improve performance on letter-series problems among fifth graders. Third graders, however, did not benefit merely from practice. These subjects, presumably, would have benefitted from direct instruction on the underlying component processes. Holzman et al.'s study lends further support to the model of underlying processing involved in solving novel series-completion problems developed by Simon and Kotovsky (1963; Kotovsky & Simon, 1973), and demonstrates a relationship between performance (i.e., error rates) and training of individual processing components.

Sternberg and Gardner (1983) studied series-completion performance among adults in three different domains: schematic pictures, verbal content, and geometric/figural content. Their series items differed from the traditional Thurstone and Thurstone (1941) letter-series items in that their items did not involve periodic relationships. Instead, subjects would induce a relationship from three serially arranged stem items and then complete the series by applying this relationship to a new term. Sternberg and Gardner found support for a model containing five component processes – encoding, reasoning, comparison, justification (needed only in forced-choice situations), and response. Reasoning was estimated as the combination of two other components, inference and application. Several of the component-speed measures (collapsed over contents) correlated with a reasoning-factor score derived from traditional paper-and-pencil tests of reasoning (encoding component with reasoning factor, $r = -.51$, $p < .05$; reasoning component with reasoning factor, $r = -.50$, $p < .05$; and comparison component with reasoning factor, $r = -.66$, $p < .01$).

The work described above yields two models of task performance on novel series completion items. One model, based on the work of Simon and Kotovsky (1963), deals with the completion of traditional, periodic, letter-series items. The other, based on the work of Sternberg and Gardner (1983), deals with less traditional series-extrapolation items. Both models find relationships between ability, as demonstrated either through low error rates (Holzman et al., 1976) or fast latencies (Sternberg & Gardner, 1983), and the hypothesized underlying component processes. In the Holzman et al. study this relationship was demonstrated through direct training of the components, while in the Sternberg and Gardner study the relationship was demonstrated through correlational analysis. The point is that at least some of the variation in traditional (e.g., paper-and-pencil) tests of intellectual functioning can be attributed to differences in the speed and error rate of the individual information processes hypothesized to underlie processing in novel tasks such as series completion. These information processes are also assumed to underlie performance on traditional intellectual tests, but novel environments may be more likely to elicit individual differences in their efficiency than routine or crystallized situations.

Classifications. Classification processing has been less well investigated than the processing in either analogies or series completions. However, two of the studies described above investigated classification processing as part of larger investigations.

Alderton et al. (1985) found that their basic model of analogical reasoning (involving encoding, inference, application, confirmation, and justification) could also be applied to the solution of classification problems. However, while analogy items showed only positive effects for the processing of answer options (that is, processing answer options sometimes aided in finding a correct solution but didn't produce distraction errors), classification items showed both positive and negative effects for processing answer options. Furthermore, the positive and negative effects for processing answer options were significantly related to ability (measured by number correct on the classification task). These two influences far outweighed contributions due to inference and application (components involved in the processing of stem terms).

Sternberg and Gardner (1983) used a four-component model (i.e., encoding, reasoning, comparison, and response) similar to the model described earlier for analogy and series processing to model latency data from classification problems. The only changes from the earlier models were that "reasoning" was assumed to consist only of inference, and that justification was not included because it could not be reliably estimated. They applied this model to subjects' performance in three domains: schematic pictures, verbal content, and geometric/figural content. The model received good empirical support, and some of the underlying component processes (collapsed over contents) were related to a reasoning factor score derived from traditional paper-and-pencil tests of reasoning (reasoning component with reasoning factor, $r = -.64, p < .01$; and comparison component with reasoning factor, $r = -.67, p < .01$).

Both of the studies cited above are notable because they used task models that could be applied across more than a single rule-induction task. This gives hope that the relationship between novel rule-induction items and intelligence can be localized in one or many of the underlying processes common to all rule-induction tasks. Indeed, in Sternberg and Gardner's study it is possible to collapse over both content domains and rule-induction item types to get an estimate of the relationship between the reasoning factor score and each component. These correlations are as follows: encoding, $r = -.37$; n.s.; reasoning, $r = -.79, p < .001$; comparison, $r = -.75, p < .001$; and justification, $r = -.48, p < .05$. Thus, three of the four basic components (response was estimated as the regression constant, and was not included in the correlational analyses) were related to intelligence, and two of these relationships were .75 or over!

An argument is sometimes made that novelty in tasks is really nothing more than spatial/figural content. Support for this comes from the fact that several of the most novel tests (e.g., Raven's Progressive Matrices, figural analogies, and the Block Design subtest of the WAIS-R) have visual/figural content. Sternberg and Gardner (1983) presented data that showed that content differences do not exert a large influence on the relationship between the processes underlying rule-induction tasks and intelligence. These correlations are presented in Table 2.2. For the two components that showed a significant relationship with the reasoning factor in all three tasks, the correlation with reasoning did not differ by more than .09! This maximal difference corresponded to a difference in shared variance of approximately 12%

Table 2.2. Correlation of component latency scores with reasoning factor scores[a]

	Content domain		
Component	Schematic pictures	Verbal	Geometric/figural
Encoding	−.46	−.02	−.25
Reasoning	−.70**	−.61*	−.67*
Comparison	−.64*	−.66*	−.65*
Justification	—	−.29	−.37

[a]Adapted from: Sternberg, R. J., & Gardner, M. K. (1983). Unities in inductive reasoning. *Journal of Experimental Psychology: General, 112,* 80–116.
*$p < .01$
**$p < .001$

($-.70^2$ minus $-.61^2$). If spatial ability were truly the controlling construct, one would expect a much larger difference between spatial and verbal tasks. Such a difference should favor spatial tasks, with their component processes strongly related to psychometrically defined reasoning, while the component processes from verbal tasks should only show modest relationships.

This is not to say that novel figural content plays no role at all. An effect for spatial content is seen in the encoding component. Here the maximal difference in correlations with reasoning was .44, corresponding to a difference in shared variance of approximately 21% ($-.46^2$ minus $-.02^2$). However, this component did not significantly correlate with reasoning for any of the three contents. The point we wish to make is that while nonverbal content, such as geometric figures, can increase the relationship between performance on a task and intelligence, *the simple theory that novelty is nothing more than spatial content is clearly wrong.* We will return to this issue when we consider Sternberg's work on novelty in verbal tasks.

Matrix problems. As shown in Figure 2.1, the Raven's (1938, 1962; 1965) Progressive Matrices is one of the best tests of general intelligence. Each problem on the test consists of a 3 × 3 matrix of geometric/figural items. One of the items is missing, and the testee must extrapolate the patterns present in the rows and columns to choose the correct completion from among a set of alternative answers. The test has been popular as an assessment device for children, the elderly, and clinical populations, in part because it requires very little verbal skill.

Carpenter, Just, and Shell (1990) performed a task analysis of the Raven's Progressive Matrices, and then instantiated their task model as a computer simulation. In developing their model, they used data derived from eye movements and protocol analyses of subjects solving matrix items. Their model was comprised of three basic categories of operations: perceptual analysis, conceptual analysis, and response generation and selection. These processes also had access to a limited-capacity working memory, and a list of stimulus descriptions (since the computer program did not actually visually encode the stimuli).

During perceptual analysis, the stimulus was encoded, and a search was begun for correspondences among sets of elements in each row. Carpenter et al. point out that correspondence finding can be a significant source of error, since many rules are operating simultaneously and the correspondence of elements is not obvious. Once correspondence was established, the program performed pairwise comparison of elements. This determined whether adjacent elements differed with regard to their individual features. Such similarities and differences served as the basic data for the conceptual-analysis stage.

The conceptual-analysis stage induced rules relating elements from each of the three figures in each of the first two rows. The basic program (known as FAIRAVEN) knew four types of rules. A higher functioning version of the program (known as BETTERAVEN) incorporated five types of rules. In addition to inducing rules within a row, the program would also attempt to generalize these rules, by finding correspondences between elements in the first and second rows, and then representing the general rule with a variable rather than a particular figural element. Carpenter et al. point out that the type of rule induced contributes to item difficulty (i.e., some rules are more difficult than others), as well as the total number of rules operating.

Response generation and selection operated by applying the generalized form of the rules induced, using knowledge of correspondences found earlier to generate an ideal solution for the missing item. The program then searched for this answer among the options presented, settling on the best matching alternative.

As stated earlier, Carpenter et al. developed an average ability program (FAIR-AVEN) and a superior ability program (BETTERAVEN). What made BETTERAVEN better? First, BETTERAVEN had one additional rule that it could induce, which FAIRAVEN did not have. This can be viewed as additional knowledge – knowledge that transformed some situations that would have been novel for FAIRAVEN into nonnovel ones for BETTERAVEN.

Second, BETTERAVEN had an ability to find more abstract correspondences among elements. It would allow one entry in a row to have a null value, if this would make sense out of the distribution of items across a row. For instance, if entries in a row are termed A, B, and C, A might have no horizontal lines (null value), while B has one horizontal line, and C has two horizontal lines. FAIRAVEN could not see the rule here, since it does not allow null values. The ability to succeed in novel environments requires an ability to construct knowledge representations that make sense out of the novel stimuli, as BETTERAVEN did. Once such a knowledge representation is constructed, the stimuli are no longer novel (i.e., they fit a pattern).

This is part of the paradox of novelty. Novel environments are, in part, good measures of intelligence because people have no preexisting knowledge structures to rely on when processing information. Thus novel situations allow us to measure information-processing ability (as we have argued with rule-induction tasks, which are measures of fluid ability). However, intelligent people are good at building knowledge representations that make sense out of novel environments. This means that there are fewer environments that are novel for intelligent people. Thus, intelligence is related to the sum of stored knowledge, or crystallized ability. Crystallized ability is an indirect measure of the ability to cope successfully with novelty; it is a measure of the number of previously novel situations that have been successfully mastered. This position is consistent with Horn and Cattell's fluid/crystallized ability theory presented earlier.

Third, BETTERAVEN exercised more direct strategic control over its processes through a new category of processes that monitored goals. The goal monitor forced BETTERAVEN to induce rules serially. This prevented conflicts among the rules induced, and allowed the program to better monitor its progress toward satisfying its goals. As BETTERAVEN demonstrates, the ability to deal successfully with novel problems requires the use of effective strategies and plans, and the monitoring of progress toward goals and subgoals.

The goal monitor in BETTERAVEN also had implications for memory management. Because parallel induction of rules took place in FAIRAVEN, it was possible for FAIRAVEN to exhaust its working memory trying to keep track of all rules simultaneously. BETTERAVEN, on the other hand, induced rules serially, and therefore conserved its memory resources. Carpenter et al. note that in Holzman et al.'s (1976) work they also found that series-completion items that imposed larger working memory loads differentiated bright- and average-IQ children. Thus, part of what relates novel problem solving to intelligence is the way in which individuals manage their limited memory resources. Indeed, there are those who believe that working-memory capacity is the single most important predictor of reasoning ability (Kyllonen & Christal, 1990).

The use of efficient strategies and plans appears to be related to fluid ability. Fluid-ability tasks typically involve novel stimuli that cannot be summarized or "chunked" by utilizing existing knowledge structures. Instead, they must be processed in terms of basic features and context-independent rules, which accumulate quickly. Keeping track of these features and rules places a great demand on working memory, and it is here that strategies and plans help, by regulating the moment-by-moment storage requirements. Individuals with better memory management avoid working-memory overload, and the consequent performance detriment that results from losing information during problem solution.

Summary. We have reviewed a number of task models of performance on rule-induction tasks. These tasks were chosen because they are both novel and related to intelligence. Because the models tend to be somewhat idiosyncratic, it is not easy to make generalizations; however, some are possible. First, the efficiency of certain underlying processes found *across* rule-induction tasks is related to intellectual ability. Sternberg and Gardner (1983) found evidence that reasoning and comparison components were related to reasoning performance as measured by paper-and-pencil measures in three different rule-induction tasks: analogies, series completions, and classifications. Their data also provided mixed evidence on the relationship of encoding and justification components to reasoning. Alderton et al. (1985) found support for a relationship between confirmation and justification components, on the one hand, and error rate on analogy and classification problems on the other.

Second, the ability to construct knowledge representations adequate for solving novel problems is an important component in successfully coping with novelty. Such representations transform the stimuli from novel to meaningful parts of previously experienced patterns. Carpenter et al.'s (1990) computer modeling of the Raven's Progressive Matrices provides evidence on this point.

Third, working-memory capacity, as implicated in Carpenter et al.'s (1990) work and Holzman et al.'s (1976) work on series-completion problems, seems to be an important variable. One reason is that working memory is used (to a greater or lesser extent) by each processing component during its operation. Thus the finding that all of Sternberg and Gardner's (1983) components bore some relationship to reasoning may be indicative of subjects' differential memory limitations (Kyllonen & Christal, 1990). Another possibility is that the memory limitations are indirect indicators of access to effective strategies for (relatively fixed) memory usage. This argument implies the importance of strategic knowledge, or, within Sternberg's (1985) triarchic theory, metacomponents (which formulate and execute strategic plans). Sternberg has presented some evidence that metacomponents (i.e., strategy formation and plan execution) are at least partially responsible for the relationship between some tasks and intelligence (e.g., Sternberg, 1981).

Novelty in verbal tasks

Sternberg (1985) has stressed the role of novelty, or nonentrenchment, in measuring intelligence. His experiential subtheory states that a task's ability to measure intelligence is in part a function of its novelty. He divides novelty into two types: (a) novelty in the comprehension of the task, and (b) novelty in acting upon one's comprehension of the task. Raaheim (1974) presents a similar dichotomy.

Tasks of the first type are difficult to perform because they are difficult to understand. Once understood, however, performing the task may be relatively simple. Tasks of the second type are difficult to solve because of constraints inherent in the task, but understanding the problem itself is simple. Naturally, a task can involve novelty of both types, but such tasks are usually too novel to provide a good measure of intelligence (see our argument at the beginning of the section on "Intelligence, psychometric theories, and rule-induction items").

Novelty in task performance. Sternberg and Davidson (1982, 1983) have studied problems generally termed "insight" problems. Insight problems require a novel solution to a problem that may or may not seem difficult. Understanding the problem is usually not the difficulty in insight problems; producing a solution that satisfies the problem's constraints is.

According to Sternberg and Davidson (1982), three underlying component processes are essential to solving insight problems: (a) selective encoding, (b) selective combination, and (c) selective comparison. Selective encoding refers to the ability to separate out the important information from a context of unimportant details. Selective combination refers to taking the important information provided by selective encoding, and organizing it into a meaningful pattern or whole. Selective comparison refers to relating new, important information to old, relevant information so that useful analogies can be formed. These analogies will provide the individual with efficient ways to use the new information instrumentally.

In an empirical study (Sternberg & Davidson, 1982), 30 adults (noncollege students) were presented with 12 insight problems to solve. These subjects also took the Henmon–Nelson IQ test (Lamke, Nelson, & French, 1973), Letter Series from the French Kit (French, Ekstrom, & Price, 1963), and Nonsense Syllogisms from the French Kit. Performance on the insight problems (number correct) was correlated .66 with the Henmon–Nelson, .63 with Letter Series, and .34 with Nonsense Syllogisms. Note that Nonsense Syllogisms, a test of deductive reasoning and therefore a less novel task, had the lowest correlation with the insight problems. A second experiment (cited in Sternberg, 1985) essentially replicated these results with new subjects. Sternberg (1985, p. 82) stated, "an examination of the point–biserial correlations between item scores and IQ revealed that the highest correlations tended to be for items that clearly measured either selective encoding, selective combination, or both."

Novelty in task understanding. Sternberg (1981, 1982a) has studied novelty in task understanding using a series of concept projection tasks. These tasks require individuals to understand concepts that are defined in novel ways, and then verify statements based upon these atypical concepts. An example of such a novel concept would be *grue:* green until the year 2000 and blue thereafter. The verification task requires the individual to relate information about the current state of affairs regarding the concept and some future state of affairs, thus the name "concept projection task" – projection to some future state of affairs. Information in the task can be either visual or verbal. The verbal information can be further subdivided into steady-state words and variable-state words. Steady-state words imply a constancy in the value of some underlying attribute over time, while variable-state words imply a change in the value of some underlying attribute over time.

On a typical trial an individual is shown either a picture or a word describing the state of affairs at the present time, and either a picture or a word describing the state of affairs at some future time. The subject must choose the alternative that correctly describes the situation portrayed by the two items (one from the present and one the future) from among three alternatives. Inconsistent descriptions of the present and future are possible, and "inconsistent" is one of the possible answer options.

Sternberg (1982a, 1985) has described an information-processing model that involves five critical processes: (a) encoding the expectation of a change in conceptual system, (b) accessing a novel conceptual system, (c) finding an appropriate concept in a new conceptual system, (d) allowing for a nonentrenched (i.e., novel) relationship, and (e) responding to a violation of an expectation of a change in conceptual system (i.e., time to recover from an incorrect expectation of change). In a series of five experiments using different instantiations of isomorphic novel concepts, Sternberg's model fit the latency data well, with the following R^2s: .94, .92, .91, .92, and .84 (Sternberg, 1982a). In addition, global task scores correlated substantially with psychometrically measured inductive reasoning ability: −.69, −.77, −.61, −.48, and −.62.

Direct manipulation of novelty. While the above studies imply that novelty is an important determinant of the relationship between task performance and intelligence, novelty was always manipulated somewhat indirectly. Sternberg and Gastel (1989) sought to manipulate novelty directly in a sentence verification task. Fifty subjects were presented with 232 statements to verify as true or false. Subjects were also presented with presuppositions which they were to treat as true when verifying the following block of sentences. In the nonnovel condition, these presuppositions were factual (i.e., true in the real world). For example, "canaries sing" might be such a presupposition. In the novel condition, presuppositions were counterfactual (i.e., not true in the real world). "Canaries play hopscotch" might be such a counterfactual presupposition. Another difference between Sternberg and Gastel's work and work reviewed to this point is that novelty was assessed in a deductive task (sentence verification) as opposed to an inductive task (e.g., matrix problems).

Sternberg and Gastel found modest support for their hypothesis that directly manipulated novelty increased the relationship between the verification times and intelligence. They created a difference score by subtracting each subject's average nonnovel verification score from her/his average novel verification score. This procedure follows the logic of the Donders' (1868-1869) subtraction method. The score was then correlated with performance on the Letter Series Test from the 1976 French Kit (Ekstrom, French, & Harman, 1976), the Syllogisms Test from the California Test of Mental Maturity, Level 5 (Sullivan, Clark, & Tiegs, 1963), and the Cattell Culture-Fair Test of g, Form A (Cattell & Cattell, 1963). The correlations of the difference score with the reasoning/intelligence tests was: Letter Series, $r = -.34$, $p < .02$; Syllogisms Test, $r = -.38$, $p < .01$; and Cattell Culture-Fair IQ, $r = -.15$, $p > .05$. Although these results are not as strong as we might like, they do provide the first *direct* evidence that manipulated novelty increases the relationship between a task and reasoning.

Summary. As we pointed out earlier, some researchers have attributed the relationship between novelty and intelligence to the spatial/figural content of certain novel tests (e.g., the Raven's Progressive Matrices). While we agree that spatial/figural content can play some role in this relationship, Sternberg and his associates' ex-

tensive work on novelty in verbal tasks demonstrates that even when the stimulus items are comprised of familiar content, as with insight problems, novelty of the processing required can have an effect. Also, Sternberg and Gastel's (1989) work found evidence for an effect due to the processing of novel relationships even though the nature of the task was held constant.

It is difficult to localize novelty effects in particular processing components in these experiments. Sternberg (1982a) attempted this in his concept-projection experiments, and some promising findings arose, but the low reliabilities associated with estimates of specific processes for individual subjects made the picture unclear. Processing associated with complexity was related to inductive reasoning in four out of five experiments, while processing associated with nonentrenchment was associated with induction in one of two experiments. Another problem in the concept-projection experiments was that it was unclear how the information-processing model of concept projection generalizes to other tasks.

Traditional reasoning and problem-solving approaches to novelty

A number of psychologists have considered the effects of novelty on information processing, but from the more traditional approach of the reasoning and problem-solving tradition. Raaheim (1974) conceives of intelligence in novel problem-solving situations (typically problems with ill-defined problem spaces [Sternberg, 1982b]) as the search for how the present problem situation fits into some previously understood series of situations. The problem situation is only a problem insofar as some elements of the problem situation deviate from the previously understood situations. The problem solver's task is to dispense with the deviations, so that the problem situation and the past situations (whose solutions are known) are equivalent.

Raaheim, like Sternberg (1985), distinguishes two different sources of novelty: (a) novelty due to difficulty in discovering what the deviation between the problem situation and past situations is; and (b) novelty due to difficulty in handling the deviation, once discovered. Also like Sternberg (1985), Raaheim believes that a problem situation may display either or both sources of novelty (or neither, in which case the problem is not novel).

Raaheim also describes his beliefs about the relationship between intelligence and problem solving. First, he notes that whether a situation is seen as a "problem" or not is heavily dependent upon the individual's past experience. Furthermore, which parts of the person's past experience are brought to bear in any situation are thought to be influenced by motivational and personality factors. Thus, Raaheim's position is similar to contextualist views that intelligence cannot be addressed independent of the physical, personal, social, and cultural milieu in which it is displayed.

Second, Raaheim believes that intelligence will influence problem solving only for that intermediate range of problems that is seen as somewhat novel (that is, they are problematic), but not too novel (they have no relationship with past situations).

Raaheim points out that as the individual's range of past experience grows, the number of problems he/she can solve using intelligence also grows, because more problems are seen as having some relationship to past experience.

Third, Raaheim notes that individuals themselves are likely to vary in intelligence, and this variation displays itself as differences in the upper range of problems that an individual can use his intelligence to solve. A more intelligent person will still see a relationship between very deviant (i.e., novel) problems and past experience, while a less intelligent person would be less likely to see any relationship at all. Thus, for the less intelligent person, the problem would be "too novel" and therefore not seen as a problem at all.

Raaheim's theoretical position bears many similarities to our earlier argument about the paradox of novelty. Raaheim views novel situations as a setting for people to display their intelligence. But he also acknowledges that as experience increases, in part through successfully overcoming novel situations, people are better able to cope with future novelty. Some problems will no longer be novel, and others will now be similar enough to past experience to allow intelligence to be employed in discovering a solution. Thus, knowledge and process are closely intertwined in Raaheim's work, just as they are in Sternberg's, Pellegrino's, and Carpenter and Just's work.

Work by Gick and Holyoak (1980, 1983) supports Raaheim's (1974) contention of the critical importance of past experience in solving novel problems. These researchers showed that a single analogous past experience is often insufficient to help individuals solve a new, but related, problem. Two analogous past experiences, however, did help people solve the new problem. Gick and Holyoak explain these findings in terms of schema theory, assuming that subjects were able to map the two analogous past experiences in an abstract schema for solving a particular type of problem. Thus quantity of relevant past experience may be a critical variable relating novelty to intelligent problem-solving performance.

As the above study shows, performance in novel environments is intimately related to the transfer literature. Presumably, when we attempt a novel task we bring with us all we have learned in the past. Whether that past learning will be beneficial (i.e., result in positive transfer), neutral (i.e., result in no transfer), or detrimental (i.e., result in negative transfer) is a function of several factors. Gick and Holyoak (1987) note that perceived similarity between past experiences and the present novel task will effect the likelihood that an individual will attempt to transfer past solutions to the current problem. The greater the perceived similarity, the greater the likelihood of attempted solution transfer. However, similarity can be due to either surface features unrelated to the true nature of the problem, or structural features important in the problem's solution. If similarity is due to common structural features between past experiences and the current novel task, transfer is likely to be positive. If similarity is based on surface features alone, then the relationship between structural features of the past and present situations will determine the direction and degree of transfer. Common structural features will lead to positive transfer, but distinctive structural features (structural features not shared by the two tasks) will lead to negative transfer. The ability to successfully transfer past learning to current problems is one reason why intelligent persons outperform less intelligent ones when coping with novelty.

We have not said much about the underlying information processing in ill-structured problems such as those studied by Raaheim (1974) and Gick and Holyoak (1980, 1983). Sternberg (1982b) has suggested that problems such as the "hatrack problem" (Maier, 1933), the "two-string problem" (Maier, 1931), and the "radiation problem" (Duncker, 1926) – all typical of the ill-structured problems studied by psychologists from the problem-solving tradition – are solved through primarily analogical means. While this would imply processes such as encoding, mapping, application, justification, and response (Sternberg, 1982b), these processes must involve selectivity, as Sternberg and Davidson's (1982, 1983) work on insight problems suggests.

Novelty and the developmental approach to intelligence

Definition of the approach

Developmental psychologists have attempted to understand how intelligent behavior evolves as the individual ages. This understanding includes both structural changes within the individual's mind, and those behaviors or functions which bring about the development of intelligence. Researchers from many fields have made contributions to research on intellectual development, but none have had the influence of Swiss psychologist Jean Piaget.

Piagetian views of novelty and intellectual development

Piaget (1952, 1970, 1977; Piaget & Inhelder, 1969, 1973) viewed intelligence from the general perspective of the biology of organisms. An essential construct in this perspective is adaptation: organisms adapt themselves to their environments. Piaget believed adaptation occurred in two complementary ways: assimilation and accommodation (Berger, 1980; Flavell, 1985; Gelman & Baillargeon, 1983). Assimilation involved incorporating environmental inputs into currently favored ways of thinking or acting (known as "schemes") with little or no modification to the scheme itself. Accommodation involved modifying the scheme so as to take account of qualities of the environmental input. An example from the nonbiological realm may help make this clear (from Berger, 1980, p. 56). When eating, the person both assimilates and accommodates the food. The food is assimilated into the body by chewing it and breaking it down into basic nutrients. But the body also accommodates different foods differently. Some foods require certain enzymes and acids for their digestion, other food require different enzymes and acids.

In adapting to novel stimuli, adaptation may be minor or major. If current schemes can assimilate and accommodate stimuli with only minor changes, intellectual development will proceed by accretion: small amounts of data (concerning the current stimulus) are added to the knowledge system. If, however, current schemes are unable to assimilate the new stimuli, and small amounts of accommodation do not help matters, the system is thrown into a state of cognitive disequilibrium. This may be resolved by equilibration majorante (Piaget, 1975), or major improvements, of the individual's schemes and cognitive systems (Gelman and Baillargeon, 1983). Thus, novel stimuli may cause a restructuring of thought processes, if these stimuli cannot be handled by current schemes.

Piaget made strong claims about the course of cognitive development. First, he claimed that the thinking of older children was qualitatively different from that of younger children. He organized the course of cognitive development into four macro-level stages, each with its own characteristic modes of thought: (a) the sensorimotor stage (from birth to approximately two years); (b) the preoperational stage (from approximately two years to six years); (c) the concrete operational stage (from approximately six years to twelve years); and (d) the formal operational stage (from approximately twelve years through adulthood). Second, he claimed that individuals moved through the stages in a fixed, immutable order. That is, individuals moved from preoperational thought to concrete operational thought, and not vice versa. It should be noted that many developmental psychologists believe Piaget's strict stage theory makes too strong a claim (Brainerd, 1978; Brown & Desforges, 1979; Flavell, 1982; Siegel & Brainerd, 1978).

Other developmental psychologists have attempted to augment Piaget's stages of cognitive development. Recently Arlin (1975) proposed that the formal operational stage can be separated into two separate stages: (a) a problem-solving stage, which is essentially equivalent to Piaget's formal operational stage; and (b) a problem-finding stage. While the mental structures of formal operations allow for convergent problem solving, Arlin proposed that the mental structures of problem finding allow for divergent thinking and formulation of abstract, general problems characteristic of creativity and scientific thinking. She further stated that problem solving is necessary for problem finding, but not sufficient.

There is a similarity between Arlin's dichotomy of problem solving and problem finding and Sternberg's (1985) two types of novelty: (a) novelty in task solution, and (b) novelty in task comprehension. It would seem that the problem-finding stage (i.e., traditional formal operations) might be associated with overcoming novelty in task solution, while the problem-finding stage might be associated with novelty in task comprehension. Arlin's theory, however, implies a stage ordering between these skills (with problem solving preceding problem finding) that Sternberg's theory does not. The mapping between theories proposed here has not been investigated empirically, but it is an interesting possibility for future research.

Arlin (1975) conducted an experiment to assess the predicted relationship between problem-solving and problem-finding skills. Problem solving was assessed using traditional Piagetian formal operational tasks, while problem finding was assessed by presenting subjects with an array of common objects and then asking subjects to raise questions about the objects. Questions were scored on their generality, using the products dimension of Guilford's (1956) structure of intellect model. Questions that were able to evoke novel connections among sets of objects resulted in higher problem-finding scores. Arlin's data indicated that all (12) subjects who were high in problem finding were also categorized as formal operational thinkers (that is, they had reached Arlin's problem-solving stage). Conversely, of those low in problem finding (10), only one was classified as having attained formal operational thought. Arlin took this as support for her distinction of a fifth stage of cognitive development – a stage closely associated with the ability to see novel relationships among common objects.

Infant information processing, temperament, and intelligence

Despite the robustness of the construct of intelligence, it has been difficult to demonstrate sizeable correlations between tests of infant intelligence and later tests of childhood intelligence (see McCall, 1979, for a review of data on this point). However, Berg and Sternberg (1985) have made a convincing argument that if intelligence is understood (at least partially) as an infant's response to novelty, a relationship can be found between infant information processing, temperament, and later intelligence.

They noted evidence from three different sources. First, they reviewed studies of infant habituation of attention (e.g., Lewis & Brooks-Gunn, 1981; Lewis, Goldberg, & Campbell, 1969; Ruddy & Bornstein, 1982). These studies were based on the fact that if an infant is repeatedly or continuously presented with a particular stimulus, the infant will display a response decrement to that stimulus. However, if a novel stimulus is presented, the infant will experience dishabituation; that is, the infant's attention to the novel experience will increase. Dependent measures in these studies include galvanic skin response, nonnutritive sucking, respiration, and heart rate.

The studies reviewed by Berg and Sternberg looked at the relationship between infant habituation of attention and both concurrent and later measures of intellectual functioning. They concluded that although infant habituation was unrelated to concurrent intellectual functioning (as measured by tests such as the Bayley scales [Bayley, 1969]), it was related to later intellectual functioning (usually tested between 6 and 24 months after the initial assessment).

The second set of studies reviewed by Berg and Sternberg concerned infant recognition memory (e.g., Fagan, 1981, April, reported in Fagan & Singer, 1983; Fagan & McGrath, 1981; Yarrow, Klein, Lomonaco, and Morgan, 1975). In these studies the infant is first familiarized with a stimulus. The stimulus is then paired with a novel stimulus. If the child looks at the novel stimulus more and/or with greater frequency, this is taken as evidence that the infant recognized the previous stimulus as old; that is, the infant has developed a memory trace for the nonnovel stimulus.

Berg and Sternberg reviewed experiments that related measures of infant recognition memory and verbal intellectual functioning (e.g., Peabody Picture Vocabulary Test and the Stanford–Binet Intelligence Test). They concluded visual-recognition memory ability in infancy was not only related to later verbal intelligence, but a better predictor of it than traditional sensorimotor scales of infant intelligence.

The third set of studies reviewed by Berg and Sternberg involved infant temperament, in particular task persistence and attention span (e.g., Goldsmith & Gottesman, 1981; Matheny, Dolan, & Wilson, 1974). These characteristics effect how an individual will approach a novel stimulus, and how much they may or may not learn from the encounter. Furthermore, temperament appears to be stable over the lifetime of the individual and across situations (Buss & Plomin, 1975; Campos, Barrett, Lamb, Goldsmith, & Stenberg, 1983). They concluded that measures of task persistence and attention span are often related to both concurrent and later mental functioning.

Berg and Sternberg took these three conclusions and interrelated them into a theory of why the response to novelty was related to intelligence. First, they associated task persistence and attention span with a motivational system that prefers novelty. This interest in novelty leads the infant, and later the child, to explore novel environments and gain new knowledge from them. Berg and Sternberg note too much preference for novelty could interfere with learning, as the infant might spend too little time gaining knowledge from each novel encounter. This is consistent with theories of infant attention that postulate intermediate degrees of novelty are most attention grabbing (e.g., McCall & Kagan, 1967) and the argument we presented earlier that intermediate degrees of novelty allow one to display one's intelligence.

Second, they associate infant habituation of attention and infant recognition memory capabilities with information processes and strategic planning abilities that are postulated to underlie intelligence (see Sternberg, 1977a, 1985). Encoding and comparison processes are proposed as necessary for both habituation and recognition memory. In addition, strategic planning in the allocation of attention between stimuli is necessary in both tasks. According to Berg and Sternberg, the reason habituation and recognition memory are better predictors of later intelligence than sensorimotor scales, such as the Bayley, is that they rely more heavily on mental processes rather than sensory and motor processes. While sensory and motor processing are integral parts of the definition of *infant* intelligence, *mental* processing is the principal defining feature of childhood and adult intelligence.

Thus, from Berg and Sternberg's perspective, responses to novelty in infancy reflects both motivational and processing characteristics that will continue to be important throughout the course of development. These characteristics increase the likelihood that individuals will encounter new situations that can serve as the basis for learning and will (mentally) profit from these encounters.

Developmental trends in fluid and crystallized intelligence

Differing developmental trends have been reported for fluid and crystallized intelligence. (This theory was presented earlier under psychometric approaches.) Performance on fluid-ability tasks, associated with the basic biologic ability to learn, is best during the earlier years of life. After young adulthood (say age 30) this ability declines, and it continues to show deterioration throughout the rest of the age span (see Cunningham, Clayton, & Overton, 1975; Horn & Hofer, 1992; McArdle & Horn, 1983, cited in Horn & Hofer, 1992). It should be remembered that fluid ability is associated with novel tests such as Raven's Progressive Matrices.

Crystallized ability, which is associated with acculturation and education, peaks much later (during the 40s [Horn & Hofer, 1992]). Some crystallized skills will either remain stable or actually increase throughout adulthood (Clark, Gardner, Brown, & Howell, 1990; Horn & Cattell, 1967). A typical marker test showing resistance to aging effects is vocabulary.

Baltes, Willis, and their colleagues have shown that the deterioration of fluid ability associated with aging is at least partially reversible (Baltes, Dittmann-Kohli, & Kliegl, 1986; Blieszner, Willis, & Baltes, 1981; Hofland, Willis, & Baltes, 1981; Willis, Blieszner, & Baltes, 1981). Adults in the 60–80 year old range have benefitted from explicit training programs aimed at improving fluid-reasoning ability. These subjects correctly answered more items at all difficulty levels, and decreased errors of commission (Baltes, Dittmann-Kohli, & Kliegl, 1986). Furthermore, training has been successful in both American and German older populations, with generalization to near-fluid ability tasks not explicitly trained. Thus, as Baltes et al. state, the elderly have a "reserve capacity" that can be tapped through explicit training.

Salthouse (1985a, 1985b) has noted that performance on most tasks, including novel fluid-ability tasks, slows with increasing age. He used this finding as basis for his processing-rate theory of aging. According to Salthouse, as the individual ages, his central cognitive processor also slows. This leads to a reduction in the individual's efficiency in performing cognitive tasks. This reduction, however, is at least partially offset by changes in the strategies used by the individual to perform these tasks. The older individual is more likely to rely on strategies that minimize his or her reliance on speedy information processing. Salthouse claims these strategic changes are difficult to detect, because they occur gradually as the individual ages. He also notes that changes in cognitive efficiency brought on by aging are likely to effect the individual's motivation to perform certain cognitive tasks. Frustration and anxiety may reduce performance in older populations over and above performance decrements that might be expected on the basis of a slowed central processor. Salthouse's theory therefore implies that novel tasks will tap a somewhat different set of variables in the elderly than they would in a young adult population.

Vygotsky and the zone of proximal development

Lev Vygotsky (1962, 1978, 1981) was a Soviet psychologist who based his theory of psychological functioning in Marxism. He believed that higher mental functions have their origins in external social interaction (Rogoff & Wertsch, 1984). The child internalizes her or his interactions with other more skilled members of society, so that eventually the child has access to these mental functions in the absence of other's support.

This led Vygotsky to distinguish between two levels of performance: actual development, or the level at which a child could function independently, and potential development, or the level at which a child could function while participating in instructional social interaction (Rogoff & Wertsch, 1984). The extension in performance that is provided by allowing a skilled member of the culture to serve as an interacting instructor is known as the "zone of proximal development."

The zone of proximal development becomes especially important when dealing with novel stimuli. For maximal learning to take place, teaching must be aimed at the zone of proximal development. Teaching aimed too low will not increase the child's skills. Teaching aimed too high will go over the child's head and not result in learning. It is only in the zone of proximal development that the child can employ his or her intelligence and profit by experience. This argument is very similar to the one we presented in the beginning of this chapter concerning the relationship between degree of novelty and intelligence: intelligence is best displayed in those situations that are somewhat novel, but which still have some grounding in past experience. Vygotsky's ideas continue to be influential, especially among educational psychologists.

Novelty and the contextualist view of intelligence

Definition of the approach

Contextual approaches to intelligence emphasize the role of context and environment in shaping and defining intelligent behavior. They may be broad, stressing the influence of culture on intelligence, or narrow, pointing out that certain results concerning intelligent behavior obtain only within certain physical or personal settings. What makes them unique is that they focus our attention on how much of intelligence is determined by things outside the individual.

Ceci's bioecological theory of intelligence

Vygotsky's theories (discussed above) are strongly contextual, as well as being developmental. In this final section we focus on another theory that is strongly contextual, as well as being developmental and information-processing in nature: Ceci's bioecological theory of intelligence. We believe it is a good representative of theories that stress the importance of context, and it is sufficiently broad to handle many empirical findings. Also, this theory shows how contextualists differ from other theorists in the importance they place on novelty.

Ceci (1990) believes that individuals begin life with a set of biologically constrained potentials. Although Ceci acknowledges that all individuals may not begin life equally endowed, he downplays these differences in favor of differences fostered by different environmental contexts, motivations, and developmental paths. For instance, Ceci believes that although much of our cognitive potentials may be the result of genetics, many of these genetically determined processing capabilities do not show substantial individual-differences variation. Thus differences in initial cognitive potentials, although they undoubtedly exist, are not seen as important determinants of later intelligent functioning, except perhaps in cases of severe mental impairment (e.g., mental retardation due to biological sources such as Down's syndrome).

Initial cognitive potentials unfold developmentally through interactions with the environment, changing themselves and the structure of knowledge in the process. Motivation plays a role, in that the individual attempts to overcome meaningful environmental challenges. These interactions develop the cognitive potentials (i.e., information processes and strategic planning), but only in relation to the knowledge domain these cognitive potentials are utilizing. That is, there is little, if any, "trans-domainal" processing and planning resources; processing and planning are intimately tied to the knowledge they are exploiting. In addition, interactions with the environment change the knowledge base itself. These interactions provide additional knowledge, as well as additional linkages and differentiation within the knowledge base. This expanded and differentiated knowledge base allows more efficient processing; processing that earlier, less well-developed instantiations of the knowledge base did not allow.

The implications of the bioecological model are manifold. First, differences in processing efficiency cannot be considered independently of the knowledge domain they are being assessed in. People may be efficient and intelligent in one domain, and inefficient and unintelligent in another domain. For instance, Ceci and Liker (1986, 1988) studied "expert" horse race handicappers: individuals who attended (and bet) on horse races frequently, and who were amazingly accurate in predicting post-time odds on horses. They found that these individuals intuitively used extremely complex models of odds estimation – models involving seven-way interactions among factors! Yet experts' IQ scores were correlated only $-.07$ with the b weight for this seven-way interaction term (a surrogate for cognitive complexity). Thus the performance of these individuals in their area of expertise could not be predicted from their performance in another domain (that of academic IQ).

Second, academic IQ is fostered by schooling. Because experience in the school environment fosters those cognitive potentials assessed by IQ tests and develops the knowledge domains these potentials use, schooling and IQ are closely related. Ceci cites studies that indicate that for each year a child's entry into formal school is delayed, IQ performance declines (Ramphal, 1962 cited in Vernon, 1969; Schmidt, 1967). In addition, IQ scores decline slightly, but reliably, during summer vacation, especially for low SES youngsters whose summer vacations are least "school-like" (Hayes & Grether, 1982; Heyns, 1978; Jencks et al., 1972).

Finally, correlations between basic information processes, such as those calculated from mental rotation (e.g., Shepard and Metzler, 1971) and letter matching tasks (e.g., Posner and Mitchell, 1967), change as a function of subjects' familiarity with the stimuli. Tetewsky (1988) demonstrated that when stimuli were unfamiliar, information-processing parameters from these tasks were correlated with fluid ability, but when subjects were familiar with the stimuli, the correlations were not significant. Ceci (1990) points out that this throws considerable doubt on the conceptualization of information processes as being "knowledge-free" or "decontextualized".

As the foregoing discussion points out, the bioecological theory envisions intelligence as a three-way interaction: person × process × context. Person factors encompass biology and motivation. Process factors relate to the information processes necessary to carry out thought. Context factors involve the particular knowledge domains on which the processes operate. The role of context in such a theory is quite strong. But what happens when we assess someone's thinking in a novel domain? In this case, the person cannot fully demonstrate his or her highest levels of functioning, since this processing would be tied to well developed knowledge domains or contexts (Ceci, personal communication, September 30, 1992). Instead, novelty would accentuate differences due to person. Novel situations would show up differences in motivation across individuals (which might be idiosyncratically tied to the particular novel situation used) and differences in biological potential. But it should be remembered that for Ceci such biological potential must be crystallized through interaction with particular contexts.

In summary, the bioecological theory does not see response to novelty as an important indicator of intelligent behavior, especially of the highest levels of performance that individuals can achieve in their most favored environments. However, the theory does allow for the possibility that performance in a novel environment *might* be an indicator of how well an individual would later perform in that same environment, after much experience (Ceci, personal communication, September 30, 1992).

Although Ceci's views are at odds with others reviewed in this chapter, there are some similarities between his position, and that of Berg and Sternberg (1985) concerning infants' response to novelty. Berg and Sternberg noted that infants' response to novelty was related to their ability to encode and compare stimuli, and their motivation to do so. Ceci's bioecological theory states that in novel situations, person variables, such as biological potential and motivation, will be emphasized. If we equate biological potential with primitive encoding and comparison processes, then the two positions coincide quite nicely, at least as a description of infant performance.

Why is performance in novel contexts related to intelligence?

Our conclusion, based on our review of the literature, is that performance in novel contexts is related to intelligence. But why is this so? We offer the following six reasons:

1. *Performance in novel contexts requires the use of widely applicable performance components.* The research reviewed earlier on rule induction problems (e.g., Alderton, Goldman, & Pellegrino, 1985; Sternberg & Gardner, 1983) implies use of certain performance components (e.g., encoding, inference, confirmation/compari-

son, and justification) over a range of novel items. Individual differences in the latency and error rate of these components appear to be related to differences in reasoning ability. Also, Berg and Sternberg (1985) found indirect evidence that the efficacy of certain performance components (encoding and comparison) during infancy was related to later early childhood measures of intelligence.

2. *Performance in novel task environments requires the use of metacomponents involved in strategic planning.* Evidence for the importance of strategic planning was found in Carpenter, Just, and Shell's (1990) analysis of performance on Raven's Progressive Matrices. Sternberg (1981) presented evidence for the importance of strategic planning in solving nonstandard analogies that could have differing numbers of missing terms and differing numbers of alternatives per missing term. Also, Gardner (1982) found evidence for strategic planning in analogical reasoning when the predictability of stimulus attributes was systematically varied.

3. *Performance in novel contexts requires working memory resources and their efficient use.* Because novel task environments do not allow access to well-developed knowledge structures, processing in these environments consumes larger than average amounts of working memory. Those individuals who either have greater working-memory capacity or who are able to manage their memory resources more efficiently are at an advantage on measures of reasoning, as Kyllonen and Christal (1990) have demonstrated. This point is obviously related to our second point, and the evidence from Carpenter, Just, and Shell's (1990) analysis of Raven's Matrices also supports the importance of memory resources. It may be a reflection of the ability to flexibly allocate attentional resources where needed (Ackerman, 1988). This also ties in with Salthouse's (1985a) theory of changing strategies as processing speed declines. With the slowing of processing speed, memory and attentional resources become more taxed, and performance on fluid-ability tests typically decline.

4. *Performance in novel tasks environments often requires selectivity in the application of performance components.* Sternberg and Davidson's (1982, 1983) work on insight problems points out that not only must performance components operate quickly and without error, but they must also work selectively on those aspects of the problem that are relevant to solution. This leads to the issue of knowledge representation.

5. *Performance in novel contexts requires establishing a knowledge representation adequate for solving the problem.* Ceci (1990) points out the importance of context in intelligent performance. But when no previous well-developed knowledge representation exists, a premium is placed on the ability to develop one from scratch, as was demonstrated in Carpenter et al.'s (1990) programs for solving Raven's Progressive Matrices. Performance on Sternberg's (1982a) concept-projection tasks required subjects to do this as well, and performance on these tasks was related to intelligence. Performance-component selectivity may also be conceptualized in this way. Performance components do not necessarily have to be "selective" if the knowledge representation has already done the selecting for them by incorporating only those aspects of the problem description that are relevant to problem solution.

6. *Motivational factors are important when facing novel problems.* Novel problems may tap intelligence in part because they measure the individual's motivation to persist in the face of frustration, their attention span, and their preference for novel situations, which, in turn, will lead to greater opportunities for new learning. This is what Berg and Sternberg (1985) concluded in their review of the infant literature, and the point may well extend to adults. Novelty may be a point of interface between personality and intellectual variables.

In sum, an understanding of intelligence requires an understanding not just of how people interact with "any old context," but an understanding especially of how they interact with relatively novel contexts. In this chapter we have reviewed some of the literature that shows just how important this interaction is to intelligent thought and behavior.

References

Ackerman, P. L. (1988). Determinants of individual differences in skill learning: An integration of psychometric and information processing perspectives. *Psychological Bulletin, 102,* 3–27.

Alderton, D. L., Goldman, S. R., & Pellegrino, J. W. (1985). Individual differences in process outcomes for verbal analogy and classification solution. *Intelligence, 9,* 69–85.

Anastasi, A. (1988). *Psychological testing* (6th ed.). New York: Macmillan.

Arlin, P. K. (1975). Cognitive development in adulthood: A fifth stage? *Developmental Psychology, 11,* 602–606.

Baltes, P. B., Dittmann-Kohli, F., & Kliegl, R. (1986). Reserve capacity of the elderly in aging-sensitive tests of fluid intelligence: Replication and extension. *Psychology and Aging, 1,* 172–177.

Bayley, N. (1969). *Bayley scales of infant development: Birth to two years.* New York: Psychological Corporation.

Berg, C. A., & Sternberg, R. J. (1985). Response to novelty: Continuity versus discontinuity in the developmental course of intelligence. In H. W. Reese (Ed.), *Advances in child development and behavior* (Vol. 19, pp. 1–47). New York: Academic Press.

Berger, K. S. (1980). *The developing person.* New York: Worth.

Blieszner, R., Willis, S. L., & Baltes, P. B. (1981). Training research in aging on the fluid ability of inductive reasoning. *Journal of Applied Developmental Psychology, 2,* 247–265.

Brainerd, C. J. (1978). The stage question in cognitive-developmental theory. *Behavioral and Brain Sciences, 2,* 173–213.

Brody, N. (1992). *Intelligence* (2nd ed.). New York: Academic Press.

Brody, E. N., & Brody, N. (1976). *Intelligence: Nature, determinants, and consequences.* New York: Academic Press.

Brown, G., & Desforges, C. (1979). *Piaget's theory: A psychological critique.* Boston: Routledge & Kegan Paul.

Burt, C. (1911). Experimental tests of higher mental processes and their relation to general intelligence. *Journal of Experimental Pedagogy, 1,* 93–112.

Buss, A. H., & Plomin, R. (1975). *A temperamental theory of personality development.* New York: Wiley.

Campos, J. J., Barrett, K. C., Lamb, M. E., Goldsmith, H. H., & Stenberg, C. (1983). Socioemotional development. In P. H. Mussen (Series Ed.) & M. M. Haith & J. J. Campos (Vol. Eds.), *Handbook of child psychology* (Vol. 2, pp. 783–917). New York: Wiley.

Carpenter, P. A., Just, M. A., & Shell, P. (1990). What one intelligence test measures: A theoretical account of processing in the Raven Progressive Matrices test. *Psychological Review, 97,* 404–431.

Cattell, R. B. (1963). Theory of fluid and crystallized intelligence: An initial experiment. *Journal of Educational Psychology, 54,* 105–111.

Cattell, R. B. (1971). *Abilities: Their structure, growth, and action.* Boston: Houghton Mifflin.

Cattell, R. B. (1973). *Culture Fair Intelligence Test.* Champaign, IL: Institute for Personality and Ability Testing.

Cattell, R. B., & Cattell, A. K. (1963). *Test of g: Culture fair, Scale 3.* Champaign, IL: Institute for Personality and Ability Testing.

Ceci, S. J. (1990). *On intelligence . . . more or less: A bio-ecological treatise on intellectual development.* Englewood Cliffs, NJ: Prentice-Hall.

Ceci, S. J., & Liker, J. (1986). A day at the races: A study of IQ, expertise, and cognitive complexity. *Journal of Experimental Psychology: General, 115,* 255–266.

Ceci, S. J., & Liker, J. (1988). Stalking the IQ–expertise relationship: When the critics go fishing. *Journal of Experimental Psychology: General, 117,* 96–100.

Clark, E., Gardner, M. K., Brown, G., & Howell, R. J. (1990). Changes in analogical reasoning in adulthood. *Experimental Aging Research, 16,* 95–99.

Cronbach, L. J. (1970). *Essentials of psychological testing* (3rd ed.). New York: Harper & Row.

Cronbach, L. J. (1984). *Essentials of psychological testing* (4th ed.). New York: Harper & Row.

Cunningham, W. R., Clayton, V., & Overton, W. (1975). Fluid and crystallized intelligence in young adulthood and old age. *Journal of Gerontology, 30,* 53–55.

Donders, F. C. (1868–1869). Over do snelheid van psychoische processen. Onderzoekingen gedaan in het Physiologisch Laboratorium der Utrechtsche Hoogeschool, *Tweede reeks, II,* 92–120.

Downing, G. L., Edgar, R. W., Harris, A. J., Kornberg, L., & Storen, H. F. (1965). *The preparation of teachers for schools in culturally deprived neighborhoods* (Cooperative Research Project No. 935). Flushing, NY: Queens College of the City of New York.

Duncker, K. (1926). A qualitative (experimental and theoretical) study of productive thinking (solving of comprehensible problems). *Journal of Genetic Psychology, 33,* 642–708.

Ekstrom, R. B., French, J. W., & Harman, H. H. (1976). *French Kit of Reference Tests for Cognitive Factors.* Princeton, NJ: Educational Testing Service.

Evans, T. G. (1968). A program for the solution of geometric-analogy intelligence test questions. In M. Minsky (Ed.), *Semantic information processing.* Cambridge, MA: MIT Press.

Fagan, J. F. (1981). *Infant memory and the prediction of intelligence.* Paper presented at the meeting of the Society for Research in Child Development, Boston, April.

Fagan, J. F., & McGrath, S. K. (1981). Infant recognition memory and later intelligence. *Intelligence, 5,* 121–130.

Fagan, J. F., & Singer, L. T. (1983). Infant recognition memory as a measure of intelligence. In L. P. Lipsitt (Ed.), *Advances in infancy research* (Vol. 2, pp. 31–78). Norwood, NJ: Ablex.

Flavell, J. H. (1982). Structures, stages, and sequences in cognitive development. In W. A. Collins (Ed.), *Minnesota symposia on child psychology* (Vol 15). Hillsdale, NJ: Erlbaum.

Flavell, J. H. (1985). *Cognitive development* (2nd ed.). Englewood Cliffs, NJ: Prentice-Hall.

French, J., Ekstrom, R., & Price, I. (1963). *Kit of factor referenced tests for cognitive factors.* Princeton, NJ: Educational Testing Service.

Gardner, M. K. (1982). *Some remaining puzzles concerning analogical reasoning and human abilities.* Unpublished doctoral dissertation, Yale University, New Haven, CT.

Gardner, M. K., & Clark, E. (1992). The psychometric perspective on intellectual development in childhood and adolescence. In R. J. Sternberg & C. A. Berg (Eds.), *Intellectual development* (pp. 16–43). New York: Cambridge University Press.

Gelman, R., & Baillargeon, R. (1983). A review of some Piagetian concepts. In P. H. Mussen (Series Ed.) & J. H. Flavell & E. M. Markman (Vol. Eds.), *Handbook of child psychology: Vol. III. Cognitive development* (4th ed., pp. 167–230). New York: Wiley.

Gick, M. L., & Holyoak, K. J. (1980). Analogical problem solving. *Cognitive Psychology, 12,* 306–355.

Gick, M. L., & Holyoak, K. J. (1983). Schema induction and analogical transfer. *Cognitive Psychology, 15,* 1–38.

Gick, M. L., & Holyoak, K. J. (1987). The cognitive basis of knowledge transfer. In S. M. Cormier & J. D. Hagman (Eds.), *Transfer of learning: Contemporary research and applications* (pp. 9–46). New York: Academic Press.

Goldsmith, H. H., & Gottesman, I. I. (1981). Origins of variation in behavioral style: A longitudinal study of temperament in young twins. *Child Development, 52,* 91–103.

Guilford, J. P. (1956). The structure of intellect. *Psychology Bulletin, 53,* 267–293.

70   Michael K. Gardner and Robert J. Sternberg

Guilford, J. P. (1967). *The nature of human intelligence.* New York: McGraw-Hill.
Guilford, J. P. (1977). *Way beyond the IQ: Guide to improving intelligence and creativity.* Buffalo, NY: Creative Education Foundation.
Guilford, J. P. (1985). The structure-of-intellect model. In B. B. Wolman (Ed.), *Handbook of intelligence: Theories, measurements, and applications.* New York: Wiley.
Guilford, J. P., & Hoepfner, R. (1971). *The analysis of intelligence.* New York: McGraw-Hill.
Guttman, L. (1954). A new approach to factor analysis: The radex. In P. F. Lazarfield (Ed.), *Mathematical thinking in the social sciences.* Glencoe, IL: Free Press.
Guttman, L. (1965). The structure of the interrelations among intelligence tests. In *Proceedings of the 1964 Invitational Conference on Testing Problems.* Princeton, NJ: Educational Testing Service.
Guttman, L. (1970). Integration of test design and analysis. In *Proceedings of the 1969 Invitational Conference on Testing Problems.* Princeton, NJ: Educational Testing Service.
Hayes, D., & Grether, J. (1982). The school year and vacations: When do students learn? *Cornell Journal of Social Relations, 17,* 56–71.
Heyns, B. L. (1978). *Summer learning and the effects of schooling.* New York: Academic Press.
Hofland, B. F., Willis, S. L., & Baltes, P. B. (1981). Fluid intelligence performance in the elderly: Intraindividual variability and conditions of assessment. *Journal of Educational Psychology, 73,* 573–586.
Holzman, T. G., Glaser, R., & Pellegrino, J. W. (1976). Process training derived from a computer simulation theory. *Memory & Cognition, 4,* 349–356.
Horn, J. L., & Cattell, R. B. (1966). Refinement and test of the theory of fluid and crystallized general intelligences. *Journal of Educational Psychology, 57,* 253–270.
Horn, J. L., & Cattell, R. B. (1967). Age differences in fluid and crystallized intelligence. *Acta Psychologica, 26,* 107–126.
Horn, J. L., & Hofer, S. M. (1992). Major abilities and development in the adult period. In R. J. Sternberg & C. A. Berg (Eds.), *Intellectual development* (pp. 44–99). New York: Cambridge University Press.
Ingram, A. L., Pellegrino, J. W., & Glaser, R. (1976). *Semantic processing in verbal analogies.* Paper presented at the meeting of the Psychonomic Society, St. Louis, MO, November.
Jencks, C., Smith, M., Acland, H., Bane, M. J., Cohen, D., Gintis, H., Heyns, B., & Mitchelson, S. (1972). *Inequality: A reassessment of the effects of family and schooling in America.* New York: Basic Books.
Joreskog, K. G. (1970). A general model for analysis of covariance structures. *Biometrika, 57,* 239–251.
Joreskog, K. G. (1971). Analyzing psychological data by structural analysis of covariance matrices. In D. H. Krantz, R. D. Luce, P. Suppes, & A. Tversky (Eds.), *Foundations of measurement* (Vol. 2). New York: Academic Press.
Kotovsky, K., & Simon, H. A. (1973). Empirical tests of a theory of human acquisition of concepts for sequential patterns. *Cognitive Psychology, 4,* 399–424.
Kyllonen, P. C., & Christal, R. E. (1990). Reasoning ability is (little more than) working-memory capacity?! *Intelligence, 14,* 389–433.
Lamke, T. A., Nelson, M. J., & French, J. L. (1973). *The Henmon–Nelson Tests of Mental Ability, 1973 Revision.* Boston: Houghton-Mifflin.
Lewis, M., & Brooks-Gunn, J. (1981). Visual attention at three months as a predictor of cognitive functioning at two years of age. *Intelligence, 5,* 131–140.
Lewis, M., Goldberg, S., & Campbell, H. (1969). A development study of information processing within the first three years of life: Response decrement to a redundant signal. *Monographs of the Society for Research in Child Development, 34*(9, Serial No. 133).
MacLeod, C. M., Jackson, R. A., & Palmer, J. (1986). On the relation between spatial ability and field dependence. *Intelligence, 10,* 141–151.
Maier, N. R. F. (1931). Reasoning in humans: II. The solution of a problem and its appearance in consciousness. *Journal of Comparative Psychology, 12,* 181–194.
Maier, N. R. F. (1933). An aspect of human reasoning. *British Journal of Psychology, 24,* 144–155.
Marshalek, B., Lohman, D. F., & Snow, R. E. (1983). The complexity continuum in the radex and hierarchical models of intelligence. *Intelligence, 7,* 107–127.
McArdle, J. J., & Horn, J. L. (1983). *Mega-analysis of the WAIS.* National Institute of Aging Grant Number AG04704 (cited in Horn & Hofer, 1992).

McCall, R. B. (1979). The development of intellectual functioning in infancy and the prediction of later IQ. In J. D. Osofsky (Ed.), *Handbook of infant development* (pp. 707–741). New York: Wiley.

McCall, R. B., & Kagan, J. (1967). Stimulus–schema discrepancy and attention in the infant. *Journal of Experimental Child Psychology, 5*, 381–390.

Matheny, A. P., Jr., Dolan, A. B., & Wilson, R. S. (1974). Bayley's infant behavior record: Relations between behaviors and mental test scores. *Developmental Psychology, 10*, 696–702.

Mulholland, T. M., Pellegrino, J. W., & Glaser, R. (1980). Components of geometric analogy solution. *Cognitive Psychology, 12*, 252–284.

Pellegrino, J. W. (1985). Inductive reasoning ability. In. R. J. Sternberg (Ed.), *Human abilities: An information processing approach* (pp. 195–225). New York: W. H. Freeman.

Pellegrino, J. W., & Glaser, R. (1979). Cognitive correlates and components in the analysis of individual differences. In R. J. Sternberg & D. K. Detterman (Eds.), *Human intelligence: Perspectives on its theory and measurement.* Norwood, NJ: Ablex.

Pellegrino, J. W., & Glaser, R. (1980). Components of inductive reasoning. In R. E. Snow, P.-A. Federico, & W. E. Montague (Eds.), *Aptitude, learning, and instruction: Cognitive process analyses of aptitude* (Vol. 1). Hillsdale, NJ: Erlbaum.

Pellegrino, J. W., & Ingram, A. L. (1977). *Components of verbal analogy solution.* Paper presented at the meeting of the Midwestern Psychological Association, Chicago, IL, May.

Piaget, J. (1952). *The origins of intelligence in children* (M. Cook, Trans.). New York: International Universities Press.

Piaget, J. (1970). *Piaget's theory.* In P. H. Mussen (Ed.), *Carmichael's manual of child psychology* (Vol. 1). New York: Wiley.

Piaget, J. (1975). *L'équilibration des structures cognitives: Problème central du développement.* Études d'épistémologie génétique, Vol. 33. Paris: Presses Universitaires de France.

Piaget, J. (1977). *The development of thought: Equilibration of cognitive structures.* New York: Viking.

Piaget, J., & Inhelder, B. (1969). *The psychology of the child.* New York: Basic Books.

Piaget, J., & Inhelder, B. (1973). *Memory and intelligence.* New York: Basic Books.

Posner, M., & Mitchell, R. (1967). Chronometric analysis of classification. *Psychological Review, 74*, 392–409.

Raaheim, K. (1974). *Problem solving and intelligence.* Oslo: Universitetsforlaget.

Ramphal, C. (1962). *A study of three current problems of Indian education.* Unpublished doctoral dissertation, University of Natal (cited in Vernon, 1969).

Raven, J. C. (1938). *Progressive Matrices: A perceptual test of intelligence.* London: Lewis.

Raven, J. C. (1962). *Advanced Progressive Matrices, Set II.* London: Lewis.

Raven, J. C. (1965). *Advanced Progressive Matrices, Sets I and II.* London: Lewis.

Rogoff, B., & Wertsch, J. V. (1984). Editors' Notes. In B. Rogoff & J. V. Wertsch (Eds.), *Children's learning in the "zone of proximal development"* (pp. 1–6). San Francisco: Jossey-Bass.

Ruddy, M., & Bornstein, M. H. (1982). Cognitive correlates of infant attention and maternal stimulation over the first year of life. *Child Development, 53*, 183–188.

Salthouse, T. A. (1985a). *A theory of cognitive aging.* New York: North Holland.

Salthouse, T. A. (1985b). Speed of behavior and its implications for cognition. In J. E. Birren & K. W. Schaie (Eds.), *Handbook of the psychology of aging* (2nd ed., pp. 400–426). New York: Van Nostrand Reinhold.

Schmidt, W. H. O. (1967). Socio-economic status, schooling, intelligence, and scholastic progress in a community in which education is not yet compulsory. *Paedogogica Europa, 2*, 275–286.

Shepard, R. N., & Metzler, J. (1971). Mental rotation of three-dimensional objects. *Science, 171*, 701–703.

Siegel, L. S., & Brainerd, C. J. (Eds.). (1978). *Alternatives to Piaget: Critical essays on the theory.* New York: Academic Press.

Simon, H. A. (1976). Identifying basic abilities underlying intelligent performance of complex tasks. In L. B. Resnick (Ed.), *The nature of intelligence* (pp. 65–98). Hillsdale, NJ: Erlbaum.

Simon, H. A., & Kotovsky, K. (1963). Human acquisition of concepts for sequential patterns. *Psychological Review, 70*, 534–546.

Snow, R. E., Kyllonen, P. C., & Marshalek, B. (1984). The topography of ability and learning correlations.

In R. J. Sternberg (Ed.), *Advances in the psychology of human intelligence* (Vol. 2, pp. 47–103). Hillsdale, NJ: Erlbaum.

Spearman, C. (1923). *The nature of "intelligence" and the principles of cognition.* London: Macmillan.

Spearman, C. (1927). *The abilities of man.* New York: Macmillan.

Sternberg, R. J. (1977a). *Intelligence, information processing, and analogical reasoning: The componential analysis of human abilities.* Hillsdale, NJ: Erlbaum.

Sternberg, R. J. (1977b). Component processes in analogical reasoning. *Psychological Review, 84,* 353–378.

Sternberg, R. J. (1981). Intelligence and nonentrenchment. *Journal of Educational Psychology, 73,* 1–16.

Sternberg, R. J. (1982a). Natural, unnatural, and supernatural concepts. *Cognitive Psychology, 14,* 451–488.

Sternberg, R. J. (1982b). Reasoning, problem solving, and intelligence. In R. J. Sternberg (Ed.), *Handbook of human intelligence* (pp. 225–307). New York: Cambridge University Press.

Sternberg, R. J. (1985). *Beyond IQ: A triarchic theory of human intelligence.* New York: Cambridge University Press.

Sternberg, R. J., & Davidson, J. E. (1982). The mind of the puzzler. *Psychology Today, 16,* June, 37–44.

Sternberg, R. J., & Davidson, J. E. (1983). Insight in the gifted. *Educational Psychologist, 18,* 51–57.

Sternberg, R. J., & Gardner, M. K. (1983). Unities in inductive reasoning. *Journal of Experimental Psychology: General, 112,* 80–116.

Sternberg, R. J., & Gastel, J. (1989). Coping with novelty in human intelligence: An empirical investigation. *Intelligence, 13,* 187–197.

Sullivan, E. T., Clark, W. W., & Tiegs, E. W. (1963). *California Test of Mental Maturity.* Monterey, CA: California Test Bureau.

Tetewsky, S. J. (1988). *An analysis of familiarity effects in visual comparison tasks and their implications for studying human intelligence.* Unpublished doctoral dissertation, Yale University, New Haven, CT.

Thurstone, L. L. (1931). Multiple factor analysis. *Psychological Review, 38,* 406–427.

Thurstone, L. L. (1938). *Primary mental abilities.* Chicago: University of Chicago Press.

Thurstone, L. L. (1947). *Multiple factor analysis.* Chicago: University of Chicago Press.

Thurstone, L. L., & Thurstone, T. C. (1941). *Factorial studies of intelligence.* Chicago: University of Chicago Press.

Toffler, A. (1971). *Future shock.* New York: Bantam Books.

Vernon, P. E. (1969). *Intelligence and cultural environment.* London: Methuen.

Vernon, P. E. (1973). Multivariate approaches to the study of cognitive styles. In J. R. Royce (Ed.), *Multivariate analysis and psychological theory.* New York: Academic Press.

Vygotsky, L. S. (1962). *Thought and language.* Cambridge, MA: MIT Press.

Vygotsky, L. S. (1978). *Mind in society: The development of higher mental processes.* Cambridge, MA: Harvard University Press.

Vygotsky, L. S. (1981). The genesis of higher mental processes. In J. V. Wertsch (Ed.), *The concept of activity in Soviet psychology.* Armonk, NY: Sharpe.

Webster's new collegiate dictionary. (1976). Springfield, MA: G. & C. Merriam.

Willis, S. L., Blieszner, R., & Baltes, P. B. (1981). Intellectual training research in aging: Modifications of performance on the fluid ability of figural relations. *Journal of Educational Psychology, 73,* 41–50.

Winston, P. H. (1977). *Artificial intelligence.* Reading, MA: Addison-Wesley.

Witkin, H. A. (1978). *Cognitive styles in personal and cultural adaptation.* Worcester, MA: Clark University Press.

Witkin, H. A., Goodenough, D. R. (1981). *Cognitive styles: Essence and origins.* Psychological Issues Monograph 51. New York: International Universities Press.

Witkin, H. A., Goodenough, D. R., & Oltman, P. K. (1979). Psychological differentiation: Current status. *Journal of Personality and Social Psychology, 37,* 327–328.

Witkin, H. A., Lewis, H. B., Hertzman, M., Machover, K., Meissner, P. B., & Wapner, S. (1954). *Personality through perception: An experimental and clinical study.* New York: Harper.

Witkin, H. A., Oltman, P. K., Raskin, E., & Karp, S. A. (1971). *A manual for the Embedded Figures Test.* Palo Alto, CA: Consulting Psychologists Press.

Woodworth, R. S., and Wells, F. L. (1911). Association tests. *Psychological Monographs, 13*(5).

Wrightstone, J. W. (1958). *A study of the Raven Progressive Matrices and the IPAT Culture Free Intelligence Test with eighth grade project pupils* (Research Report No. 17). New York: New York City Board of Education, Bureau of Educational Research.

Yarrow, L. J., Klien, R. P., Lomonaco, S., & Morgan, G. A. (1975). Cognitive and motivational development in early childhood. In B. X. Friedlander, G. M. Sterritt, & G. E. Kirk (Eds.), *Exceptional infant* (Vol. 3, pp. 491–502). New York: Brunner/Mazel.

3 The effects of context on cognition: postcards from Brazil

Stephen J. Ceci and Antonio Roazzi

The history of cognitive-development research underscores the relative importance given to "process" over "context" by most psychologists. With only a few exceptions (e.g., Berry, 1983; Charlesworth, 1979; Cole & Scribner, 1974; Irvine & Berry, 1988; Sternberg, 1985), the major psychological theories of cognitive development (in contrast to anthropological and sociological theories) have downplayed the importance of context in cognition, preferring instead to emphasize the role of basic cognitive and biological processes. This is just as true for structuralist accounts of development, such as Piaget's (Piaget & Inhelder, 1969; though neo-Piagetians like Case, 1985, have acknowledged a somewhat greater role for context), as it is for nonstructuralist accounts, such as information processing (Jackson & McClelland, 1979), neurophysiological (Eysenck, 1986), and psychometric (Bayley, 1970). Elsewhere, one of us has reviewed each of these accounts, pointing out the processing assumptions that are implicit in them, and the manner in which they short-shrift context (Ceci, 1990).

For most psychologists, the idea that context can differentiate cognitive processing is akin to acknowledging the fragility of our theories. In the search for universal truths, it is a disappointment to learn that a phenomenon is situationally specific. At the same time that we are told how important context is for development – in dictating the rate at which a child passes through stages or acquires some concept – we are simultaneously told that context is superfluous to a developmental account because it influences performance in trivial ways. So, while Piaget came to concede the influence of the physical context on the speed with which a child traversed his stages (Piaget, 1977), he never acknowledged that this was due to anything deeper than mere familiarity with the materials and procedures.

Thus, the overriding message in developmental theories is that, if one is to get at the essence of development and chart the trajectories of various processes, then context is a form of noise to be controlled, deleted, or covaried. In nearly all

Portions of this research were supported by a Senior Fullbright-Hayes Award and Grants from the National Institutes of Child Health and Human Development, RO1HD22839 and KO4HD00801, to S. J. Ceci.

developmental accounts of cognitive growth, context is viewed as an adjunct to cognition, rather than as a constituent of it.

Recently, however, there has been a growing recognition among researchers (of both human and animal cognition) of the importance of context. These researchers have discovered that aspects of the physical, mental (e.g., the memory representation), and social context contribute to many of the cognitive developments that were once thought to be the result of age-related changes in processes. Recognition of the power of context on cognition can be seen in many areas of developmental research; for example, Keil (1984) argued that metaphorical reasoning is context-specific, occurring much earlier in some content domains than others, and Chi and Ceci (1987) suggested that many types of problem solving are under the direct influence of the structure of the mental representation, that is, the mental context the child brings to the task. Perhaps the area has received the most attention from researchers in this regard has been that of memory development. It is here that researchers studying developmental processes in humans and animals have seen the need to acknowledge the importance of context, not merely as a type of background that can influence task performance, but as an inextricable aspect of cognition:

There is a "new look" in memory development research, and it is decidedly contextual. The crux of the current view, in fact, is that memory processes cannot be adequately understood or evaluated acontextually: To think about memory without considering the contexts that lead children to remember is akin to thinking about smiles independently of the faces on which they appear. Different contexts not only evoke different strategies to aid recall, but they also differentially shape an individual's perception of the recall task itself. Depending on the context in which remembering takes place, children may recall everything or nothing; their level of performance speaks as much to the power of context as to their native mnemonic processing capacity. (Ceci & Leichtman, 1992, p. 223)

In this chapter we report on some recent research from Brazil that provides a "window" through which the importance of context in cognition can be viewed. But before describing this research we provide a glimpse into some of the evidence from North American research for the role of context in cognition.

In principle, it is possible to distinguish three types of context: 1) the social context, 2) the mental context, and 3) the physical context. Each of these can exert powerful influences on the efficiency of the developing organism's cognitive ability. For example, one physical context may elicit strategies that are not elicited by another; moreover, the context in which a cognitive attainment is made can itself serve as an elicitor of it subsequently. This is because, initially, most cognitive attainments are tied to the physical contexts in which they are acquired, and as a result the child benefits from context reinstatement when trying to solve a problem. Thus, the 3-year-old child has a contextually limited understanding of the "halving rule," which states that half of any entity results from its division by 2. The child knows that if you cut an apple in half you get two pieces, and that if you cut an orange in half, you get two pieces. But when asked how many pieces will result from cutting a watermelon in half, 3-year-olds will frequently reply in a manner that belies the importance of their acquisition context (e.g., claiming that it will depend on how large the melon is). With development, some individuals learn to extricate mental operations from the contexts of their original acquisition, though the degree to which we as adults are truly context-independent is probably much less than we believe (see Ceci, in press, for numerous examples of context dependency among adults).

And the same is true for the social and mental contexts of thinking. As we shall show below, if the social valence of a task is altered, for example by changing its sex-role expectation or changing the incentive for its successful completion, this can lead to pronounced differences in outcomes even though the cognitive processing demands of the task have remained unchanged (e.g., Ceci & Bronfenbrenner, 1985). Finally, the manner in which an individual represents the problems at hand is a type of context, too – the mental context. And it is intimately linked to cognitive performance, as the literature on expertise demonstrates (e.g., Chi, Hutchinson, & Robins, 1989; Means & Voss, 1985). An elaborate knowledge representation in a specific content domain allows for more sophisticated solutions in that domain, because it determines how the problems are coded and the types of strategies that will be deployed (e.g., Staszewski, 1989). So, these three types of context (physical, social, and mental) play a powerful role in cognitive development, simultaneously limiting and facilitating performance, creating both continuities and discontinuities – to the extent that these contexts are consistent across tasks.

Even though all three types of contexts can be logically identified and separated, cognition usually occurs simultaneously in social, mental, and physical contexts. An alteration to the physical context, for example, can result in a change in both the social and mental contexts. Thus, the problem of low cross-context correlations on cognitive tasks (or ostensible discontinuities in development) is not easy to localize at the level of a single contextual variable because physical, social, and mental contexts are interwoven. Moreover, individuals are engaged in a multiplicity of different contexts in which occasions for problem solving emerge. Whether and how they use or transfer knowledge constructed in one context to solve a problem in another context is a critical question for researchers. This concern can be expressed in the following questions: How does context affect behavior? How is it possible to ensure that an experimental context is functionally identical for different groups?

An attempt to answer these questions implies a need to integrate the environmental dimensions into a more comprehensive theoretical framework of organism–environment interaction. This implies a reconceptualization of the role of both the environment and the organism. It also implies the necessity for a more detailed model of the influence of external conditioning on cognitive processes. The elaboration of this model will depend especially on comparative studies which permit us to detect the intersection in development of an individual's biological background and the sociocultural environment in which the individual grows up.

Having stated the problem, we turn now to a brief description of the North American research on contextual influences on cognitive development, and follow this with a more detailed description of the new work being done in Brazil, as this latter work is unknown to most monolingual Anglophones. These Brazilian studies shed some light on the above questions as well as on the sometimes contradictory conclusions about children's capabilities that have been reached in North American research on low SES children, although they are not in themselves sufficient to provide a conclusive answer.

Altering the contexts of cognition

Ceci and Bronfenbrenner (1985; Ceci, 1990) have conducted a series of studies into the importance of the physical and social contexts on cognition, employing a dual-context paradigm. In all of this work, children are asked to perform the same task in two or more contexts. The idea behind using two contexts is that some settings are postulated to result in more effective forms of cognition than others because they elicit different strategies or activate different knowledge structures that allow for more efficient processing. For instance, if a task is perceived as a video game it may help recruit a set of strategies that children have acquired to conquer video games that might not be recruited if the same task is perceived as a type of test. Or, to take another possibility, if a task is perceived as related to a domain of knowledge that is well structured, it will result in more efficient processing than if it is seen as belonging to a less elaborated domain (e.g., Coltheart & Walsh, 1988; Means & Voss, 1985; Walker, 1987). It has been shown, for instance, that if material is presented as part of a house-buying context it will instantiate different knowledge structures in professional burglars than if it is presented as part of a home-buying context for prospective purchasers, and significantly different memory performance will result (Logie & Wright, 1988). Similarly, depending on whether the material is presented as part of a baseball game, a bird-watching exercise, or a Star Wars game, it can have dramatic consequences because it will recruit different levels of knowledge that can be used to draw inferences and set up expectations (Coltheart & Walsh, 1988; Means & Voss, 1985; Walker, 1987). This much seems noncontroversial, as these kinds of alterations in the mental context of a task have been the grist for an entire tradition of research on expert systems. But can changes in the physical and social contexts of a task alter the strategies that a child uses? The answer, as will be seen, is that it can. Moreover, one would have no reason to believe that children even possessed the strategy if they were evaluated in only one type of context.

Capturing butterflies

Ceci and Bronfenbrenner (1985; Ceci, 1990) asked 10-year-olds to guess in which direction a geometric shape that appeared in the center of a computer screen would migrate. The shape (circle, square, or triangle) always appeared in the center of the screen but it would migrate to another location. Children were instructed to point to the location on the screen where they thought the shape would migrate. These children were not informed of the algorithm that determined where the shape would migrate. For example, an algorithm might simply specify the following: 1) SHAPE indicates left/right directionality (e.g., if it is a square it will move rightward; if it is a circle it will move leftward; if it is a triangle it will remain unchanged); 2) COLOR indicates up/down directionality (e.g., if the shape's color is dark it will move upward; if the shape's color is light it will move downward); and 3) SIZE indicates distance (e.g., if the shape is large it will go a short distance; and small shapes will go a long distance). This would be an example of a "main effects" type of reasoning wherein one needs only to add the various features to determine where a specific shape will migrate on the screen. A large, dark circle, for instance, should move UPWARD, LEFTWARD, and a SHORT distance from the center.

Ten-year-olds are not very proficient at figuring out such rules on their own. Even after 750 trials they still seem to be confused about where the shape will migrate. As can be seen in Figure 3.1, they are slightly above chance after 750 trials, but this is accomplished entirely by having memorized a few specific combinations of features, and not by having solved the underlying rule. They may have learned, for example, that a large, dark circle migrates to a certain spot on the screen, but they have no understanding of the values associated with color, shape, or size, and this is why they are still performing near chance after 750 trials. Lest one imagine that these 10-year-olds were slow learners, it is important to understand that they are doing exactly what university students do on similar laboratory tasks of multicausal reasoning. In fact, the decision-science literature is strewn with examples of university students failing similar laboratory reasoning tasks (see Klayman, 1984).

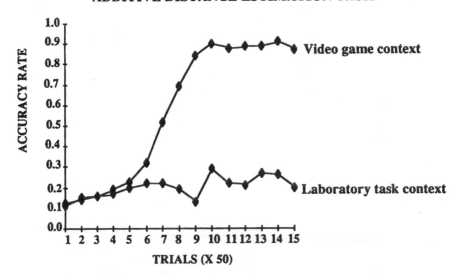

Figure 3.1. Children's mean proportion of accurate estimates of a moving object in game versus laboratory contexts (simple main-effects algorithm).

After making a slight alteration to the task, children's performance dramatically improved. The three shapes (square, circle, and triangle) were replaced with animals (birds, bees, and butterflies) and sound effects were added, thus making the context resemble a video game. The algorithm was unchanged; the only difference was one of surface transformation. Thus, the laboratory setting of predicting geometric shapes was substituted with a new context, a video-game setting, and children were asked to place a cursor that looked like a butterfly net at the spot on the screen where they thought the bird, bee, or butterfly would migrate. In other words, they were invited to capture the animals in the net. As can be seen in Figure 3.1, this contextual change resulted in nearly perfect performance after three hundred trials.

Ceci and Bronfenbrenner repeated this same experiment with a variety of algorithms, including complex curvilinear functions, and the result has been the same: Children solve the algorithms in the video-game context far better than they solve them in the disembedded laboratory context. The decision-science literature would lead to the expectation that neither children nor adults could internalize these algorithms because it is claimed that the ability to engage in complex multicausal reasoning is beyond the ability of most people. However, any parent who accompanies her 10-year-old to the video arcade at the local mall knows this to be untrue. To do well on games such as Galactia requires the appreciation of algorithms more complex than the ones devised by Ceci and Bronfenbrenner.

In a follow-up experiment, ten-year-olds were given the video-game context; then, after working on it, they were given the more abstract laboratory context in order to determine whether they would transfer the knowledge that they gained in the former to the latter. The answer seems to be that they can do so, but only if the laboratory context is presented immediately after solving the video-game context, and only if the testing room is unchanged and the same computer and mouse are used. Thus, their reasoning is tightly bounded by the psychological context in which it is deployed. Similar boundaries also have been observed in the adult cognitive literature whenever transfer between contexts is observed (Nisbett, Fong, Lehman, & Cheng, 1988; Schooler, 1989).

The racetrack vs. the stock market

In a case study of two men who were known to employ a certain form of reasoning at the racetrack, Ceci and Ruiz asked them to solve a stock market prediction task that was isomorphic in structure to the one they routinely used at the racetrack (Ceci & Ruiz, 1991; in press). The type of reasoning these men used at the racetrack requires a specific multiplicative interaction term to predict outcomes, and it is the use of this specific interaction term that is the basis of their success at the racetrack (see Ceci & Liker, 1986a,b, for validation of this term). Yet, when they were given the opportunity to deploy this same interactive term in a novel context (a stock market simulation that was similarly structured to the racetrack problem), they failed to do so. After 611 trials they were still only slightly better than chance (see Figure 3.2). Interestingly, the man

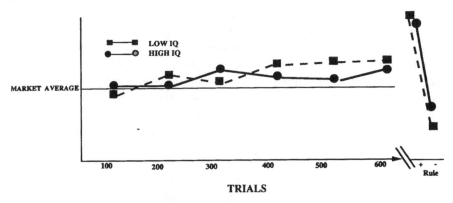

Figure 3.2. Probability of predicting whether a stock will exceed the market average. "Rule" refers to provision of information that the task was analogous to the racetrack task (+), and subsequently altering the correct racetrack weightings (−) without warning.

with the IQ of 125 was no better than the man with the IQ of 80 at transferring his knowledge. If this could be replicated on a more representative sample of individuals and tasks, it would carry important implications for the use of measures of general intelligence in employment screening, diagnosis and remediation.

After 611 trials both men in the stock market simulation were given a hint: They were told that predicting the price–earning ratio at the stock market is similar to predicting post-time odds at the racetrack. As can be seen in Figure 3.2, this hint resulted in immediate transfer of their racing knowledge to near-perfect performance in the stock market context. To insure that they were indeed using the racetrack solution and not some other strategy, the algorithm was then changed to a different one to determine whether their performance would plummet, thus suggesting they were using the racing strategy. As can be seen in Figure 3.2, their performance did indeed plummet when the algorithm was changed. In short, these gamblers realized that a form of reasoning deployed in one context could be applied in another context – but only after the instructions were "rigged" to make the transferability salient! Context was all-important in determining how efficiently they would reason.

Charging batteries and baking cupcakes

In another set of studies, Ceci and Bronfenbrenner (1985) asked 10- and 14-year-old children to either charge a motorcycle battery or bake cupcakes for exactly 30 minutes. While they waited to remove the battery cables or the cupcakes from the oven, the children were allowed to play a video game that was positioned in such a manner that each time they checked the clock to see if the 30 minutes had elapsed, the experimenter could record it. Some children were asked to charge the battery or bake the cupcakes in their homes and others were asked to do so in a university laboratory.

As can be seen in Figure 3.3, the children who performed these tasks in their homes exhibited a U-shaped pattern of clock checking during the 30 minute waiting period. They checked the clocks a lot during the first ten minutes, then they hardly looked at the clock again until the waning minutes, when they would look incessantly at the clock. In contrast, the children who performed these tasks in the laboratory exhibited a completely different pattern of clock-checking, one that was ascending and linear over the 30 minute period. These two patterns of clock checking reflect different cognitive strategies and different efficiencies.

The U-shaped pattern of clock checking in Figure 3.3 indicates that the children who charged the battery or baked the cupcakes in their homes deployed an early calibration strategy. They checked the clock every few minutes during the early part of the period in order to confirm their estimation that a few minutes had elapsed, no more and no less. Once they received multiple confirmations of their subjective assessment of the passage of time, they were free to immerse themselves in the video game without concern for watching the clock. Their mental clocks had been "set" by these early clock checks and they now were on "auto-pilot" until the final minutes. Support for this interpretation was obtained in a follow-up study in which the clocks were programmed to run faster or slower than real time and the children were able to recover similar U-shaped patterns unless the clocks ran 50% or more faster or slower than real time. In other words, children as young as 10 years old spontaneously calibrated their mental clocks and this is reflected in the U-shaped pattern of clock checking.

What is so strategic about a U-shaped pattern of clock checking? There are two useful purposes that this pattern serves. First, it results in the same level of punctuality that was seen in children who performed the task in a laboratory setting, but with one

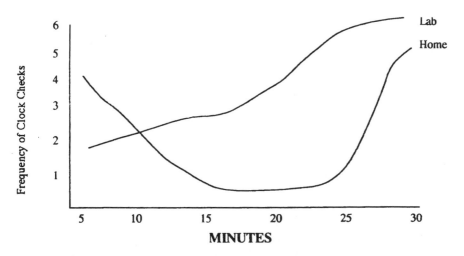

Figure 3.3. Mean frequency of checking the lock in home and lab contexts.

third fewer clock checks. So, this strategy is more economical in terms of energy expended. Second, the U-shaped pattern allowed the children to immerse themselves in the video game once they calibrated their mental clocks. This meant that they were able to invest all of their conscious resources in improving their scores in the game instead of worrying about the time. Thus, a coefficient representing the U-shaped quadratic was associated with superior video-game performance.

In summary, the home setting allowed children to engage in a relaxed, yet strategic form of time monitoring that had significant advantages. If one had only observed these children in the laboratory setting, there would be far less evidence that they possessed such a strategy. It was only on the female sex-typed task (baking cupcakes), that any evidence was found for the use of this strategy in the laboratory context. It was on this task that the older boys displayed the U-shaped strategy in the laboratory that was seen only in the home for the male sex-typed task. The reason for this departure seems to be that teenage boys did not regard the baking task as serious, thus they were more relaxed in the way they monitored the passage of time – even when they were in the lab setting. In contrast, older girls did not behave in the more relaxed manner in the laboratory when the task was male sex-typed, thus demonstrating the contextual subtleties of cognitive development.

Transfer of learning across contexts appears to be quite limited (Ceci, in press). In fact, outside the case of those rare individuals who are recognized as brilliant (e.g., Feynman, 1986), the norm is for subjects not to transfer. Depending on how much knowledge one possesses about the theme in question, and the social implications of various aspects of the physical context, cognitive processes will be deployed with differential efficiency.

The failure to transfer learning from one context to another is pervasive, including both the young and old, educated and uneducated, and high and low IQ. If true, then it would be surprising to learn that students in schools and universities acquired a general ability to solve problems. Based on the available research, it appears that even those students at good universities who take ample science, statistics, and math courses do not transfer the principles they learn in these courses to novel contexts. Leshowitz (1989) recently reported that University of Arizona students who had been amply exposed to scientific reasoning in their math, statistics, and science courses were, nevertheless, scientifically illiterate. Principles such as control groups, counterbalancing, and so on go unappreciated in everyday contexts despite the students' appreciation of them in their courses:

Of the several hundred students tested, many of whom had taken more than 6 years of laboratory science in high school and college and advanced mathematics through calculus, almost none demonstrated even a semblance of acceptable methodological reasoning. (Leshowitz, 1989, p. 1160)

Later, we will return to why we think people do not transfer their knowledge, and what we, as educators, can do about it. Prior to doing so, however, we will add one last piece of information to complete this story of context specificity in cognition, before turning to the new Brazilian work on this topic.

Problem isomorphs

In a vague way, the context-specific reasoning examples that we have been describing are special instances of what are called "problem isomorphs." An isomorph is an analog of the same problem but couched in different terminology or in a different context. For example, the famous problem about missionaries and cannibals, wherein a single missionary cannot be left alone with more than one cannibal, can be converted into an analogous problem about wives and jealous husbands, in which a wife cannot be left alone with more than one man unless her husband is present (Gholson, Eymard, Long, Morgan, & Leeming, 1988). General questions that these problem isomorphs pose are: to what extent does experience in functionally relevant domains of one's culture promote ability in other areas?; and can intellectual abilities easily be transferred or generalized to a broader range of abilities? The general finding in the cognitive literature is that cross-task correlations between a problem and its isomorph are usually low: knowing how well individuals can solve one problem is little help in predicting how well they will solve the same problem in another context, even when it is isomorphic to it.

Sometimes subjects in psychology experiments will gain insights by answering one version of a problem that helps them answer its isomorph. For example, Schliemann and MagalhÜes (1990) gave unschooled Brazilian maids proportional-reasoning problems in familiar contexts (cooking, purchasing foods) and unfamiliar contexts (mixing medicinal herbs). They found that answering problems in the familiar food-purchasing context improved the maids' ability to answer similar problems in the familiar cooking context as well as in the unfamiliar medicinal-herbs context. This becomes understandable when one considers the problems themselves. Food-purchasing problems require an exactness that is not true of cooking and medicinal herbs. Thus, when asked "If 2 kilograms of rice cost 6 cruzados, how much will one have to pay for 3 kilograms?" these maids frequently exhibited exact proportional reasoning, whereas when they were asked isomorphic problems having to do with how much water to add to a recipe they usually estimated answers – the same way they do when actually cooking. As a result, their answers on cooking questions gave no evidence that they could engage in accurate proportional reasoning. When the purchasing problems preceded the cooking and medicinal-herbs problems, this resulted in significantly greater proportional-reasoning accuracy because it alerted the maids to the isomorphism between the tasks. In Detterman's (in press) framework, placing the purchasing task immediately before the cooking and herbs tasks "rigged" the results. He would probably argue that exposing the ten-year-olds in our studies to the video-game context immediately prior to the geometric shape task also rigged the results, and that no real degree of transferability is demonstrated in such studies. While we agree with this argument in principal, we think that these studies of limited transfer may hold a clue as to how more genuine transfer may be nurtured. It may be that the use of proximal examples and explicit instructions are a necessary first step to inculcating transfer, at least in most people. As Schliemann and Carraher (in press) note in their discussion of the Brazilian maids research:

These findings ... suggest that proportionality reasoning may develop first in a limited range of contexts and about particular contents. Given the proper conditions, similarities of relations can be detected and transfer and generalization become possible. This recognition may then act as a bridge for transfer of procedures to the unknown contexts. (Schliemann & Carraher, in press, p. 16)

Before we attempt to nurture transfer by juxtaposing examples from different contexts, it is important to keep in mind that the order in which problems are solved can be a complicated matter, as seen in the work by Gholson et al. (1988). The three jealous husbands and two women problem helped subjects transfer their solution to an isomorph that involved three cannibals and two missionaries, whereas the reverse was not true. On the other hand, answering a version of this problem that involved only two missionaries helped produce transfer to an isomorph involving two jealous husbands, whereas the reverse was not true! In this regard, Stroud's classic transfer studies (1940) of Latin grammar to English grammar, of classical of physics to the mechanical problems of daily life, and of Euclidean geometry to everyday reasoning problems, found extremely small levels of transfer. In short, problem solving can be exceedingly context-dependent. Slight changes in the problem format, the order of solving a problem, or in the wording of the problem can lead either to success or failure to transfer a solution process. It suggests we abandon the idea that one can instill an ability through sheer exercise of a general habit.

Perhaps the best-known case of a failure to transfer in isomorphic reasoning is that of Wason and Johnson-Laird's well-known selection task (Wason, 1966, 1968; Wason & Shapiro, 1971; Wason & Evans, 1972; Johnson-Laird, 1983; Johnson-Laird, Legrenzi & Sonino-Legrenzi, 1972; Johnson-Laird & Wason, 1972). In this task subjects are asked to decide whether some rule is true. For example, the rule might be: "If a card has a vowel on one side, it will have an even number on its other side." Then subjects are shown the following four cards:

A, B, 2, 5

and are asked to turn over only those cards that are critical to verifying the rule. In this example, the best decision is to turn over the 5 and A, as these allow one to disconfirm the rule with the minimum number of card turns. Although university students have great difficulty with this problem, they do much better when the isomorph is framed in terms of a travel game in which one must decide whether to turn over cards that have a picture of a type of transportation on them or to turn over the ones that have the name of a town on them. From a cognitive perspective, there is nothing in the travel isomorph to make it easier than the number-letter task. Its underlying structure is identical to the task involving the numbers and letters. And yet, performance on one is vastly different from performance on the other (Johnson-Laird, 1983).

Such findings show that thinking skills developed in one context often do not transfer to other contexts, so that cognitive abilities learned in one specific context may well have little impact on performance in connected areas. They also call into question the presumption that only a limited number of mental faculties need to be trained, and that once they have been trained they can be used in a wide range of situations. This presumption has led American researchers to become pessimistic about the limits of training and the generalizability of cognitive operations. For instance, Schooler (1989) concluded his review of the cognitive training literature by noting that:

The question for which we do have some empirical answers has to do with how generalizable cognitive training is from one subject area to another. As of now, the answer is not very much. (Schooler, 1989, p. 11)

And Detterman (in press) concludes his analysis of the transfer literature by claiming that even college students fail to transfer unless the experiment is so obvious as to make the term transfer meaningless:

What is truly amazing about all these studies is not that they really do not produce transfer . . . (but) the extent of similarity it is possible to have between two problems without subjects realizing that the two situations are identical and require the same solutions. Evidently the only way to get subjects to see the similarity is to tell them or to point it out in some not-so-subtle way" (p. 20)

Cognition in and out of school: research from Brazil

"E' preciso saber como o cenario seRa' montado antes de iniciar a peÄa" (It is necessary to know how the stage is set before the play may begin – Brazilian proverb)

By now you might justifiably be wondering: What are children learning in school, if not to transfer their knowledge to novel contexts? And are the failures that we have been describing pervasive or are they limited to those students who are low in intelligence or without motivation? Although we have already alluded to the fact that IQ does not seem to predict transfer in complex tasks (Ceci & Ruiz, 1991), and that formal schooling does not seem to matter (Schliemann & Carraher, 1989), there is direct support for these views from cross-cultural research carried out in Brazil by a group of developmental psychologists (the second author is a member of this group).

Researchers at the Federal University of Pernambuco in Northeast Brazil have carried out a series of experiments, comparing poor and middle-class children who possess differing levels of formal schooling. The main manipulation has been to study the influence of various experimental contexts on poor and middle-class children's problem solving.

Some information about the social background of poor Brazilian children is indispensable in order to understand the reason Brazilian researchers have included working experience as a variable in their designs. Poor childrens' families generally dwell in urban shanty towns, called "favelas." In Recife, the capital of Northeast Brazil, approximately one million individuals (or 50% of the entire population) live in favelas. (Although this is the highest percentage in the country, Sao Paulo and Rio de Janiero have greater numbers of favela residents than Recife because of their greater sizes.)

The management of money is one of the most pressing problems faced by favela families. Generally, the basic wages earned by the parents of favela children are insufficient to cover even the most basic daily subsistance needs, let alone saving for unexpected emergencies. Thus, many informal activities are employed within favela families to meet their financial needs, for example, providing services, food, etc. These informal activities are carried out in the neighborhood by most of its members to ensure the flow of resources. In a favela environment these activities form systems or devices that are used to survive, considering the low level of skills involved. For example, housewives take on various domestic tasks such as babysitting for another family's children, performing some practical job, like mending, washing clothes, and preparing sweets or pastries to be sold in the market by one of their own children. Favela children are forced to go out to work at a very early age in order to aid the family. Thus, a family with many children is at an advantage because of the extra income the children can earn; their cooperation is permanently available and their maintenance cost is insignificant. Children squeeze into whatever space is left over in the small favela rooms, they wear any used clothing that can be found, and they eat whatever food is available. They will skip school whenever the economy of the household needs them, and a sizable number of them do not attend school at all beyond first grade: Generally, the number of children who quit school rises precipitously around 10 to 11 years of age, a period in which a large number start working in order to contribute to the family financially. Only 12% of children who attend the first year of school finish the last year of compulsory education.

Poor children from the favelas begin their work careers at an early age in a range of unskilled occupations, such as selling fruits in the market or peanuts, ice cream, suntan oil on the beach, sweets, coffee, needles, coconuts, corn on the cob, or other items at sidewalk stands; watching over parked cars in front of restaurants and shops for a tip; collecting choice bits of garbage or begging for left-over food from door to door for themselves or for their chickens, pigs, or other domestic fowl at home in the backyard; shining shoes in the town center; cleaning windshields and selling popcorn at the traffic lights; gathering waste paper, plastic containers, metal and other waste products that can be sold for scrap. Even when they do not go outside to work, favela children are expected to help their mother with domestic chores.

Thus, children represent an important mechanism of survival for poor families living in favelas. However, social life in the favela unfolds in a manner that is more complex than might appear from this synopsis.

The decision to focus on social class was motivated by the desire not only to document class differences in cognitive processes as a function of different forms of task presentation and in different settings, but also to provide an empirical and theoretical understanding of the influence of sociocultural factors on the cognitive functioning of different social classes, and to reflect on what this means for cognitive developmental psychology more generally. This latter point carries with it several methodological implications for comparative research that we address in the conclusion.

Below, we describe three studies concerned with the manner in which cognitive abilities are affected by contextual factors across social classes. The first study investigated street-vendor children from favelas as they were engaged in solving arithmetic problems. Some of these problems were embedded in academic tasks and others were embedded in everyday situations that the children confront in their jobs.

The second study consisted of two experiments. Both of these dealt with the influence of the context in which a "class-inclusion" problem is presented for middle-class vs. poor children. In the first experiment of this study the class-inclusion problem was presented in both a formal context and an informal context (a sales-transaction context). The poor children in this experiment worked as street vendors, so the informal sales-transaction context was familiar for them. These children unwittingly participated in the research during the normal course of a customer–vendor transaction in which the customer was one of the researchers. For middle-class children this "same" context (in which they were asked to role-play vendors in a game situation) was rather unfamiliar. None of them had worked in this capacity before, unlike the poor children. In the second experiment of this study an attempt was made to test middle-class children in an informal context that was more familiar to them. As with the poor children in the first experiment, the middle-class children were not made aware that they were participating in an experiment.

The third study assessed, across social classes, the potential influence of communicative context on cognition, by comparing children's performance on a standard "conservation" task with a series of modified versions in which social intelligibility and communicative interactions were varied.

Mathematics in the street and in the school

Carraher, Carraher, and Schliemann (1985) carried out a study of daily uses of mathematics by young Brazilians (9–15 years old) working in commercial activities. Their sample was composed of sons and daughters of poor migrant workers who had moved to favelas in Recife. In the course of their daily jobs as street vendors, their work requires them to carry out mental arithmetic, such as subtraction, addition, multiplication, and sometimes division. The intriguing point is that despite their limited formal education – in general, these children attend school for fewer than five years – they can easily calculate how much certain goods costs and how much change a customer should receive, given a certain amount of money.

Carraher, Carraher, and Schliemann (1985) compared the performance in mathematical problems embedded in real-life situations (Informal Test) and context-free computational isomorphs of these problems (Formal Test). The results indicated that problems presented in the context of customer–vendor transactions (e.g., "If a large coconut costs 76 cruzeiros, and a small one costs 50, how much do the two cost together?") were much more easily solved than the same problems presented in the decontextualized Formal Test (e.g., "How much is 76 + 50?"). In fact, 98% of the 63 problems presented in the Informal Test involving practical questions were correctly solved; on the other hand, only 37% of the decontextualized math questions were answered correctly. At an intermediate level of context, there were Formal Test word problems which provided some descriptive setting for the subjects but were not couched in the language or content of their specific jobs (e.g., "If an orange costs 76 cruzeiros and a passion fruit cost 50, how much do the two cost together?"). The rate of correct answers on these intermediate problems was 74%. Clearly, children bring different aspects of their knowledge to bear in different problem-solving contexts.

How is it possible that subjects are able to solve a computational problem in a natural context and yet fail to solve the same problem when it is disconnected from that context?[1] An answer is suggested by the findings of a qualitative analysis of these children's protocols. This analysis indicates that the problem-solving routines used may have been different in the various experimental settings. In the two natural settings children tended to reason by using what can be termed "convenient groupings," while in the formal setting school-taught routines were more frequently, although not exclusively, observed.

Thus, mathematical ability was demonstrated to be dependent on the situations in which it is elicited. It is interesting to note that the exactly complementary result was reported by Perret-Clermont (1980) who, in an investigation of second-grade children (probably from a middle-class milieu), found that they had no difficulty in solving paper-and-pencil arithmetical exercises, such as $5 + \ldots = 8$, which they were accustomed to solve in school. However, using the same types of addition problems in a different context (bunch of flowers, counting of sweets), they observed little transfer of the previous knowledge. So, the context-specificity of unschooled children's arithmetic is not unique: schooled children often fail to solve isomorphs of school problems that are couched in nonschool language and content.

These findings (Carraher et al., 1985) show how the inferior performance of poor children in formal tasks cannot always be taken as indicative of their arithmetical competence in everyday life, which requires the use of elaborate cultural knowledge and abilities. Thus, on the basis of these findings, it is possible tentatively to suggest that (1) an individual's ability to demonstrate a competence is, at least to some extent, dependent on the social and cultural situations in which he or she has the opportunity to use it. In comparative research, behavior is most appropriately observed in a functional context (ecological setting) in which it naturally occurs; to adopt a different approach is to risk making ethnocentric and, therefore, mistaken evaluations; (2) the social setting determines, in part, the level of difficulty of the tasks and problems; it means that an identical problem may assume different meanings for individuals or sociocultural groups when it is embedded in different social contexts; (3) we can more reliably assess an individual's pattern of cognitive competencies when the sample of informative life tasks for his or her group has been classified and defined with respect to a number of descriptive features and everyday experiences. In fact, the social ecology in which individuals carry out their lives greatly influences performance by determining the problems that are important to solve and the strategies appropriate to solving them. To sum up, the findings from this first Brazilian study suggest that when we try to appraise practical capacities that may be enhanced by everyday life experiences, it is necessary to consider the context carefully, not only as a general setting for development, but also as a setting for the display of the ability in question. The way in which individuals tackle intellectual problems may change radically with the social context.

Class inclusion

The above study suggests that a discrepancy between formal and informal testing situations often exists when comparing children from diverse sociocultural backgrounds. To explore this further, Roazzi and his colleagues (Roazzi, 1987; Roazzi & Carraher, 1991; Roazzi and Bryant, 1991; Roazzi, Bryant and Schliemann, 1988) examined variations to two Piagetian tasks: class inclusion and conservation.

In the first study, Roazzi (Roazzi, 1987) analyzed the performances of 60 poor and middle-class 6- to 9-year-old children from Recife, Brazil, on class-inclusion problems, first in an informal context, and then in a formal one (Roazzi, 1986a).

Street-vendor children unknowingly participated in the research during the normal course of a customer–vendor interaction. The interviewer, posing as a casual purchaser, searched among the goods for two classes of things or foods (e.g., mint and strawberry chewing gum) of the same price per unit and that are included in a superordinate class (e.g., two flavors of chewing gum).

Next, the researcher verified that the child understood the two subclasses (mint and strawberry chewing gum) as a part of a larger class (chewing gum) asking questions such as "What kinds of chewing gum do you have?" and "How much is this one?" If the child demonstrated how to include the two subclasses of the chewing gum in the superordinate class, then the researcher divided 4 units of one subclass (i.e., mint chewing gum), 2 units of the other subclass (i.e., strawberry chewing gum), and displaying them, asked: "Do I pay more for the mint chewing gums or for the strawberry chewing gums? Why?" "For you to get more money is it better to sell me the mint chewing gum or is it better to sell me the strawberry chewing gum? Why?"

So, in the Informal Test, working-class children were studied in a context in which they work and solve daily challenges (shop, street kiosk, or market stall) without knowing that they were being tested. Furthermore, they were tested in an activity that was meaningful to them, something significant for their daily survival.

Afterwards, the same children were given a formal test (called Formal Test 2), approximately similar to that described by Piaget and Inhelder (1969), which has the same logical structure as the Informal Test ("Are there more yellow balls or are there more balls? Why?").

In addition, middle-class children were tested in the same way in these two kinds of class-inclusion tests. The Informal Test was called Formal Test 1 because, in spite of the same questions and the same logical problem structure, for these children the context was not the one in which they met their daily challenges. As part of a game context, these middle-class children were invited to pretend they were chewing-gum vendors and the examiner was a purchaser. After giving him chewing gum to sell, the same series of questions was asked as in the Informal Test.

Results showed a significant interaction between social class and context; differences between poor and middle-class children were found in each of the contexts. Street-vendor children were more successful at the class-inclusion task in the natural (Informal) context than in the Formal one ($\chi^2 = 9.38$; d.f. 2; $p < 0.05$); middle-class children, on the other hand, were more prone to success in the classical (Formal) version of the task ($\chi^2 = 7.5$; d.f. 2; $p < 0.05$).

Furthermore, a comparison of poor and middle-class children in the two kinds of tests, Formal 2 and Informal (for poor children) and Formal 1 (for middle-class children), indicate that the superiority of the Informal context is disproportionately greater for the poor children.

These data indicate that there are social-class differences in the ability to understand and perform a logical task. Performance varied according to the degree of similarity between the usual situations of a subject's daily life and the type of experimental situation used by the researcher.

In the above experiment the context was not varied for the middle-class children; in fact, Formal Test 1 cannot be considered as a natural (i.e., Informal) test. Thus, a second experiment was conducted to examine their performance on an informal test. In this experiment an attempt was made to test middle-class children in a natural context. Consequently, in this new experiment a special effort was made to make one of the two class-inclusion tasks as natural as possible for the middle-class children ($N = 50$). Their mean ages were 6.4 years, 7.3 years, and 8.5 years.

In the Informal Test, children participated in 30-minute play sessions. During these sessions, games were organized by the examiners and children with the specific aim of getting the latter accustomed to the former, the place (a room especially adapted for the purpose in the children's school), and the context of the game. The context

Table 3.1. Distribution of poor and middle class children (MCC) by level of performance in Formal Test 2 of the class-inclusion task*

Class	Level of performance			
	NC	I	C	N
Poor	11	12	7	30
	37%	40%	23%	
MCC	10	4	16	30
	33%	13%	54%	
Total	21	16	23	60

*NC = no class inclusion; I = intermediate; C = class inclusion; $\chi^2 = 7.5$; $p < 0.05$.

Table 3.2. Distribution of poor and middle class children by level of performance respectively in the Informal Test and in the Formal Test 1 of the class-inclusion task*

Class	Level of performance			
	NC	I	C	*N*
Poor	4	8	18	30
	13%	27%	60%	
MCC	14	8	8	30
	46%	27%	27%	
Total	18	16	23	60

*NC = no class inclusion; I = intermediate; C = class inclusion; χ^2 = 9.38; $p < 0.05$.

of one of these games was a sales transaction in which children role-played vendors and the examiner role-played a customer. The first five sessions were preparatory for the actual testing of the subjects in an informal context. This informal test followed the identical procedure and questioning of the informal test that was used with poor street vendors above.

The Formal Test was the same Formal Test 2 used in the above experiment. It took place in a special room set aside for the purpose in the school. The order of administration of the Informal Test and Formal Test 2 was counterbalanced across subjects.

A series of comparisons of the results of this experiment with the above experiment were conducted. The comparison of the performance of the middle class children in the Informal condition of this experiment with the performance of poor children in the above experiment, revealed no difference (χ^2 = 0.516; d.f. 2; p = n.s.).

These findings demonstrate that context is as relevant for middle-class children as it is for poor ones. In fact, in the comparisons of middle-class children of this

Table 3.3. Distribution of poor children by level of performance in the Formal Test 2 and in the Informal Test of the class-inclusion task*

Test	Level of performance			
	NC	I	C	*N*
Informal	4	8	18	30
	13%	27%	60%	
Formal 2	11	12	7	30
	37%	40%	23%	
Total	15	20	25	60
	25%	33%	42%	

*NC = no class inclusion; I = intermediate; C = class inclusion; χ^2 = 8.9; $p < 0.05$.

Table 3.4. Distribution of middle class children by level of performance in the Formal Test 2 and in Formal Test 1 of the class-inclusion task*

	Level of performance			
Test	NC	I	C	N
Formal 1	14	8	8	30
	46%	27%	27%	
Formal 2	10	4	16	30
	33%	13%	54%	
Total	24	12	24	60

*NC = no class inclusion; I = intermediate; C = class inclusion; χ^2 = 4.66; p = N.S.

experiment with the poor children in the above one, the superior performance of the latter over the former disappeared when the performance of middle-class children in the Informal Test was considered.

Hence, the contextual aspects became important components in the type of experimental methodology adopted, making it difficult to infer a competence directly from a single performance. It is not possible to make inferences about cognitive differences between a class of children for whom a certain task is more familiar than it is for another class of children (Gay & Cole, 1967; Labov, 1972; Roazzi, 1986b, 1987).

In this research we can see that poor children behave differently: in the informal context they perceive themselves as street vendors in the exercise of their occupation. Since their survival depends on this occupation, a mistake in the sales transaction would be very costly. In the formal context, which is more similar to a school setting, they frequently become passive, and the examination does not make much sense to them; moreover the purpose of the game is not always clear to them. In the two

Table 3.5. Distribution of poor and middle class children by level of performance in the Informal Tests, of the class-inclusion task*

	Level of performance			
Test	NC	I	C	N
Poor	4	8	18	30
	13%	27%	60%	
MCC	6	8	16	30
	20%	27%	53%	
Total	10	16	34	60

*NC = no class inclusion; I = intermediate; C = class inclusion; χ^2 = 0.516; p = N.S.

contexts we have an exchange of parts, different frames of reference, a changed interpretation of the situation, and the social meaning of the event. It is this distinction between natural and formal contexts which explains the varying performances found in the two test conditions; and this is the reason it is untenable to attempt inferences about the level of competence of the poor children on the class-inclusion task when considered apart from its context. Instead we obtain only a performance in a specific context, at a precise moment, from which we cannot always generalize an underlying competence.

Thus, we cannot conclude that children lack certain cognitive abilities just because they do not exhibit them in a given context. These abilities could be expressed in other contexts. In this example, poor children demonstrated in a daily context a performance significantly superior to the one they exhibited in a more formal testing context, even though the two tasks had the same logical structure. Thus, methodological features, rather than a child's deficiencies, may be responsible for some of the social-class differences that have been reported in the cognitive-developmental research.

This consideration allows us better to comprehend why it is unwarranted to assume that cognitive operations are deployed transcontextually with equal efficiency; presenting children belonging to different sociocultural backgrounds with the same context without first considering differences in their respective interests, levels of motivation, and their interpretation of the context, render an assessment of their competence problematic.

Conservation

The third and final study from Brazil that we will describe in detail examined conservation ability across social classes (Roazzi, Bryant & Schliemann, 1988; Roazzi & Bryant, 1991). This work suggests that wrong answers on the traditional conservation task may be due to misinterpretation of the crucial conservation question by the poor children (i.e., due to a lack of explicitness), rather than to a delayed acquisition of this logical ability.

In the traditional conservation task children are first asked to compare two quantities that are identical in appearance. After the children judge them to be equal, the experimenter then transforms the perceptual appearance of one of the quantities and asks the child to compare the two quantities again. Preoperational children usually claim that the two quantities are now unequal, a finding exacerbated among economically disadvantaged and culturally different children. An incorrect response on this task led Piaget to claim that children have not grasped the principle of invariance of quantity and therefore they wrongly treat a mere perceptual change as a quantitative change.

This conservation procedure can be criticized for not making it clear to subjects that the judgment that they are being asked to make is a quantitative one and not a perceptual one. In fact, in the traditional form of the task, children are first simply asked to look at and compare two quantities which are identical both quantitatively and perceptually. The fact that the two quantities also look exactly alike may mislead the child into thinking that the initial, pretransformation, question and also the question asked for the transformation, are about the perceptual appearance of the two quantities (e.g., height of beakers) and not about their actual amounts. So, when the experimenter transforms the appearance of one of the two quantities in front of the child, the child, seeing that they are different and thinking the question to be a perceptual one, answers that they are no longer the same. In other words, this type of procedure may lead to a misinterpretation of the conservation question, and consequently to children's failure to answer correctly. If the traditional sequence of questions may lead children to incorrectly assume that what the examiner really wants is a perceptual and not a quantitative comparison, then a stress on the quantitative comparison from the beginning should lead to more frequent conservation answers, especially among economically disadvantaged children who do so poorly on this task.

To test this hypothesis, Brazilian researchers have carried out three studies modifying the traditional Piagetian procedure to assess conservation. Carraher, Carraher, and Schliemann (1985) examined four groups of four- or five-year-old Brazilian children in two versions of the conservation of discrete quantities task and two of the conservation of continuous quantities task. Two groups were given the traditional Piagetian versions of each task and, accordingly, first established the equality between the quantities through perceptual comparison. The other two groups underwent a modified version of each task where, instead of a perceptual comparison, the child was first asked to make a quantitative comparison between the two quantities. Results revealed a significantly higher performance in the modified version among five-year-olds (60% and 45% conservation answers for discrete and continuous quantity, respectively, in the modified version versus 27% and 0% in the traditional version).

Roazzi compared Brazilian children of different social classes in two types of conservation tasks: liquid and length. In the conservation of liquid task, where the traditional perceptual comparison of the two quantities was asked in the first phase of the task, middle-class Brazilian children performed much better than their poorer peers. In the length conservation task, which from the beginning laid more emphasis on a quantitative comparison, no differences were found. The fact that the poor children did not differ from middle-class children when the aim of the task – a quantitative comparison – was made explicit from the beginning suggests that the difference usually found may be due to misunderstandings about what it is that the examiner wants and not to any deficit in logical reasoning.

On the basis of these two studies, Roazzi, Bryant, and Schliemann (1988) conducted a third study to determine whether differences between social classes in the conservation task can be explained in terms of differences in the need for explicitness. We will delve into this study in some detail.

The performance of 192 poor and middle class 5-, 6-, 7- and 8-year-old children was studied in liquid conservation tasks under three conditions: Control, Quantity, and Money (each child was tested in only one condition).

In the Control condition the initial comparison was made through a perceptual estimate. Part 1 – The examiner suggests to the child that they play a vendor–purchaser game in which the experimenter takes the role of the purchaser and the subject adopts the role of a vendor. "Let's play a game. I am a customer and you are selling lemonade. Here is the jug with the lemonade and the glasses (A and A'). All right. You sell the lemonade in these glasses and after we have drunk it we take the glass back. How much are you going to charge me for the lemonade in this glass?" "I would like to have a lemonade. How much is it? Give me one, please."

Part 2 – After the child pours the lemonade into one of the glasses (A), the experimenter says: "I want to buy another lemonade for a friend of mine. Pour the same amount of lemonade here into this glass (A')." After this the experimenter puts the two glasses (A and A') next to each other and asks: "Do you think that my friend and I are going to drink the same amount of lemonade, or is one of us going to drink more than the other?" "How do you know? How did you guess?"

Part 3 – If the child replies that one glass contains more lemonade than the other, the experimenter says: "So, pour more lemonade into the other one where you think there is less lemonade so that the two glasses have the same amount of lemonade." "And now, is there the same amount of lemonade in the two glasses?" When the child agrees that the two glasses have the same amount, the experimenter asks: "How much does this lemonade cost?" (pointing to glass A). "And how much does this one cost?" (pointing to glass A').

Part 4 – The experimenter then pretends to be surprised to find that glass A' is dirty, and, producing a new glass which is clean (B), says: "This glass (pointing to A') is dirty. Let's change it for this other one (B), which is clean." "Now I am going to pour the lemonade from this glass (A') into this one (B)." "And now, do my friend and I still have the same amount to drink or is one going to drink more lemonade than the other? How do you know? How did you guess? Why?" Part 5 – "And about the price, do my friend and I pay the same price or is one going to pay more than the other? Why?"[2]

In the Quantity condition the child was not allowed to make a perceptual comparison. The initial comparison to establish the equality between the two glasses was obtained through measurement. The instructions were more explicit about the quantitative nature of the task than is the case in the Control condition, and involved measurement in the initial part of the problem. In the Quantity condition the children first had to dispense the lemonade in the two glasses with a ladle ("Each glass of lemonade that you sell must be filled four times with this ladle and the ladle must always be full"). Thus, they were explicitly asked to put 4 ladle-fulls of lemonade into each glass. One of the two glasses was covered, in order to preclude a perceptual comparison. The child had to judge the two amounts as equal on the basis of having put the same number of ladle-fulls into each glass. Thereafter the procedure was exactly the same as in the control condition.

The Money condition was exactly the same as the Quantity condition except that the child was told that he would have to sell the lemonade and that each ladle-full was worth 1 cruzeiro. The child was asked to put 4 cruzeiros worth of lemonade in each glass. So the emphasis here was as much on the price as on the number of ladles.

Two scores were analyzed: the number of correct responses, and children's success in justifying their responses. Table 3.1 shows the pattern when children are divided into the usual Piagetian categories (Szeminska, 1965): Nonconservers, Intermediate conservers (i.e., children who were either inconsistent or who gave the correct answer but could not justify it), and Conservers (children who gave the correct answer and produced the correct explanation for it).

The two Measurement conservation tasks (Quantity and Money) differed only in terms of their emphasis, and both focused the child's attention at the time of the pretransformation question on a comparison between quantities and not on perceptual appearance.

It is clear from Figure 3.4 that poor children benefited from the introduction of explicit quantitative instructions. Many more poor children were classified either as Intermediate conservers or as Conservers when they were given the Quantity and the Money task than when given the Control task ($\chi^2 = 9.93$ with 4 d.f., $p < .05$). The difference between the Quantity and the Control task was mainly in the number of Intermediate conservers, while in the Money task the difference was in the number of Conservers.

Among middle-class children differences emerged between the three conditions, but they assumed a different pattern from that seen for the poor children ($\chi^2 = 12.25$ with 4 d.f., $p < 0.01$). Middle-class children were no better in the Quantity task than in the Control task, but in the Quantity conditions, more of them were classified as Intermediate conservers while at the same time fewer of them were classified as Conservers than was true in the Control condition. There was some evidence that they benefited from the instructions in the Money task vis-à-vis the Control task, because just as many were classified as Conservers but more of them were classified as Intermediate Conservers in the Money task.

The differences between social classes reached significance only in the Control condition ($\chi^2 = 6.93$ with 2 d.f., $p < 0.05$). Social-class differences in the other two measurement conditions disappeared (quantity condition $\chi^2 = 0.14$ with 2 d.f., p = n.s. and money condition $\chi^2 = 1.40$ with 2 d.f., p = n.s.). These data indicate that it is not a question of having or not having a logical ability that differentiates poor and middle-class children, but a difference in the ability to detect without confusion the communicative message transmitted by the language and the procedure. This finding is most parsimoniously viewed as due to a social difference between poor and middle-class children rather than to a cognitive difference.

The results of this experiment not only show a strong link between context and performance on a logical ability task, but they give us some ideas about how contexts are related to one another. Children's failures to give conserving answers may not be caused by the child's concentration on a particular perceptual feature, such as the different levels of lemonade in the two different glasses (this is the position defended by Piaget),[3] but by the experimenter's failure to take into account the child's assump-

PERCENTAGE

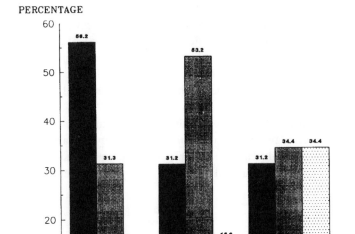

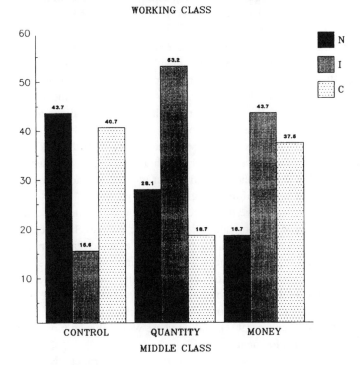

Figure 3.4.

tions about the task, and the interaction of these assumptions and the linguistic and communicative aspects of the task. The data can also be viewed as a reflection of an inadequate communicative competence of the child to understand the real intention of the experimenter. This mutual misunderstanding of child and experimenter is apparently a function of the context in which the task is embedded, the mental operations demanded by the task itself, and the meaningfulness of the goal implicit in the traditional conservation task.

Social-class differences found in the control condition but not in the two other measurement conditions indicates that the explicit stress on quantity has an appreciably stronger effect on poor children than on middle-class ones. The former benefitted most from this explicitness, particularly when money is involved.

Conclusion

Our review of work that spans continents, social classes, and levels of formal education shows that the context in which learning occurs has an enormous influence on cognition, by serving to instantiate specific knowledge structures, by activating context-specific strategies, and by influencing the subject's interpretation of the task itself. Neither context nor cognition can be understood in isolation; they form an integrated system in which the cognitive skill in question becomes part of the context. To try to assess them separately is akin to trying to assess the beauty of a smile separately from the face it is part of.

It follows that cognitive-developmental research must, if it aims to probe an individual's underlying competence, take into consideration both the social environment of the subjects and the meaning of the experimental context as a consequence of this environment. This means that it is necessary to consider the social situation in which the task is embedded, the task materials, the mental operations demanded by the task, and the meaningfulness of the goal of the activity. Before planning an experimental procedure, researchers should ask: Which features of the task situation facilitate the assessment of competence and which features may obstruct it? To accomplish this it may become necessary to know far more about the ecology of our subjects' lives than we have heretofore thought necessary.

An implication of the research we have been discussing is that there is a need to merge both observational and experimental methods in the quest to chart the development of cognitive competence. Observational methods (in order to reach a more exact understanding of the social milieu and the subject's comprehension of the situation), and experimental approaches (for precision and disentanglement of variables that are confounded in everyday settings) can complement each other. Elsewhere we have argued that approximations to scientific truth have to make a link between these two methods (Ceci & Bronfenbrenner, 1991), and nowhere would this be more true than in the field of cognitive development.

To conclude, the performance of an individual in an experiment is inherently grounded in the social situation of their performance. The studies presented in this chapter highlight the need for a fine-grained examination of the context of the experimental situation, especially for children from poor and/or culturally different backgrounds. This point underscores the need to consider methodological issues before beginning any individual assessment.

Although a large number of investigations (such as our own studies) have shown changes in performance as a function of changes in context, our understanding of the processes underlying such effects is far from complete. We have only a very limited knowledge of the nature of the interaction between context and performance or its development, and it should be the goal of future research to explore this interface in greater detail.

Notes

1 Investigators should look more seriously at this question, especially if the goal of the research is to draw inferences about the underlying cognitive ability of poor or culturally different youngsters. For instance, sometimes inferences are made about the limits of the abilities of the groups being studied – e.g., "economically disadvantaged children lack complex abstract reasoning processes," when the observed failure may be limited to a particular context and not reflective of a general deficit.

2 After Part 5, the conservation task continued in the same way in all three conditions (Control, Quantity, and Money) as a function of the type of answer obtained. It followed this procedure: Part 6 – if the child has given a correct answer to the quantity question and a correct price, the experimenter draws his attention to the different levels of liquids in the two glasses. "But here (showing glass A) the lemonade is only up to here ... don't you think that someone who is going to drink this glass is going to drink less lemonade and that the glass has to be cheaper?" The test is terminated after the child has given a logical justification for his/her answers. Part 7 – if the subject has given a wrong answer to the quantity question but a correct price, the examiner asks "Didn't you say before that this one has less lemonade? Why does it cost the same now?" If he changes his judgment the experimenter poses the corresponding question. If he does not change his judgment the experimenter asks for a justification and ends the session. Part 8 – if the subject has given a right answer to the quantity question but a wrong price, the experimenter asks "Didn't you say before that both had the same amount of lemonade? So why does one cost more than the other now?" Part 9 – if the child has given a wrong answer and a wrong price, the experimenter says "But before, when you poured the lemonade into these glasses (A and A'), did not you say that my friend and I were going to drink the same amount of lemonade? Why does this glass (B) now have more lemonade than this one (A)?"

3 For Piaget, young children fail the conservation task, which implies reversible thought, because, while they are dominated by salient perceptual cues, reversibility entails going beyond the use of such cues. In Piaget's words: "Suppose a child estimates that there are more beads in B than in A because the level has been raised. He thus 'centers' his thought, or his attention, on the relation between the heights of 'B' and 'A', and ignores the widths." (Piaget, 1950b, pp. 130–131)

References

Bayley, N. (1970). Development of mental abilities. In P. H. Mussen (Ed.), Carmichael's manual of child psychology (Vol. 1, pp. 1163–1209). New York: Wiley.

Berry, J. W. (1983). Textured contexts: Systems and situations in cross-cultural psychology. In S. H. Irvine & J. W. Berry (Eds.), Human assessment and cultural factors. (pp. 117–125). Amsterdam: North Holland Press.

Carraher, T. N., Carraher, D., & Schliemann, A. D. (1985). Mathematics in the streets and in the schools. *British Journal of Developmental Psychology, 3*, 21–29.

Case, R. (1985). Intellectual development from birth to adulthood. Orlando, FL: Academic Press.

Ceci, S. J. (1990). On intelligence . . . more or less: A bioecological treatise on intellectual development. Englewood Cliffs, NJ: Prentice-Hall.

Ceci, S. J. (in press). "Now you see it, now you don't": The effects of context on cognition. In H. Rosselli (Ed.), The Edyth Bush Symposium on intelligence.

Ceci, S. J., & Bronfenbrenner, U. (1985). Don't forget to take the cupcakes out of the oven: Strategic time-monitoring, prospective memory and context. *Child Development, 56*, 175–190.

Ceci, S. J., & Bronfenbrenner, U. (1991). On the demise of everyday memory: Rumors of my death are greatly exaggerated. *American Psychologist, 46*, 27–31.

Ceci, S. J., & Leichtman, M. (1992). Memory cognition, and learning. (pp. 223–240). In S. Segalowitz & I. Rapin (Eds.), Handbook of neuropsychology. Amsterdam: Elsevier.

Ceci, S. J., & Liker, J. (1986a). A day at the races: A study of IQ, expertise, and cognitive complexity. *Journal of Experimental Psychology: General, 115*, 255–266.

Ceci, S. J., & Liker, J. (1986b). Academic and nonacademic intelligence: An experimental separation. In R. J. Sternberg & R. Wagner (Eds.), Practical Intelligence: Origins of competence in the everyday world. New York: Cambridge University Press.

Ceci, S. J., & Ruiz, A. (1991). Cognitive complexity and generality: A case study. (pp. 41–55) In R. Hoffman (Ed.), The psychology of expertise. New York: Springer-Verlag.

Ceci, S. J., & Ruiz, A. (in press). Transfer, abstractness, and intelligence. In D. Detterman & R. J. Sternberg (Eds.), Transfer on Trial: Intelligence, cognition, and instruction. Norwood, NJ: Ablex.

Charlesworth, W. (1979). An ethological approach to studying intelligence. *Human Development, 22*, 212–216.

Chi, M. T. H., & Ceci, S. J. (1987). Content knowledge: Its restructuring with memory development. In H. Reese (Ed.), *Advances in Child Development and Behavior, 20*, 91–146.

Chi, M. T. H., Hutchinson, J., & Robins, A. (1989). How inferences about novel domain-related concepts can be constrained by structural knowledge. *Merrill Palmer Quarterly, 35*, 27–62.

Cole, M., & Scribner, S. (1974). *Culture and thought: A psychological introduction.* New York: Wiley.

Coltheart, V., & Walsh, P. (1988). Expert knowledge and semantic memory. In M. M. Gruneberg, P. Morris, & P. Sykes (Eds.), Practical aspects of memory, Vol. 2. London: Wiley Interscience.

Detterman, D. K. (in press). The Case for the Prosecution: Transfer as an epiphenomenon. In D. Detterman & R. J. Sternberg (Eds.), Transfer on Trial: Intelligence, cognition, and instruction. Norwood, NJ: Ablex.

Eysenck, H. J. (1986). The theory of intelligence and the psychophysiology of cognition. In R. J. Sternberg (Ed.), Advances in the psychology of human intelligence (Vol. 3; pp. 1–34). Hillsdale, NJ: Erlbaum.

Feynman, R. P. (1986). Surely you're joking, Mr. Feynman! New York: W. W. Norton.

Gay, J., & Cole, M. (1967). The new mathematics and an old culture. New York: Holt, Reinehart, & Winston.

Gholson, B., Eymard, L., Long, D., Morgan, D., & Leeming, F. (1988). Problem solving, recall, isomorphic transfer, and nonisomorphic transfer among third grade and fourth grade children. *Cognitive Development, 3*, 37–53.

Irvine, S. H., & Berry, J. W. (1988). The abilities of mankind: A reevaluation. In S. H. Irvine & J. W. Berry (Eds.), Human abilities in cultural context (pp. 3–59). New York: Cambridge University Press.

Jackson, M., & McClelland, J. L. (1979). Processing determinants of reading speed. *Journal of Experimental Psychology: General, 108*, 151–181.

Johnson-Laird, P. N., & Wason, P. C. (1972). A theorical analysis of insight into a reasoning task. In P. N. Johnson-Laird & P. C. Wason (Eds.), Thinking: Readings in Cognitive Science. Cambridge: Cambridge University Press (originally published in *Cognitive Psychology, 1*, 134–148).

Johnson-Laird, P. N. (1983). Mental models: Toward a cognitive science of language, inference, and consciousness. Cambridge, MA: Harvard University Press.

Johnson-Laird, P. N., Legrenzi, P., & Sonino-Legrenzi, M. (1972). Reasoning and a sense of reality. *British Journal of Psychology, 63*, 395–400.

Keil, F. (1984). Mechanisms in cognitive development and the structure of knowledge. In R. J. Sternberg (Ed.), Mechanisms of cognitive development. (pp. 81–100). New York: W. H. Freeman.

Klayman, J. (1984). Learning from feedback in probabilistic environments. Unpublished manuscript. University of Chicago Graduate School of Business.

Labov, W. (1972). The study of language in its social context. In P. P. Giglioli (Ed.), Language and social context. Hammondsworth: Penguin.

Leshowitz, B. (1989). It is time we did something about scientific illiteracy. *American Psychologist, 44,* 1159–1160.

Logie, R., & Wright, R. (1988). Specialised knowledge and recognition memory in residential burglars. In M. M. Gruneberg, P. Morris, & P. Sykes (Eds.), Practical aspects of memory, Vol. 2. London: Wiley Interscience.

Means, M., & Voss, J. (1985). Star Wars: A developmental study of expert and novice knowledge structures. *Memory* & Language, 24, 746–757.

Nisbett, R. E., Fong, G., Lehman, D., & Cheng, P. (1988). Teaching reasoning. Unpublished manuscript. University of Michigan. Ann Arbor.

Perret-Clermont, A. N. (1980). *Social interaction and cognitive development in children.* London: Academic Press.

Piaget, J., & Inhelder, B. (1969). The psychology of the child. New York: Basic Books.

Piaget, J. (1977). The development of thought: Equilibration of cognitive structures. New York: Viking.

Roazzi, A. (1986a). Implicacoes methodologicas na pesquisa transcultural: A influencia do contexto social em tarefas logicas. *Arquivos Brasileiros de Psicologia, 38,* 71–91.

Roazzi, A. (1986b). Social context in experimental psychology. *Ricerche di Psicologia, 4,* 24–45.

Roazzi, A. (1987). Effects of context on cognitive development. In J. F. Cruz & R. A. Goncalves, P. P. (Eds.), Psicologia e Educao: Investigacao e intervencao. (pp. 91–115) Porto: Associacao dos Psicologos Portugueses.

Roazzi, A., & Bryant, P. (1991). Social class, context, and cognitive development. In P. Light & G. Butterworth (Eds.), Context and cognition: Ways of learning and knowing. Hemel Hampstead: Harvester Wheatsheaf.

Roazzi, A., Bryant, P., & Schliemann, A. D. (1988). Context effects on children's performance of conservation tasks. Paper presented at the Annual Conference of the British Psychological Society: Developmental Section. Coleg Harlech, Wales. Sept. 16–19.

Schliemann, A. D., & Carraher, D. W. (in press). Proportional reasoning in and out of school. In P. Light, & G. Butterworth (Eds.), Context and cognition: Ways of learning and knowing. Hemel Hamstead: Harvester Wheatsheaf.

Schliemann, A. D., & MagalhÜes, V. P. (1990). Proportional reasoning: From shops, to kitchens, laboratories, and, hopefully, schools. Proceedings of the XIV International Conference for the Psychology of Mathematics Education. Oaxtepec, Mexico.

Schooler, C. (1989). Social structural effects and experimental situations: Mutual lessons of cognitive and social science. In K. W. Schaie & C. Schooler (Eds.), Social structure and aging: Psychological processes. Hillsdale, NJ: Erlbaum.

Staszewski, (1989). Exceptional memory: The influence of practice and knowledge on the development of elaborate encoding strategies. In W. Schneider & F. Weinert (Eds.), Interactions among aptitudes, strategies, and knowledge in cognitive performance. New York: Springer-Verlag.

Sternberg, R. J. (1990). Metaphors of mind. New York: Cambridge University Press.

Stroud, J. B. (1940). Experiments on learning in school situations. *Psychological Bulletin, 37,* 777–807.

Szeminska, A. (1965). The evolution of thought. In P. Mussen (Ed.), European research in cognitive development. *Monographs of the Society for Research in Child Development, 30,* 47–57.

Walker, C. H. (1987). Relative importance of domain knowledge and overall aptitude on acquisition of domain-related information. *Cognition and Instruction, 4,* 25–42.

Wason, P. C. (1966). Reasoning. In B. Foss, (Ed.), New Horizons in Psychology. Harmondworth: Penguin Books.

Wason, P. C. (1968). Reasoning about a rule. *Quarterly Journal of Experimental Psychology, 20,* 273–281.

Wason, P. C., & Evans, J. St B. T. (1972). Dual Process in Reasoning? *Cognition, 3,* 141–154.

Wason, P. C., & Shapiro, D. (1971). Natural and contrived experience in a reasoning problem. *Quarterly Journal of Experimental Psychology, 23,* 63–71.

Part II

Everyday tasks

4   The role of problem interpretations in understanding the development of everyday problem solving

Cynthia A. Berg and Katerina S. Calderone

Imagine the following conversation between an 11-year-old and a 14-year-old. The two are fighting over how best to solve a problem that the 14-year-old experienced while working on a project at school. The problem involved completing the project so that it would be competitive for the class prize. The project partner no longer wishes to work with the 14-year-old as the partner thought the student was too bossy. The 11-year-old indicates that buckling down and doing the things that are needed to finish the project and win the prize is the best course of action. The 14-year-old, however, states that the best way to solve the problem is to talk with the project partner and convince the partner that you will be less bossy.

Research on the development of everyday problem solving has focused on how children and adults individually solve such everyday problems, describing developmental differences as due to individuals' experience and intellectual abilities (e.g., Berg, 1989; Cornelius & Caspi, 1987; Klaczynski, Laipple & Jurden, 1992; Spivack & Shure, 1982). As research has indicated that individuals' strategies are sensitive to the specific features of particular everyday problems (e.g., Berg, 1989; Cornelius & Caspi, 1987; Scribner, 1986), the role of context as an important influence on the form and function of everyday problem-solving skills across development has been acknowledged. Our research suggests that developmental differences in everyday problem solving may be due, in part, to variability in the ways that individuals interact with their context, with this interaction reflected in individuals' interpretations of everyday problems. That is, in the specific example above, the two individuals do not share the same interpretation of this problem: the 11-year-old interprets the problem as completing the project, whereas the 14-year-old interprets the problem as an interpersonal conflict with the project partner. These two different interpretations of the problem, then, have consequences for many aspects of the problem-solving process, including the strategies that are perceived as effective for solving the problem.

The primary goal of this chapter is to examine how individuals' interpretations of everyday problems are critical to understanding individuals' interactions with their context throughout development. As our perspective on intelligence as interaction is

105

heavily influenced by a contextual perspective on intellectual development, we will begin with a brief discussion of contextual perspectives. We will then translate this contextual perspective into a set of principles that guide our work more specifically in everyday problem solving and present a tentative framework that we use in our research in this area. Next, we discuss the results from two studies that illustrate the utility of our framework. Finally, we summarize and describe the implications of our framework for research in everyday problem solving and more generally on intellectual development.

Contextual perspectives to intellectual development

Several theories of intellectual or cognitive development within the last two decades adopt, at least loosely, a contextual perspective on development (e.g., Baltes, Dittmann-Kohli, & Dixon, 1984; Ceci, 1990; Laboratory of Comparative Human Cognition, 1982; Rogoff, 1982; Sternberg, 1984; see Dixon, 1992 and Wertsch & Kanner, 1992 for reviews). Although an extensive discussion of the tenets and philosophical assumptions of a contextual perspective is beyond the scope of this paper (see Altman & Rogoff, 1987; Lerner & Kauffmann, 1985; Pepper, 1942; Rosnow & Georgoudi, 1986), we will outline features common to many contextual models of intellectual development. Central to most of these theories is the view that intelligence or cognition is dependent on both the person and the context. The focus of many contextual perspectives on intellectual development is to understand how the intellectual activities of the individual are influenced by the demands and opportunities afforded by the context (Berry, 1984; Laboratory of Comparative Human Cognition, 1982). Intelligence, specifically, is concerned with the mental activity involved in providing an optimal fit between the individual and the demands of particular contexts (e.g., Baltes et al., 1984; Berg & Sternberg, 1985). Development is described not as a passive adaptation of an individual to a stable context, but as an active shaping and altering of both the individual and the context: "Just as the context changes the individual, the individual changes the context" (Lerner, Hultsch, & Dixon, 1983, p. 103).

As contextual perspectives to intellectual development view intelligence as tied to specific contexts (see Laboratory of Comparative Human Cognition, 1982), it has become important to examine contexts across development in order to make meaningful comparisons of intelligence across development. The implication has been "that intelligence will be different across cultures (and across contexts within cultures) insofar as there are differences in the kinds of problems that different cultural milieus pose their initiates" (Laboratory of Comparative Human Cognition, 1982, p. 710). Although no extensive developmental analyses have been conducted of the specific contexts that children and adults inhabit and the demands and opportunities of those contexts, some empirical work is present for certain developmental periods (e.g., Barker and associates, 1978 for children and Baltes, Wahl, & Schmid-Furstoss, 1990 for older adults) and theorists have speculated for other periods. For instance,

Barker and his colleagues (1978) conducted detailed observations of the behavior settings that elementary school children inhabit on a daily basis and found that children most frequently occupy settings dealing with school and family.

Although no such detailed analyses exist of the contexts that adults occupy across the life span, work on developmental life tasks suggests that the contexts of adults differ in a variety of ways across the life span. For instance, the work of Cantor and colleagues (e.g., Cantor, Norem, Niedenthal, Langston, & Brower, 1987) suggests that college students' tasks center around succeeding academically, getting along with others, developing an identity, and being separate from family. Havighurst (1972) and Neugarten, Moore, and Lowe (1968) characterized the developmental tasks of adults as changing from starting a family and an occupation in young adulthood to adjusting to impairments of health and to retirement during late adulthood. Baltes et al. (1984) argue that development tasks during adulthood move from the academic sphere during late adolescence/early adulthood to the more pragmatic sphere during middle and later adulthood.

Research on laypeople's conceptions of intelligence has been used to illustrate that the perceived intellectual demands required by these changing contexts may differ. People's conceptions of intelligence have been posited as providing an insider's perspective on the mental activity it takes to adapt to life contexts (e.g., Berg, 1990; Berry, 1984; Neisser, 1979; Sternberg, 1984). For instance, research by Siegler and Richards (1982) and Yussen and Kane (1983) indicates that adults and children agree that the characteristics that constitute intelligence during child development shift from sensorimotor and language skills in infancy to academic and social skills in grade school and then to social, motivational, and cognitive factors in young adulthood. Berg and Sternberg (1992) find that perceived intellectual demands change across the adult life span from an emphasis on more academic types of intellectual demands during young adulthood (e.g., interest in and ability to deal with novelty) to more pragmatic demands during late adulthood (e.g., everyday competencies).

Contextualists, then, are interested in how individuals adapt to and shape these changing environmental contexts and intellectual demands across the life span. As contexts do not remain the same across development nor across individuals within a given developmental period, contextualists maintain that there is no single outcome or endpoint to intellectual development (e.g., Rogoff, 1982; see Kessen, 1984 for a discussion). That is, the intellectual demands present in one context may require different mental processes and products than another context. The adaptation that occurs, then, occurs with respect to a specific context and may be construed as "local adaptation." An implication of this perspective is that there are no set measures or criteria for assessing intelligence that are optimal across development or across contexts with different intellectual demands.

Although contextual theorists share the notion of the importance of the context as an instigator of developmental change, they differ in their unit of analysis (e.g., Rogoff, 1982). Those coming from the Soviet tradition have emphasized the inseparability of the individual and the context (e.g., Lave, 1989; Rogoff, 1982), whereas others have found it important to understand the separate role of the individual and the context as they interact, at least for the purposes of empirical research (e.g., Baltes, 1987; Berg, 1990; Klaczynski & Reese, 1991; Sternberg, 1984). We have found that our particular position on the separability of the individual and the context has moved from an interactional perspective (examining the ways in which individual and contextual features interact) to a more transactional perspective, in which individual and contextual features are fused in the individuals' interpretation or perspective of the problem environment.

Contextual perspective on everyday problem solving

Such contextual perspectives on intellectual development have brought attention to the types of intellectual tasks and problems individuals face in their familiar, natural settings, in addition to those that they face in the laboratory testing setting (e.g., Poon, Rubin, & Wilson, 1989; Rogoff & Lave, 1984; Sternberg & Wagner, 1986). This interest in intelligence and cognition in context has fostered examinations of how children and adults solve everyday or practical sorts of problems (e.g., Berg, 1989; Cornelius & Caspi, 1987; Sinnott, 1989). Our work on everyday problem solving across the life span utilizes a contextual perspective and is guided by a set of principles derived from this perspective. We shall first outline these principles, noting how this perspective and our work derived from it departs from much of the other work on everyday problem solving. We will then present a tentative framework that guides our current research on everyday problem solving.

Principles guiding our perspective

Everyday problem-solving context and the demands present in those contexts differ across development. The first principle derived from a contextual perspective is that the everyday problem-solving context may change across the life span, so that individuals of different ages are presented with different demands and opportunities for problem solving. In an ongoing study of everyday problems, we have started to examine aspects of the everyday problem-solving context (e.g., Sansone & Berg, 1993; Sansone, Berg, Weir, Calderone, Harpster, & Morgan, 1991). For the purposes of the present paper, we will present some preliminary results from four different age groups: kindergarten and first graders ($N = 73$, mean age = 6.1 years), fifth and sixth graders ($N = 96$, mean age = 10.92 years), college students ($N = 128$, mean age = 21.55 years), and older adults ($N = 118$, mean age = 72.6 years). We asked individuals to describe a recent problem (hassle, conflict, challenge, etc.) they had experienced and to describe the problem in as much detail as possible. This very open-ended method was chosen so that individuals could select the types of problems that were most salient to them and thereby give us a sense of what had prominence in their own view of the context of everyday problem solving (e.g., Higgins, King, & Mavin,

1982; McGuire & Padawer-Singer, 1986). We were interested in whether the types of domains of problems would remain constant across development or whether different types of problems would appear for different age groups.

Consistent with a contextual perspective, we did find that the everyday problem-solving context differed across development, as perceived by everyday problem solvers. The everyday problem-solving context for 5–6-year-olds consisted predominantly of problems dealing with family (e.g., fights with siblings, conflicts with parents) and with work (e.g., chores around the house). For 11–12-year-olds, however, the context shifted to the school environment (e.g., working on projects, having to work hard for a grade) and to activities dealing with free time (e.g., fixing a flat bicycle tire, working on hobbies). For our college students, no one context assumed primacy, with numerous contexts mentioned dealing with free time, work, friends, family, and romantic relationships. For our older adults, the family context and problems dealing with health were most frequently mentioned. Although this study cannot address whether such frequencies reflect the actual incidences of these sorts of everyday problem-solving contexts across development, they certainly demonstrate that the problems that are most salient to everyday problem solvers differ across the life span.

Further research in this project suggests that what problem solvers perceive to be required to achieve adaptation to their everyday problems differs across these contexts. To assess such perceived demands, we asked participants to describe attributes of the individual that they felt would best have been able to solve the problem that they mentioned (i.e., abilities, personality, talents, etc.). Our coding scheme, developed empirically from the attributes that participants mentioned, included a broad array of characteristics encompassing achievement motivation, cognitive abilities, experience, personality, social skills, and the mentioning of specific individuals. We found that individuals perceived such attributes to be differentially effective in solving problems depending on the domain in which the problem occurred. For instance, problems dealing with friends and family were perceived as relying more on social skills, whereas problems at school and work were perceived as relying more on cognitive abilities and experience.

Our research suggests that problem solvers perceive that aspects of their everyday problem-solving context differ across development and what is required to achieve adaptation to the demands present in those contexts differ. This work has implications for everyday problem-solving research. Much of the past research presents children and adults with hypothetical problem-solving scenarios that are couched in a particular context (e.g., Berg, 1989; Cornelius & Caspi, 1987; Sinnott, 1989). Although researchers typically justify the selection of such contexts on the basis of ecological validity, given the research described above, the importance or salience of such domains might differ across developmental groups. For example, Cornelius and Caspi (1987) presented young, middle-aged, and older adults with everyday problems drawn from six distinct life domains: economic/consumer, managing the home, interpersonal conflicts with family, interpersonal conflicts with friends, and conflicts with co-workers. Clearly, some of these domains were of differential salience to participants in our study. Whether the differential salience of such contexts impacts aspects of the problem-solving process has yet to be demonstrated.

Strategies that accomplish adaptation may differ across contexts. As the contexts and demands differ across development, the strategies and abilities individuals may use to adapt to those contexts may differ. Much of the research in the everyday problem-solving literature has been aimed at investigating the different sorts of strategies that children and adults perceive to be effective or actually use in dealing with everyday problems and charting developmental trends. Implicit behind much of this work is that a particular type of strategy (e.g., one involving problem-focused action) is overall more effective than other sorts of strategies (e.g., those involving reliance on others) in solving a broad array of everyday problems (see Denney, 1989; Folkman, Lazarus, Pimley, & Novacek, 1987).

However, research suggests that a particular type of strategy is not perceived to be overall more effective in solving everyday problems, but that strategies are differentially effective depending on the context in which the everyday problem is placed (e.g., Berg, 1989; Ceci & Bronfenbrenner, 1985; Cornelius & Caspi, 1987; Scribner, 1986). For instance, Cornelius and Caspi (1987) found that four different types of strategies (i.e., problem-focused action, cognitive problem analysis, passive–dependent behavior, and avoidant thinking and denial) were viewed as differentially effective by the domain of the problem (e.g., consumer, information, home, family, etc.) as well as by the specific problem presented within each domain. Mischel (1984) noted that such sensitivity to specific contexts may actually be preferable to the use of solutions that are consistent across situations and that, in many cases, consistency across situations may be maladaptive. Thus, everyday problem solving across the life span may not be best characterized as a process whereby individuals become more likely to use "optimal" strategies that are effective across contexts. Rather, the process of development may be better construed as individuals becoming more able to modify their strategies to the specific contextual features of everyday problems (see Berg, 1989; Rogoff, Gauvain, & Gardner, 1986).

Although strategies have been found to differ depending on the context, just what in the context produces such differences has not been clear (see Ceci, 1990). Part of the difficulty lies in the multiple uses of the word context. For instance, the term context has been used to refer to the place in which an activity occurs (e.g., Ceci & Bronfenbrenner, 1985; Wertsch, Minick, & Arns, 1984), the domain or content of the activity (e.g., Cornelius & Caspi, 1987), the functioning or meaning of the task (e.g., Scribner, 1986), the way in which a task is framed (e.g., Rogoff & Waddell, 1982), the presence or absence of others (e.g., Goodnow, 1986; Meacham & Emont, 1989), familiarity of stimulus items (e.g., Denney & Palmer, 1989), etc. However, even when context is further specified in these terms, the effects of context on cognitive strategies have not always been consistent for any one of these variables. Our use of the word context draws on this literature, but has come to mean how context is represented in the psychological environment of the individual (see also Lewin, 1951). As will be discussed later, although the actual context might include the fact that a particular problem occurs at home, if this contextual feature is not salient to the individual, then this particular contextual factor might not impact the strategies the individual uses.

Strategies that accomplish adaptation may differ across individuals. Strategies are not only affected by the context and the demands and opportunities present in those contexts, but also by features that the individual brings to the problem-solving environment. Such individual features include the individual's developmental level, experience, and underlying intellectual abilities. Most of the everyday problem-solving literature focuses on these individual differences, positing that some combination of these individual features leads to more optimal problem-solving performance (e.g., Band & Weisz, 1988; Ceci & Liker, 1986; Denney, 1989; Willis & Schaie, 1986).

The most prominent individual factor investigated in the developmental literature on everyday problem solving has been the effect of age on the strategies individuals use to approach everyday problems. For instance, Band and Weisz (1988) found that older children were more likely to use secondary control strategies (i.e., efforts to modify the individuals' own subjective psychological state to fit better with the present conditions of the problem), whereas younger children were more likely to use primary control strategies (i.e., efforts to influence the problem by bringing the problem conditions more in line with the problem solver's wishes). Folkman et al. (1987) found that older adults were more likely to use passive and emotion-focused coping, whereas young adults were more likely to use active problem-focused coping strategies. Denney and Palmer (1981) also found adult age differences in strategies, with older adults relying more on others than younger adults, who were more likely to solve problems on their own initiative.

Other individual features that have impacted strategy use, but have received somewhat less attention, include an individual's underlying cognitive abilities and actual experience. Individuals who differ in underlying cognitive abilities have been found to differ in how they solve everyday problems, with more cognitively advanced individuals utilizing more advanced everyday problem-solving strategies (Brotman-Band, in press; Kuhn, Pennington, & Leadbetter, 1983). Experience has also been found to lead individuals to adopt more complex strategies for solving everyday problems (e.g., Ceci & Liker, 1986), to search through relevant problem information in a more goal-directed fashion (e.g., Charness, 1981; Walsh & Hershey, in press), and to lead to more effective solutions (e.g., Ceci & Liker, 1986; Walsh & Hershey, in press).

Numerous other individual features exist that might impact strategy utilization, such as gender, individual differences in personality, social skills, and achievement motivation. Although the individual could be described with all of these individual features, all such features may not be important for understanding individual differences in strategy use within a particular task. That is, everyday problem-solving tasks may elicit different individual features that are involved in the problem-solving process. Thus, this interaction between contextual and individual features is important to understanding aspects of the problem-solving process.

Optimality of everyday problem-solving performance depends on the interaction of individual and context. As the everyday problem-solving context differs across development and the strategies needed to adapt to these contexts differ, what defines an optimal strategy for any given problem is a function of what the individual brings to it in terms of his or her abilities, experiences, and developmental level, and his or her representation of the context. An implication of this perspective is that there is no a priori criterion for optimal everyday problem-solving performance that exists across development or across contexts, much as there is no telos to which intellectual development is directed in the larger contextual perspective. Such a conclusion may seem like radical relativism in light of a number of studies that do impose a set criterion for everyday problem solving across contexts and development (e.g., Denney, 1989; Folkman, Lazarus, & Pimley, 1987; Willis & Schaie, 1991).

In our large life-span study of everyday problem solving, we have found that strategies that are often viewed by researchers as ineffective for solving problems are not necessarily viewed as ineffective by the problem solver's themselves (Berg, Calderone, & Gunderson, 1990). In this study, individuals' strategies for solving their everyday problems were coded as representing primary, secondary, or relinquishing (i.e., no apparent attempt to deal with the problem) control strategies, after distinctions advanced by Rothbaum, Weisz, and Snyder (1982) and Band and Weisz (1988), discussed above. In examining individuals' ratings of the effectiveness of their strategies, we found that overall primary and secondary control strategies were viewed as equally effective, with relinquishing control viewed as less effective. However, even within the relinquishing-control category, we found a wide range in the perceived effectiveness of such strategies, with some individuals rating the effectiveness of their solutions quite high. For instance, one young adult reported a recurring interpersonal problem that she was having at work where co-workers were rude to her and reported that she had done nothing to deal with the problem. When she was queried as to why she had done nothing to deal with the problem, she indicated that she had tried several active problem-focused strategies in the past that did not seem to be effective.

We interpret such results to mean that the effectiveness of a problem-solving strategy depends on the demands present in the context and what the individual brings to the problem-solving situation in terms of his or her history (e.g., experiences and abilities). Thus, a particular type of strategy (e.g., primary, secondary, or relinquishing control) cannot be deemed a priori to be more effective across all contexts or for all individuals (c.f. Band & Weisz, 1988), as is often done (e.g., Denney & Palmer, 1981; Folkman, Lazarus, & Pimley, 1987).

Framework for examining everyday problem solving

Our view that the everyday problem-solving process is dependent on how the individual, with his or her abilities and experiences, interacts with the demands and opportunities of his or her context, might at first glance seem nearly chaotic. That is, there seem to be no general strategies that individuals might employ optimally across situations and across development. However, we have found that such an organizing construct may be found in the individual's perspective, definition, or interpretation of the problem, which captures the transaction of the individual with his or her context. Our notion of problem interpretation (see also Sansone & Berg, 1993) is similar to Sinnott's "essence" of a problem (1989), Leont'ev's object of an activity (1981), Newell and Simon's (1972) idea of problem space, and Lewin's (1936, 1951) activated portion of the life space. Such interpretations might include the content of the problem (e.g., whether it be interpersonal or task-oriented), the category or type of problem (e.g., logical problem, pragmatic problem), and the extent of the problem space (e.g., confined within the constraints of the problem versus enlarged to include experiential components of the person's life).

As can be seen in Figure 4.1, an individual's problem interpretation involves the transaction of the individual with his or her context. This interpretation derives from features of the individual and of the context and yet may not include all of those individual and contextual features that are present in the problem situation. For instance, the individual could draw on his or her experience, age, gender, and

EVERYDAY PROBLEM-SOLVING FRAMEWORK

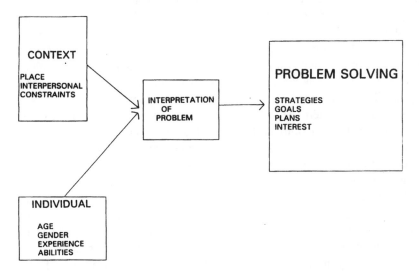

Figure 4.1. Everyday problem-solving framework.

underlying intellectual abilities to approach the problem and yet all of these features may not be reflected in the individual's interpretation of the problem. Similarly, the context of the problem might contain aspects of the physical environment, interpersonal constraints, and time pressure and yet such features may or may not be relevant to an individual's interpretation. In fact, such individual and contextual features may be differentially relevant at various points in development, contributing to developmental differences in problem interpretations.

We view the individual's problem interpretation as an important factor in influencing aspects of the problem-solving process, as opposed to what an outside perceiver might see as relevant to the context or the individual solving the problem. An individual's problem interpretation is posited to influence many aspects of the problem-solving process, including the strategies an individual perceives to be effective and actually uses in solving everyday problems. We view such problem interpretations as potentially important in understanding developmental differences in how individuals solve everyday problems, in that differences in performance may be due to individuals of various ages interpreting problems in a disparate fashion.

Several very recent examinations of problem solving lend support to the view that an individual's problem interpretation will influence aspects of the problem-solving process and that such differences in interpretation may be useful in understanding developmental differences in performance. For instance, Sinnott (1989) found that older adults interpret Piagetian logical combination problems, particularly those couched in an everyday context (e.g., allocating pairs of relatives to sleeping quarters), in a greater variety of ways than younger adults. Older adults placed more emphasis on the social and interpersonal components of the problem than the younger adults, who emphasized the formal and logical components of the problem. Sinnott suggested that many of the older adults performed poorly on these tasks because they interpreted the problems in a different fashion than young adults. Stronger evidence for the mediational role of problem interpretations in understanding developmental differences in problem-solving performance comes from work by Laipple (1991). Laipple found that older adults were less likely to interpret logical problems with the meaning intended by the experimenter (i.e., staying within the logical confines of the problem), but instead imputed elements of their own experience in the problem context. Such different interpretations were able to account for all of the age differences in problem-solving performance between the young and old adults.

Thus, these two recent studies point to the relation between individuals' problem interpretation and their subsequent performance and to the role of problem interpretation in explaining developmental differences in performance. As will be discussed below, this work has important implications for much of the current and past research examining developmental differences in problem-solving tasks both in and outside of the laboratory setting. We will now turn to a discussion of two studies that illustrate the importance of examining individuals' interpretations of everyday problems in understanding how individuals across development and across different contexts deal with such problems.

Developmental differences in everyday problem solving

The first study to be described was an initial attempt to examine the knowledge that children and adolescents have of the effectiveness of strategies for dealing with everyday problems. Very little work had been conducted prior to or after this study of children's everyday problem solving, although work in social problem solving (e.g., Spivack & Shure, 1982) and coping (e.g., Band & Weisz, 1988) was relevant. This study nicely illustrates how the perceived effectiveness of strategies differs by features of the context (and situation within context) and by features of the individual (e.g., age and gender). However, what the first author had perceived to be chaos in the contextual and individual specificity of strategy effectiveness we now see as potentially organized by the individual's interpretation of each problem. That is, we speculated that the contextual and individual specificity of strategy effectiveness might be mediated by the fact that individuals of different ages and genders were interpreting individual problems in different ways. The second study examined whether children and adolescents differed in their interpretations of everyday problems and whether such interpretations could relate to differences in strategy knowledge.

Study 1. Knowledge of strategies for dealing with everyday problems

The primary purpose of this study (Berg, 1989) was to examine the knowledge that children and adolescents have of the strategies that are effective for dealing with everyday problems. First we examined whether different types of strategies were perceived as differentially effective by children and adolescents for approaching everyday problems couched in two different settings (i.e., school context or outside of the school context). Of particular interest was whether the strategies that children and adolescents viewed as effective would be similar across contexts or would differ depending on the context. Problem analogs were constructed that were very similar in content across the two contexts, school and outside of school, and individuals rated the effectiveness of six different types of strategies. Second, we examined whether there were developmental differences in children's and adolescent's strategy knowledge. Optimal strategy knowledge was viewed as resemblance to a prototype of a good everyday problem solver. The optimality of strategy knowledge was operationalized by comparing students' responses to teachers' responses and to a group of students who had been nominated by their teachers and themselves to be "good" everyday problem solvers. Third, the relation between students' ability to use strategy knowledge and measures of school achievement (e.g., grades and achievement scores) was explored, in order to understand whether everyday problem solving was distinct from more traditional measures of academic achievement.

Method. Participants included 217 fifth-grade ($N = 87$, M age = 11 years, 5 months; SD = 5.6 months), eighth-grade ($N = 64$, M age = 14 years, 1 month; SD = 4.2 months), and eleventh-grade ($N = 66$, M age = 17 years, 4 months; SD = 6.7 months) students drawn from public schools in the Greater New Haven area in southeastern Connecticut.

Students' everyday problem solving was assessed through a questionnaire consisting of 20 everyday problems. One-half of the students solved problems that were couched in the school setting (e.g., dealing with teachers, meeting school deadlines, and receiving unanticipated grades); the other half solved problems that occurred outside of the school setting (e.g., dealing with parents and siblings, hobbies, and chores around the house). The problems for these questionnaires came, in part, from surveys of the daily hassles and life events that face individuals of these ages (e.g., Clabby & Elias, 1986; Coddington, 1972a,b; Compas, 1987; Metcalf, Dobson, Cook, & Michaud, 1982). Five situations on the School and Outside of School Questionnaires were written to have similar content. Although the same problems were used for all participants, small adjustments were made in some aspects of the problems across the three grade levels to make them relevant for a particular grade level (e.g., in the sample problem below, we adjusted the curfew times).

Each questionnaire presented problems that contained a conflict that could be reduced by taking one of six courses of action. Individuals read a given problem and then rated six strategies on a 1 (very bad) to 7 (very good) scale as to how good they thought the option would be in solving the problem. These six strategies consisted of the following categories of dealing with problems: *plan* to take action sometime in the future; *seek* more information about the problem; *change perception* of the problem by redefining elements of the problem so that it was seen in a new light; *adapt* to the problem through self-initiated action that would make the problem solver's behavior conform better to the demands of the problem; *shape* the environment to change elements of the problem situation so that it would fit better with the problem solver's needs and goals; and *select* another environment by removing oneself from the problem environment in order to avoid the conflict inherent in the problem. These six strategies were drawn from the work of contextual theorists of intellectual development (e.g., Sternberg, 1985), research examining everyday intellectual skills in the work place (e.g., Fredericksen, 1986), and research on coping and stress (e.g., Lazarus & Folkman, 1984). A sample problem on the outside of school questionnaire is listed below.[1]

Sample questionnaire

Your parents have become more strict about what time you must be home at night. On Friday and Saturday nights you have to be home by 10:30. You and your friends want to go out to a movie on Friday night that will not be over until 11:00, so you wouldn't be home until 11:30. You find out from the movie theater that the movie will be showing at the theater for one more week. Rate how good each of the answers is in *allowing you to see the movie and be home by 10:30*.

   a. Ask your friends if they have a strict time that they must be home at night (seek).
   b. Decide that seeing the movie is really not worth causing problems with your parents (change perception).

    c. Wait to see the movie on Saturday afternoon (adapt).

    d. Persuade your parents that the new rule is not fair (shape).

    e. Spend Friday night at the house of a friend who does not have to be home so early (select).

    f. Plan how you could both see the movie and be home by 10:30 (plan).

Students then turned the page over and on the back of the sheet were again presented with the same problem but with additional information that either added a new constraint or obstacle in the problem or removed one. The results of this manipulation will not be discussed here as the manipulation did not interact with age or strategy in any theoretically meaningful way (see Berg, 1989, for full results).

Eighteen teachers also completed the Everyday Problems Questionnaire: 5 fifth-grade teachers, 10 eighth-grade teachers, and 3 eleventh-grade teachers. They were asked to rate the strategies as to how effective they would be in solving the problem for a student. Internal consistency reliability (coefficient alpha) for teachers was .86 on these ratings, indicating a high degree of consistency within the group of teachers in their profile of ratings.

Results. The first question to be addressed was whether certain strategies were perceived as differentially effective across the two contexts (school and outside school) and by individuals of different ages. Analyses of variance directed toward this question were restricted to the set of five problems that were written to be analogues on the School and Outside School Problems Questionnaires (see Table 4.1 for the means). Certain strategies were perceived to be more effective than others ($F(5, 965)$ = 261.09, $p < .01$), with the strategy of adapting to the problem seen as the most effective option, planning viewed as next most effective, seeking more information, changing one's perception, and shaping viewed as next most effective, and selecting out of the environment seen as the least effective strategy. However, this main effect was qualified by an interaction between strategy and type of questionnaire ($F(5, 965)$ = 27.02, $p < .01$), indicating that certain strategies were perceived as more effective in the school setting than outside of the school setting. For instance, the strategies of planning, seeking more information, and adapting to the environment were seen as more effective outside of the school setting than in it. In addition, a significant interaction among strategy, type of questionnaire, and grade level ($F(10, 965) = 3.0$, $p < .05$) indicated that the differences in perceived effectiveness of strategies on the School and Outside School Questionnaires were more marked for the eighth and eleventh graders than for the fifth graders.

These effects of strategy differences were further examined by including the actual problem situation as a factor in the design. The results of this analysis illustrate how strategy effectiveness differed as a function of the context of the specific problem. The problem type by strategy interaction was highly significant, $F(20, 3860) = 65.9$, $p < .01$), indicating that certain strategies were perceived as more or less effective for certain problems than for others. In addition, a significant problem type by strategy by grade level interaction ($F(40, 3860) = 3.62$, $p < .01$), indicated that the strategy by problem situation interaction differed by grade level. A similar interaction was

Table 4.1. Means of the six strategies for the everyday-problems questionnaires: analogous problems

Subjects	Strategy					
	Plan	Seek	Change	Adapt	Shape	Select
School questionnaire						
5th graders						
Male	4.8	4.5	4.2	4.8	4.3	3.4
Female	5.1	4.8	4.7	5.0	4.9	3.4
8th graders						
Male	4.5	4.4	4.8	4.7	4.1	3.3
Female	4.8	4.3	4.8	5.1	4.6	3.1
11th graders						
Male	4.2	4.1	4.4	4.4	3.5	2.9
Female	4.7	4.5	5.1	4.9	4.4	3.0
Overall school	4.7	4.4	4.7	4.8	4.3	3.2
Outside-school questionnaire						
5th graders						
Male	5.3	4.9	4.3	5.5	4.5	3.3
Female	4.9	4.4	4.2	5.4	4.1	2.8
8th graders						
Male	5.1	4.8	4.1	5.9	4.7	3.2
Female	5.4	5.2	4.2	6.0	4.7	3.1
11th graders						
Male	5.1	4.7	4.3	5.8	4.5	3.0
Female	5.0	4.6	4.2	5.8	4.3	2.6
Overall outside school	5.1	4.7	4.2	5.7	4.4	3.0
Overall	4.9	4.6	4.4	5.2	4.4	3.1

found among problem situation, strategy, and gender, $F(20, 3860) = 4.51, p < .01$), indicating that differences in strategy effectiveness across problems differed by gender.

In sum, the perceived effectiveness of these six strategies was highly dependent on the overall context in which the problem occurred (i.e., school or outside of school) and the specific demands presented by each individual problem. In addition, gender and age modified these context effects in subtle, and not always interpretable ways.

Our second question was to address whether developmental differences would occur in an overall measure of children's and adolescents' strategy knowledge. Strategy knowledge was quantified by correlating the students' profile of responses across all twenty items with the profile of ratings that teachers gave these responses. Good strategy knowledge scores were indicated by high correlations between the students' ratings and the ratings of the teacher group; poor strategy knowledge scores were indicated by low and sometimes negative correlations between the students' ratings and the ratings of the teacher group. Another approach to defining an expert group of individuals was used, namely using students who had been rated by their teachers and themselves as much better than other students in their ability to solve everyday problems. Using this group to compute strategy knowledge scores yielded results that were similar to those reported here.

Grade level of the student did relate to strategy knowledge scores (F (2, 193) = 10.72), with eleventh graders scoring significantly higher (.54) than eighth graders (.47), who scored higher than fifth graders (.42). In addition, a significant effect of gender (F (1, 193) = 10.53, $p < .05$), indicated that females scored higher (.50) than did males (.43). The domain of the questionnaire did not impact strategy knowledge scores. Thus, the results indicated that older students' and females' profiles of strategy knowledge were more consistent with the teacher profile of strategy knowledge than were younger students and males.

Finally, we examined the relation between strategy knowledge scores and more traditional measures of academic achievement (composite achievement test scores and grade-point average (GPA)). As can be seen in Table 4.2, correlations between mean strategy knowledge scores and academic achievement were highest for the fifth graders and were more moderate for the eighth- and eleventh-grade students. These

Table 4.2. Relations among strategy-knowledge score, achievement score, and grade point average (GPA)

Subjects	N	M, strategy-knowledge score
School forms		
5th graders		
Achievement test	41	.57**
Semester GPA	40	.38**
8th graders		
Achievement test	33	.15
Semester GPA	33	.24
11th graders		
Achievement test	30	.18
Semester GPA	31	.32
Outside-school forms		
5th graders		
Achievement test	45	.44**
Semester GPA	45	.24
8th graders		
Achievement test	31	.29
Semester GPA	31	.41*
11th graders		
Achievement test	30	.26
Semester GPA	34	.37*

*$p < .05$
**$p < .01$.

relations indicate that although strategy knowledge scores are related to the domain of intelligence, they do measure something different than what is tapped by achievement scores and other measures of academic success.

Two important conclusions can be drawn from these results. First, the effectiveness of strategies depends on the domain in which the problem is embedded, the specific conditions of the actual problem context, and the grade and gender of the students rating such strategies. These findings confirm one of our guiding principles that the strategies that are perceived as accomplishing adaptation may differ across context and across development. Given a contextual perspective, it would not seem likely that the strategy that will provide a better fit with the demands of one's environment will be the same across problems that may present different demands. We had not anticipated, however, that the perceived effectiveness of strategies would vary with the conditions present in each problem and thus contextual specificity seemed overwhelming. This contextual specificity was more apparent in the responses of the eighth and eleventh graders than in those of the fifth graders, indicating that older students may have been more sensitive to the context in which the problems were presented.

Second, strategy knowledge, as quantified in terms of how closely students matched a prototype of "good" everyday problem solving, increased with age and differed by gender, favoring females. This study was not able to capture why these groups outperformed other students. That is, developmental and gender differences were not attributable to the level of familiarity or experience students had with these problems.

A closer examination of the everyday problems used in this study revealed a possible mechanism that might help to explain the variability in strategy effectiveness across problems and developmental and gender differences in strategy knowledge. Many of the problems used in the study could be interpreted in a variety of different ways and such interpretations often had consequences for the sorts of strategies viewed as effective in solving the problem. For instance, one of the problems used involved competing against a friend for the office of class president. Such a problem could be interpreted in at least two ways. One interpretation focuses on the interpersonal theme of maintaining the friendship in spite of the competition. A second interpretation is more task-oriented and involves winning the election. These different interpretations of the problem inherent in the situation could influence the types of strategies perceived as effective in solving the problem. For instance, if one's interpretation is to "win the election," then an effective strategy might be to talk to friends to persuade them to vote for you. Such a strategy might not be perceived as most effective if one's interpretation is to maintain the friendship. These two different classes of interpretations, task-oriented and interpersonal, seemed to run across a number of the problems used in the Berg (1989) study. Thus, a second study was designed to examine whether problem interpretations could impact strategy knowledge and whether developmental and gender differences in interpretations might contribute to overall differences in everyday problem-solving performance.

Study 2: The role of problem interpretation on strategy knowledge

A second study was conducted in order to examine whether problem interpretations might be useful for understanding developmental and gender differences in rated strategy effectiveness. First, we examined whether individuals of different ages and genders would interpret problems differently. We presented children and adolescents with everyday problem scenarios that contained interpersonal and task components. Individuals then interpreted what the "real" problem was in the scenario and such interpretations were coded as to whether they contained an interpersonal or a task focus. Second, we examined whether individual differences in problem interpretation were related to strategy-effectiveness ratings. Strategy options were written so that they dealt either with the interpersonal component or the task component of the problem scenario. We predicted that individuals who interpreted the problem as being task oriented would rate the strategies that dealt with the task element of the problem higher than strategies that dealt with the interpersonal component. Similarly, individuals who interpreted the problem as being interpersonally oriented would rate the strategies that dealt with the interpersonal elements of the problem higher than strategies that dealt with the task component.

Method. Participants were 163 students from public schools in the Greater Salt Lake City area in Utah and included fifty-nine fifth graders (*M* age = 10.8, *SD* = .49), forty-six eighth graders (*M* age = 13.6, *SD* = .49), and fifty-eight eleventh graders (*M* age = 16.7, *SD* = .06).

Students' interpretations of problems and strategy knowledge were assessed through a questionnaire consisting of eight analog pairs of problems making a total of 16 everyday problems. The problems were derived from Berg (1989) and from children's actual reports of their own everyday problems in the larger life-span study of everyday problem solving discussed above (Berg, Calderone, & Gunderson, 1991; Sansone & Berg, 1993). The eight analog pairs presented to students were designed so that one problem in each pair was embedded in a school context and the other problem in the pair was embedded in a family context. The analog problem pairs were nearly identical. For instance, students were asked to think about a problem dealing with a friend's broken calculator at school, and to think about a problem dealing with a sibling's broken mountain bike at home.

Problems were constructed so that they could involve at least two different interpretations: a task-oriented interpretation, in which a specific task not involving others is approached; and an interpersonally oriented interpretation, in which some sort of enduring problem with another individual is described. These two interpretations were chosen as such definitions spontaneously emerge when children and adolescents describe their own everyday problems (see Sansone, Berg, & Weir, 1991) and may have impacted strategy knowledge ratings in Berg (1989). In the above example, a task-oriented interpretation of the problem would focus on dealing with the calculator or bike, and an interpersonally oriented interpretation would focus on dealing with the upset friend or sibling. Students' interpretations of the 16 problems were collected by asking them to, "Please write down what you think is the real problem."

Interpretations of the problems were categorized into groups by two trained coders. Coders made judgments on 25% of the protocols and achieved an overall reliability of 85%. Discrepancies were resolved through discussion. After achieving reliability, one of the coders completed the rest of the protocols. Four categories of interpretations were found. They included the anticipated task-oriented (focus was on accomplishing a specific task) and interpersonally oriented interpretations (focus was on another person), as well as self-oriented interpretations (focus was on some aspect of the self), interpretations that were combinations of the three, and other interpretations (typically these did not include interpretations, but rather strategies for how to solve the problem).

After students defined the problem, they were presented with four alternative strategies for dealing with the problem and rated these strategies on a 1 (very bad) to 7 (very good) scale. Two of the four strategies were designed to be a good fit with a task-oriented interpretation, and the other two strategies were designed to be a good fit with an interpersonally oriented interpretation. The two strategies provided for each of the two interpretations were of different types. One was a primary strategy and the other was a secondary strategy, after distinctions made by Rothbaum, Weisz, & Snyder (1982) and Band and Weisz (1988), discussed above. An example of a specific problem and strategies provided for the problem dealing with a broken calculator at school are listed below.

Sample questionnaire. You have borrowed your friend's brand new calculator to try it out. You were being rough with it, and you accidentally dropped it on the hall floor. The display window is cracked. Your friend really looked forward to getting this calculator and will probably be very upset that you damaged it.

- a. Pay for the calculator repairs (strategy is primary and task oriented).
- b. Decide that, since it was an accident, the calculator is no big deal (strategy is secondary and task oriented).
- c. Talk to your friend so that your friend won't be too upset (strategy is primary and interpersonally oriented).
- d. Realize that the two of you will not fight about it (strategy is secondary and interpersonally oriented).

Results. The primary question to be addressed in this study was whether age and gender-related differences in problem interpretations might relate to differences in strategy knowledge. We first examined age- and gender-related differences in the four types of problem interpretations. Separate chi-square analyses for grade level and gender were both significant ($\chi^2 = 239.79$, df = 8, $p < .01$ for grade level; $\chi^2 = 111.08$, df = 4, $p < .01$ for gender). These analyses were followed up with one sample chi-square analyses. As can be seen in Table 4.3, younger children were more likely to interpret the problems in a task-oriented fashion than older children. Also, older adolescents had higher percentages of interpretations that were self oriented and that

Table 4.3. *Relationships between developmental level and problem interpretation*

Problem interpretation	Developmental level		
	5th grade	8th grade	11th grade
Task-oriented	32%	24%	17%
Interpersonal-oriented	42%	45%	47%
Self-oriented	9%	12%	13%
Mixed	8%	9%	13%
Other	9%	9%	10%

were mixtures of the self, task, and interpersonal orientations than younger children. With regard to the gender difference (see Table 4.4) males were slightly, but not significantly, more likely to interpret problems in a task-oriented fashion than females, who were more likely to interpret problems in an interpersonally oriented fashion, self-oriented fashion, and using mixtures of the categories than males. In addition, problem interpretations differed by domain ($\chi^2 = 20.9, p < .01$) such that self and mixed interpretations were more likely in the school domain.

Given that there were gender- and age-related differences in the ways in which problems were interpreted, we were interested in the relation between such interpretations and students' ratings of strategy effectiveness. Two repeated measures ANOVAs, one for problems in the family domain and the other for problems in the school domain,[2] were conducted with grade level, gender, interpretation of the problem, strategy orientation (interpersonal or task), and strategy type (primary or secondary) as the independent variables and strategy effectiveness ratings as the dependent variable. We will only mention the effects that are relevant to the primary questions addressed in this paper (see Calderone, 1993 for full results).

For the analysis of the family problems, the anticipated interaction between interpretation of the problem and strategy orientation was significant ($F (4, 421) = 7.01$, $p < .01$). This effect was modified by a significant strategy type by strategy orientation

Table 4.4. *Relationships between gender and problem interpretations*

Problem interpretation	Gender	
	Female	Male
Task-oriented	23%	26%
Interpersonal-oriented	46%	42%
Self-oriented	12%	11%
Mixed	12%	8%
Other	8%	12%

by interpretation of the problem interaction $(F (4, 421) = 11.7, p < .01)$. This interaction revealed that our predicted relation between task- and interpersonally oriented interpretations and strategy orientations was restricted to the primary strategies and did not hold for secondary strategies. As was predicted (see Table 4.5) and confirmed through planned comparisons, individuals who interpreted problems in an interpersonal manner rated the effectiveness of strategies dealing with interpersonal components of the problems higher than they did strategies dealing with task components. Likewise, individuals who interpreted problems in a task manner rated the effectiveness of strategies dealing with task components higher than they did strategies dealing with interpersonal components. An additional five-way interaction between strategy type, strategy orientation, problem interpretation, grade level, and gender $(F (8, 421) = 2.65, p < .05)$ revealed that the predicted interaction was more prominent for certain ages and genders than others. More specifically, the relation between problem interpretation and strategy orientation for primary strategies was not as pronounced for fifth-grade males and eighth-grade females.

The same predicted interaction between problem interpretation and strategy orientation holds for performance on the school problems $(F (4, 461) = 5.66, p < .01)$. Again, this interaction was modified by a significant problem interpretation by strategy orientation by strategy type interaction $(F (4, 461) = 12.3, p < .01)$. That is, for primary strategies only, individuals who interpreted problems in interpersonal or task terms rated higher those strategies that were congruent with their task definitions (i.e., interpersonal interpretations resulted in higher effectiveness ratings for interpersonally oriented strategies than task-oriented strategies).

Table 4.5. Means of the four strategies by problem interpretation

| | Type of strategy | | | |
| | Primary | | Secondary | |
	Interpretation	Task	Interpersonal	Task
School				
Task	4.87	5.78	3.34	2.17
Interpersonal	5.48	4.97	3.37	2.36
Self	5.16	5.87	3.19	2.08
Garbage	5.08	5.14	3.56	2.49
Mixed	5.32	5.65	3.44	2.32
Family				
Task	4.92	5.44	3.06	2.37
Interpersonal	5.42	4.98	3.22	2.21
Self	5.03	5.64	2.99	2.12
Garbage	5.02	5.46	3.21	2.52
Mixed	5.31	5.69	3.06	2.08

Discussion

Consistent with our framework, this study revealed that problem solvers interpret the same everyday problem in a variety of ways, that individuals of different ages and genders may focus on different interpretations, and that different domains may pull for different interpretations. With age, there was a decrease in the frequency of task interpretations and an increase in interpersonal, self, and mixed interpretations. The large decrease with age in the frequency of task interpretations may be related to developmental changes in the self system, moving from a system that is concrete and specific to one that incorporates psychological constructs and is more abstract and integrated, incorporating emotions and cognitions (see Harter, 1983 for a review). The increase in frequency of mixed orientations with age may suggest that older adolescents interpret problems in a more complex fashion than younger children, integrating multiple aspects of the problem. The finding that females focused more on interpersonal issues than males is consistent with a growing body of literature on the greater sensitivity to interpersonal issues among females (e.g., Gilligan, 1982; Tannen, 1990). In addition, problem interpretations differed by domain with school drawing for more self and mixed interpretations than the family domain. Consistent with our framework for everyday problem solving, then, individuals' interpretations of everyday problems were influenced both by aspects of the context and features of the individual.

In addition, these different interpretations had implications for how individuals thought about potential strategies for dealing with the problem. Specifically, individuals who interpreted the problem with either an interpersonal or task orientation perceived that strategies that were consistent with their interpretations were more effective than strategies that were inconsistent with their interpretations. The finding that the fit between problem interpretations and strategy ratings was localized to only one type of strategy, those that dealt with primary control but not with secondary control, is in need of further investigation. Secondary control strategies were perceived to be far less effective in dealing with the problem than were primary strategies. However, such a result has not always been found (see Band & Weisz, 1988; Berg, Calderone, & Gunderson, 1990). It is possible that the secondary control strategies included in this study were simply less effective than other secondary control strategies that could have been used and that other such strategies might show a relation between interpretations and strategy effectiveness.

One of the motivations for this study was to examine whether problem interpretations would be useful in explaining domain differences in strategy effectiveness and age and gender interactions with domain as were found in Berg (1989). Although the analyses reported here do not allow us to compare domains directly, there was no indication that domain impacted the relation between problem interpretation and strategy orientation. Subsequent hierarchical loglinear analyses, in which we were able to test for differences in domain, also confirmed that domain did not alter the relation between problem interpretation and strategy orientation and that older students were no more likely to fit their strategies to their interpretations than younger individuals. Thus, it appears that the individual and contextual specificity of strategy effectiveness ratings found in Berg (1989) may have been due to domain and developmental and gender differences in problem interpretations.

This study and its approach at investigating problem interpretations is not without its limitations, which we are currently addressing in ongoing research. First, the assessment of problem interpretations relied heavily on verbal report and, as such, findings that older students were more likely to interpret problems in a more complex fashion (i.e., greater incidence of mixed interpretations) could be due to older students' greater verbal facility. Second, having students explicitly define problems may have made the strategies they rated that fit with those interpretations more salient. Clearly other methodologies need to be employed to investigate problem interpretations. We are currently examining problem interpretations through an in-depth interview so that individuals can be probed as to the extensiveness of their interpretations. In addition, problem interpretations can be investigated in a more implicit manner through differential memory for problem information, endorsement of statements regarding the problem situation, and priming techniques about problem components.

Summary and conclusions

In this paper, we have argued that individuals' interpretations of everyday problems are critical to understanding the development of everyday problem solving. A framework for examining everyday problem solving was presented, based on a contextual perspective to intellectual development. This framework presented a potential mechanism for understanding developmental differences in everyday problem-solving strategies, namely, an individual's interpretation of everyday problems. We view such interpretations as representative of the transaction of the individual with his or her context.

Two studies were presented that examined the influence of individual and contextual features on problem solvers' perceived effectiveness of strategies for dealing with everyday problems. In the first study, great individual and contextual specificity was found in individuals' strategy knowledge. In the second study, the role of individuals' interpretations in addressing such individual and contextual specificity was examined. This study revealed that individuals of different ages and genders interpret problems differently, interpretations that have consequences for the perceived effectiveness of strategies for dealing with everyday problems.

These results hold important implications for much of the work on everyday problem solving. First, the finding that individuals interpret problems differently and such interpretations have consequences for strategy knowledge is critical, as most of the work on everyday problem solving assumes that problem solvers hold a similar interpretation of the problem, most notably, the interpretation that the experimenter has in mind. For instance, in Berg (1989) strategy options were written primarily with the idea that individuals would interpret problems as dealing with specific tasks.

Although the problems in Berg were not written to have such an explicit tension between interpersonal and task components, many of the problems in Berg could have been interpreted with an interpersonal or self focus, as is true for problems used by Denney (see 1989 for a review) and Cornelius and Caspi (1987).

Our results caution investigators against assuming that problem scenarios can be written so that they draw exclusively for one particular orientation of interpretation or that even one kind of interpretation will best capture the everyday problem-solving process. That is, although the everyday problem scenarios in our second study were written to be interpreted with primarily a task or interpersonal focus, other interpretations emerged as well. Further, other types of interpretations that do not focus on the content or orientation of the interpretation may also be important in understanding the development of everyday problem solving. Other dimensions of interpretations could include concreteness versus abstraction, specificity, and the extent to which interpretations are constrained within the problem environment or rely on experience outside of the problem environment. For instance, in our current work (Berg & Klaczynski, in prep.) we have found that older adults' greater experience-based interpretations may relate to their inability to generate alternative problem solutions, as they state that in their experience only their given strategy will work.

The relation between interpretations and strategy effectiveness further cautions investigators not to view one particular type of strategy as overall more effective than others. Strategies may differ in both perceived and actual effectiveness, given an individual's interpretation of an everyday problem. Such results may call for a reinterpretation of developmental work on everyday problem solving. For example, Denney and Palmer (1981) found age differences, favoring young adults, in everyday problem-solving strategies. Older adults used strategies that involved reliance on others more so than young adults, which were coded as less effective than strategies that involved solving the problem by relying on one's own initiative. However, if older individuals in Denney and Palmer's study interpreted problems as interpersonally oriented, then strategies that relied on others may have been best fitted to solving the problem rather than strategies that relied on one's own initiative. Thus, such developmental differences could not necessarily be interpreted as representing deficiencies in one group versus another.

Future research is needed in order to understand the role of problem interpretations in the everyday problem-solving process. First, we need to understand the contextual and individual features that lead individuals to different interpretations. Variables such as an individual's perception of control (Klaczynski & Berg, 1992), perceived and actual experience (Elbaum, Berg, & Dodd, 1993), and an individual's underlying cognitive abilities may relate to their interpretations in predictable ways. Second, we need to understand the transactional process whereby individual and contextual features combine to create different interpretations of everyday problems. Third, the process by which different problem interpretations result in differential strategy effectiveness is an important area for future research. That is, in Newell and

Simon's (1972) terminology: Do different interpretations set up different problem spaces in which the problem solver operates? Do such interpretations restrict or constrain the type of information available in memory for the problem solver to use? Detailed analyses of individual's problem-solving processes are needed to address such questions. Fourth, research is needed to examine whether such relations between problem interpretations and strategies would hold when individuals solve their actual everyday problems.

Individuals' problem interpretations may not only be useful in understanding the development of everyday problem solving, but developmental differences in other types of cognitive and intellectual performance as well. The possible role of developmental differences in problem interpretations in explaining developmental differences in cognitive performance have been suggested for differences in childhood development in Piagetian tasks (e.g., Perret-Clermont, Perret, & Bell, in press), adult age differences in text processing (e.g., Adams, Labouvie-Vief, Hobart, & Dorosz, 1990; Gould, Trevithick, & Dixon, 1991), and decision making (e.g., Johnson, 1990). Such work points out that not all subjects interpret the intellectual and cognitive tasks that we present to them in the way that we as experimenters interpret such tasks (see also Lave, 1989).

The relation between problem interpretation and strategy effectiveness suggests a reorientation of research away from ordering individuals across development as to who is most effective against some apriori criterion, but rather understanding how it is that individuals across development adapt to the constraints of their environments. Such a reorientation focuses attention on the process of how individuals adapt to their everyday environments, rather than exclusively on the product. By focusing on the process, we will be better able to understand how individuals with their own individual histories (e.g., abilities and experience) interact with the demands and opportunities of their context.

Acknowledgments

Study 2 was supported by a University of Utah Research Committee Grant and the preparation of this chapter was supported by grant HD 25728 from the National Institute of Child and Human Development and the National Institute of Aging, both awarded to Cynthia A. Berg.

Notes

1 Note that information regarding the type of problem-solving strategy indicated in parentheses was not presented to subjects.
2 Two repeated measures ANOVAs were conducted rather than one ANOVA containing domain as a factor, for multiple reasons. First, the preferred method for conducting such an analysis through both SAS and SPSS requires that the setup of the analysis be appropriate for MANOVA. However, because the interpretation of a problem was a between-subjects variable that did not necessarily contain all levels for all subjects, MANOVA was not an appropriate procedure. Second, the univariate means of analyzing

the data was attempted, although virtual-memory limitations of the supercomputer were not sufficient to complete this analysis.

References

Adams, C., Labouvie-Vief, G., Hobart, C. J., & Dorosz, M. (1990). Adult age group differences in story recall style. *Journal of Gerontology: Psychological Sciences, 45,* 17–27.

Altman, I., & Rogoff, B. (1987). World views in psychology: Trait, interactional, organismic, and transactional perspectives. In D. Stokols & I. Altman (Eds.), *Handbook of environmental psychology* (Vol. 1, pp. 7–40). New York: Wiley.

Baltes, P. B. (1987). Theoretical propositions of life-span developmental psychology: On the dynamics between growth and decline. *Developmental Psychology, 23,* 611–626.

Baltes, P. B., Dittmann-Kohli, F., & Dixon, R. A. (1984). New perspectives on the development of intelligence in adulthood: Toward a dual-process conception and a model of selective optimization with compensation. In P. B. Baltes & O. G. Brim, Jr. (Eds.), *Life-span development and behavior* (Vol. 6, pp. 33–76). New York: Academic Press.

Baltes, M. M., Wahl, H. W., & Schmid-Furstoss, U. (1990). The daily life of elderly humans: Activity patterns, personal control, and functional health. *Journal of Gerontology: Psychological Science, 45,* 173–179.

Band, E., & Weisz, J. R. (1988). How to feel better when it feels bad: Children's perspectives on coping with everyday stress. *Developmental Psychology, 24,* 247–253.

Barker, R. G. and associates (Eds.), *Habitats, environments, and human behavior.* San Francisco: Jossey-Bass.

Berg, C. A. (1989). Knowledge of strategies for dealing with everyday problems from childhood through adolescence. *Developmental Psychology, 25,* 607–618.

Berg, C. (1990). What is intellectual efficacy over the life course?: Using adults' conceptions to address the question. In J. A. Rodin, C. Schooler, & K. W. Schaie (Eds.), *Self-directedness: Causes and effects throughout the life course,* (pp. 155–181). Hillsdale, NJ: Erlbaum.

Berg, C. A., Calderone, K., & Gunderson, M. (1990). *Strategies young and old adults use to solve their own everyday problems.* Paper presented at the meeting of the Gerontological Society, Boston, MA, November.

Berg, C. A., & Klaczynski, P. A. (in prep.) *Young and older adults' interpretations of everyday problems and strategy generation.*

Berg, C. A., & Sternberg, R. J. (1985). A triarchic theory of intellectual development during adulthood. *Developmental Review, 5,* 334–370.

Berg, C. A., & Sternberg, R. J. (1992). Adults' conception of intelligence across the life span. *Psychology and Aging, 7,* 221–231.

Berry, J. W. (1984). Towards a universal psychology of cognitive competence. In P. S. Fry (Ed.), *Changing conceptions of intelligence and intellectual functioning.* Amsterdam: North-Holland.

Brotman-Band, E. (in press). Stress-coping among children with diabetes. *Journal of Pediatric Psychology.*

Calderone, K. S. (1993). *What is the real problem: The impact of children's and adolescent's definitions of everyday problems on strategy effectiveness ratings.* Unpublished Master's Thesis, University of Utah, Salt Lake City, UT.

Cantor, N., Norem, J. K., Niedenthal, P. M., Langston, C. A., & Brower, A. M. (1987). Life tasks, self-concept ideals, and cognitive strategies in a life transition. *Journal of Personality and Social Psychology, 53,* 1178–1191.

Ceci, S. J. (1990). *On intelligence . . . more or less: A bio-ecological treatise on intellectual development.* Englewood Cliffs, NJ: Prentice Hall.

Ceci, S. J., & Bronfenbrenner, U. (1985). Don't forget to take the cupcakes out of the oven: Strategic time-monitoring, prospective memory, and context. *Child Development, 56,* 175–190.

Ceci, S. J., & Liker, J. (1986). Academic and nonacademic intelligence: An experimental separation. In R. J. Sternberg & R. K. Wagner (Eds.), *Practical intelligence: Nature and origins of competence in the everyday world* (pp. 119–142). New York: Cambridge University Press.

Charness, N. (1981). Search in chess: Age and skill differences. *Journal of Experimental Psychology: Human Perception and Performance, 7,* 467–476.

Clabby, J. F., & Elias, M. J. (1986). *Teach your child decision making.* Garden City, NY: Doubleday.

Coddington, R. D. (1972a). The significance of life events as etiological factors in the diseases of children: I. A survey of professional workers. *Journal of Psychosomatic Research, 16,* 7–18.

Coddington, R. D. (1972b). The significance of life events as etiological factors in the diseases of children: II. A survey of a normal population. *Journal of Psychosomatic Research, 16,* 205–213.

Compas, B. E. (1987a). Coping with stress during childhood and adolescence. *Psychological Bulletin, 101,* 393–403.

Compas, B. E. (1987b). Stress and life events during childhood and adolescence. *Clinical Psychology Review, 7,* 1–28.

Cornelius, S. W., & Caspi, A. (1987). Everyday problem solving in adulthood and old age. *Psychology and Aging, 2,* 144–153.

Denney, N. W. (1989). Everyday problem solving: Methodological issues, research findings, and a model. In L. W. Poon, D. C. Rubin, & B. A. Wilson (Eds.), *Everyday cognition in adulthood and late life* (pp. 330–351). New York: Cambridge University Press.

Denney, N. W., & Palmer, A. M. (1981). Adult age differences on traditional and practical problem-solving measures. *Journal of Gerontology, 36,* 323–328.

Dixon, R. A. (1992). Contextual approaches to adult intellectual development. In R. J. Sternberg & C. A. Berg (Eds.), *Intellectual Development* (pp. 350–380). New York: Cambridge University Press.

Elbaum, B., Berg, C. A., & Dodd, D. H. (1993). Previous learning experience, strategy beliefs, and task definition in self-regulated foreign language learning. *Contemporary Educational Psychology, 18,* 318–336.

Folkman, S., Lazarus, R. S., Pimley, S., & Novacek, J. (1987). Age differences in stress and coping processes. *Psychology and Aging, 2,* 171–184.

Frederiksen, N. (1986). Toward a broader conception of human intelligence. *American Psychologist, 41,* 445–452.

Gilligan, C. (1982). *In a different voice: Psychological theory and women's development.* Cambridge, MA: Harvard University Press.

Gould, O. N., Trevithick, L., & Dixon, R. A. (1991). Adult age differences in elaborations produced during prose recall. *Psychology and Aging, 6,* 93–99.

Goodnow, J. J. (1986). Some lifelong everyday forms of intelligent behavior: Organizing and reorganizing. In R. J. Sternberg & R. K. Wagner (Eds.), *Practical intelligence: Nature and origins of competence in the everyday world.* Cambridge: Cambridge University Press.

Harter, S. (1983). Developmental perspectives on the self-system. In P. H. Mussen (Ed.), *Handbook of child psychology, Vol. IV.* New York: Wiley.

Havighurst, R. (1972). *Developmental tasks and education.* New York: Van Nostrand.

Higgins, E. T., King, G. A., & Mann, G. H. (1982). Individual construct accessibility and subjective impressions and recall. *Journal of Personality and Social Psychology, 43,* 35–47.

Higgins, E. T., & Eccles-Parsons, J. (1983). Social cognition and the social life of the child: Stages as subcultures. In E. T. Higgins, D. N. Ruble, & W. Hartup (Eds.), *Social cognition and social development* (pp. 15–62). Cambridge: Cambridge University Press.

Johnson, M. M. S. (1990). Age differences in decision making: A process methodology for examining strategic information processing. *Journal of Gerontology, 45,* 75–78.

Kessen, W. (1984). Introduction: The end of the age of development. In R. J. Sternberg (Ed.), *Mechanisms of cognitive development* (pp. 2–17). New York: Freeman.

Klaczynski, P. A., & Berg, C. A. (1992). *What's the real problem? Age, perceived control and perceived difficulty as predictors of everyday problem definitions.* Presented at *Cognitive Aging Conference,* Atlanta, GA, April.

Klaczynski, P. A., Laipple, J. J., & Jurden, F. H. (1992). Educational context differences in practical problem-solving during adolescence. *Merrill-Palmer Quarterly, 38,* 417–438.

Klaczynski, P. A., & Reese, H. W. (1991). Educational trajectory and "action orientation": Grade and track differences. *Journal of Youth and Adolescence, 20,* 441–462.

Kuhn, D., Pennington, N., & Leadbeater, B. (1983). Adult thinking in developmental perspective. In P. B. Baltes & O. G. Brim (Eds.), *Life-span development and behavior, Vol. 5.* New York: Academic Press.

Laboratory of Comparative Human Cognition (1982). Culture and intelligence. In R. J. Sternberg (Ed.), *Handbook of human intelligence* (pp. 642–719). Cambridge: Cambridge University Press.

Laipple, J. S. (1991). *Problem solving in young and old adulthood: The role of task interpretation.* Unpublished doctoral dissertation, West Virginia University.

Lave, J. (1989). *Cognition in practice.* New York: Cambridge University Press.

Lazarus, R. S., & Folkman, S. (1984). *Stress, appraisal, and coping.* New York: Springer.

Leont'ev, A. N. (1981). The problem of activity in psychology. In J. V. Wertsch (Ed.), *The concept of activity in Soviet psychology.* Armonk, NY: Sharpe.

Lerner, R. M., Hultsch, D. F., & Dixon, R. A. (1983). Contextualism and the character of developmental psychology in the 1970's *Annals of the New York Academy of Sciences, 412,* 101–128.

Lerner, R. M., & Kauffman, M. B. (1985). The concept of development in contextualism. *Developmental Review, 5,* 309–333.

Lewin, K. (1936). *Principles of topological psychology.* New York: McGraw-Hill.

Lewin, K. (1951). *Field theory in social science: Selected theoretical papers* (D. Cartwright, ed.). New York: Harper & Row.

McGuire, W. J., & Padawer-Singer, A. (1976). Trait salience in the spontaneous self-concept. *Journal of Personality and Social Psychology, 33,* 743–754.

Meacham, J. A., & Emont, N. C. (1989). The interpersonal basis of everyday problem solving. In J. D. Sinnott (Ed.), *Everyday problem solving: Theory and applications* (pp. 7–23). New York: Praeger.

Metcalfe, R. J. A., Dobson, C. B., Cook, A., & Michaud, A. (1982). The construction, reliability, and validity of a stress inventory for children. *Educational Psychology, 2,* 59–71.

Mischel, W. (1984). Convergences and challenges in the search for consistency. *American Psychologist, 39,* 351–364.

Neisser, U. (1979). The concept of intelligence. In R. Sternberg & D. Detterman (Eds.), *Human intelligence: Perspectives on its theory and measurement* (pp. 179–189). Norwood, NJ: Ablex.

Neugarten, B. L., Moore, J. W., & Lowe, J. C. (1968). Age norms, age constraints, and adult socialization. In B. L. Neugarten (Ed.), *Middle age and aging* (pp. 22–28). Chicago: University of Chicago Press.

Newell, A., & Simon, H. A. (1972). *Human Problem Solving.* Englewood Cliffs, NJ: Prentice-Hall.

Pepper, S. C. (1942). *World hypotheses.* Berkeley, CA: University of California Press.

Perret-Clermont, A. N., Perret, J. F., & Bell, N. (1991). The social construction of meaning and cognitive activity in elementary school children. In J. M. Levine, L. B. Resnick & S. Behrend (Eds.), *Perspectives on socially shared cognition.* Washington, DC: A.P.A. Press.

Poon, L. W., Rubin, D. C., & Wilson, B. A. (1990). (Eds.). *Everyday cognition in adulthood and late life.* New York: Cambridge University Press.

Rogoff, B. (1982). Integrating context and cognitive development. In M. E. Lamb & A. L. Brown (Eds.), *Advances in developmental psychology* (Vol. 2, pp. 125–169). Hillsdale, NJ: Erlbaum.

Rogoff, B., Gauvain, M., & Gardner, W. (1987). Children's adjustment of plans to circumstances. In S. L. Friedman, E. K. Scholnick, & R. R. Cocking (Eds.), *Blueprints for thinking* (pp. 303–320). Cambridge: Cambridge University Press.

Rogoff, B., & Lave, J. (1984). (Eds.) *Everyday cognition: Its development in social context.* Cambridge, MA: Harvard University Press.

Rogoff, B., & Waddell, K. J. (1982). Memory for information organized in a scene by children from two cultures. *Child Development, 53,* 1224–1228.

Rosnow, R. L., & Georgoudi, M. (1986). *Contextualism and understanding in behavioral science.* New York: Praeger.

Rothbaum, F., Weisz, J. R., & Snyder, S. S. (1982). Changing the world and changing the self: A two-process model of perceived control. *Journal of Personality and Social Psychology, 42,* 5–37.

Sansone, C., & Berg, C. A. (1993). Adapting to the environment across the life span: Different process or different inputs? *International Journal of Behavioral Development, 16,* 215–241.

Sansone, C., Berg, C. A., & Weir, C. (1991). What are we adapting to? Perceived environments across the lifespan. In C. Sansone and C. A. Berg (Chairs) *Competence in context: Social-developmental lifespan perspectives in everyday competence.* Symposium presented at the meetings of the American Psychological Association, San Francisco, CA, August.

Sansone, C., Berg, C. A., Weir, C., Calderone, K., Harpster, L. L., & Morgan, C. (1991). Assessing normative contexts across the life span. Presented at the biannual meeting of the Society for Research in Child Development, Seattle, WA, April.

Scribner, S. (1986). Thinking in action: Some characteristics of practical thought. In R. J. Sternberg & R. Wagner (Eds.), *Practical intelligence: Origins of competence in the everyday world.* (pp. 143–162). New York: Cambridge University Press.

Siegler, R. S., & Richards, D. D. (1982). The development of intelligence. In R. J. Sternberg (Ed.), *Handbook of human intelligence.* New York: Cambridge University Press.

Sinnott, J. D. (1989). A model for solution of ill-structured problems: implications for everyday and abstract problem solving. In J. D. Sinnott (Ed.), *Everyday problem solving: Theory and applications.* New York: Praeger.

Sinnott, J. D., & Guttmann, D. (1978). The dialectics of decision making in older adults. *Human Development, 21,* 190–200.

Spivack, G., & Shure, M. B. (1982). The cognition of social adjustment: Interpersonal cognitive problem-solving thinking. In B. Lahey & A. E. Kazdin (Eds.), *Advances in clinical child psychology* (Vol. 5). New York: Plenum.

Sternberg, R. J. (1984). A contextual view of the nature of intelligence. In P. S. Fry (Ed.), *Changing conceptions of intelligence and intellectual functioning: current theory and research* (pp. 7–34). Amsterdam: North-Holland.

Sternberg, R. J. (1985). *Beyond IQ: A triarchic theory of human intelligence.* New York: Cambridge University Press.

Sternberg, R. J., & Wagner, R. K. (Eds.) (1986). *Practical intelligence.* New York: Cambridge University Press.

Tannen, D. (1990). Gender differences in topical coherence: Creating involvement in best friends' talk. *Discourse Processes, 13,* 73–90.

Walsh, D. A., & Hershey, D. A. (in press). Mental models and the maintenance of complex problem solving skills into old age. In J. Cerella & W. Hoyer (Eds.), *Adult information processing: Limits on loss.* New York: Academic Press.

Wertsch, J. V., & Kanner, B. G. (1992). A sociocultural approach to intellectual development. In R. Sternberg & C. Berg (Eds.), *Intellectual development.* New York: Cambridge University Press.

Wertsch, J. V., Minick, N., & Arns, F. J. (1984). The creation of context in joint problem-solving. In B. Rogoff & J. Lave (Eds.), *Everyday cognition: Its development in social context.* Cambridge, MA: Harvard University Press.

Willis, S. L., & Schaie, K. W. (1986). Practical intelligence in later adulthood. In R. Sternberg & R. Wagner (Eds.), *Practical intelligence* (pp. 236–270). New York: Cambridge University Press.

Willis, S. L., & Schaie, K. W. (1991). Everyday cognition: Taxonomic and methodological considerations. In J. M. Puckett & H. W. Reese (Eds.), *Life-span developmental psychology: Mechanisms of everyday cognition.* Hillsdale, NJ: Erlbaum.

Yussen, S. R., & Kane, P. T. (1983). Children's ideas about intellectual ability. In *The child's construction of social inequality.* New York: Academic Press.

5 Context counts: the case of cognitive-ability testing for job selection

Richard K. Wagner

Cognitive-ability tests are solid predictors of school performance, particularly when the measure of school performance is an achievement test that is similar in many respects to cognitive-ability tests. But even for other indices of school performance, such as grades and frequency of retention, respectable correlations are observed. More controversial is the question of how valuable cognitive-ability tests are for predicting performance in out-of-school contexts. If cognitive-ability tests are uniformly good predictors of performance regardless of context, the rationale for the present book on contextual aspects of intellectual functioning becomes questionable, at least for the kind of intellectual functioning measured by cognitive-ability tests.

The out-of-school context that has received the most attention from researchers seeking to validate cognitive-ability tests for predicting performance outside the classroom is job performance. The question that has motivated much of this research is the value of cognitive-ability tests for job selection. According to some recent accounts, cognitive-ability tests not only predict job performance, but they are so valuable for job selection that their widespread use is believed to be the key to economic prosperity and the well-being of society at large (see, e.g., Ree & Earles, 1992; Schmidt & Hunter, 1992; Hunter & Schmidt, 1983).

One way to quantify the value of cognitive-ability measures for job selection is to apply the methods of utility analysis. Utility analysis is an approach for estimating the savings in personnel costs that would be achieved by using a selection device such as a cognitive-ability measure (Cronbach & Gleser, 1957; Hunter & Schmidt, 1983; Schmidt, Hunter, McKenzie, & Mudrow, 1979). If performance on the selection device is related to job performance, then selecting those who score well on the selection device should improve employee performance. With improved employee performance, fewer individuals can accomplish the same amount of work that a larger group of unselected employees would accomplish. Fewer workers mean savings in personnel costs, and an estimate of these savings is what is referred to as a test's utility. Purportedly, conservative estimates of the utility of cognitive-ability measures for job selection are mind boggling, ranging from $376 million over 10 years if the federal government would use an IQ test to select computer programmers (Schmidt et al., 1979) to $80 billion per year for the economy as a whole were IQ testing to be used universally for job selection (Hunter & Schmidt, 1982). As a former chairman of the Senate budget appropriations committee once observed, "a billion here and a billion there, and pretty soon we're talking real money."

Of course, the utility of cognitive-ability tests depends upon their validity when used for job selection. A test with no validity has no utility because performance on the test will not predict performance on the job. According to some recent accounts, the validity of cognitive-ability tests for job selection is nothing short of phenomenal: Cognitive-ability tests are valid predictors of job performance for a wide range of job settings (Barrett & Depinet, 1991) or even for all job settings (Schmidt & Hunter, 1981; see also Gottfredson, 1986; Hawk, 1986). The implications of such views for policy on job selection is obvious: "If an employer were to use only intelligence tests and select the highest scoring applicant for each job, training results would be predicted well regardless of the job, and overall performance from the employees selected would be maximized" (Ree & Earles, 1992, p. 88).

Are these kinds of claims correct or are they exaggerated? This chapter, which is divided into three parts, is one attempt to answer this question. In the first part, I consider claims about the remarkable validity of cognitive-ability tests for job selection. In the second part, I consider claims about the remarkable utility of the tests. In the third part, I consider how the actual validity and utility of selection procedures might be enhanced by acknowledging differences between academic and nonacademic contexts, and incorporating these differences in measures used for selection.

The validity of cognitive-ability tests for job selection

Opinions about the validity of cognitive-ability tests for job selection run the gamut from " . . . measures of cognitive ability have substantial validity for all jobs . . . " (Hunter & Schmidt, 1983, p. 477) to " . . . the evidence for their validity is by no means so overwhelming as most of us, rather unthinkingly, had come to think it was" (McClelland, 1973, p. 1). Despite such diversity of opinion, some basic empirical facts are undisputed.

The average validity coefficient or correlation between cognitive-ability test scores and job performance is about .2 (Wigdor & Garner, 1982). Squaring the validity coefficient gives us the percentage of variability in job performance that is accounted for by test scores, which in this case is only 4%. With 96% of the variability in job performance unaccounted for, McClelland's (1973) pessimism about the worth of the cognitive-ability testing enterprise for job selection is understandable. However, it is possible that the average validity coefficient underestimates the true magnitude of the validity of cognitive-ability tests for job selection. When validity coefficients are corrected for measurement artifacts such as restriction of range and error – a topic that will be considered shortly – the average validity coefficient increases from the .2 level to about the .5 level. With this level of validity, roughly 25% of the variability in job performance is accounted for by scores on cognitive-ability tests. Whether one's inclination is to view the glass as one-quarter full or three-quarters empty, room for improvement exists. In any case, validity coefficients provide limited and biased information about the true validity of general cognitive-ability measures for selection, for at least three reasons.

1. Validity coefficients overestimate the unique predictive validity of tests for job selection

A maxim in selection that routinely is followed in practice is to rely on multiple sources of information. Thus, college students in the United States are selected on the basis of Scholastic Aptitude Test (SAT) scores, high school grades, and, often, letters of recommendations and interviews. Similarly, companies routinely ask job applicants to provide information about their schooling, previous work experience, and letters of recommendation, in addition to having them take one or more employment tests. If each of the multiple sources of information is predictive of criterion performance, and if each contributes something to prediction that is not completely redundant, then the validity of the combined sources of information will be greater than that of any of the sources of information used in isolation.

Because validity coefficients associated with individual sources of information such as test scores are correlation coefficients, they only tell us about what would happen if a source of information were used by itself, ignoring overlap with the other sources of information used to make a selection decision. When the predictive power of a test score overlaps with that of other sources of information, as it normally does in practice, the test's validity coefficient presents an inflated picture of the test's unique contribution to prediction. Consider a fictitious but representative example.

A biomedical research company hires computer programmers on the basis of a verbal-ability test – the Miller Analogies Test – college grades, and letters of recommendation that describe an individual's programming experience. Correlations among these variables are presented in Table 5.1. By squaring the validity coefficient for verbal ability (.4), we learn that this predictor apparently accounts for 16% of the variability in job performance as a computer programmer. This is more than the variability in job performance accounted for by college grades (9%) or letters of recommendation (4%), so we might be tempted to simply use verbal ability when deciding whom to hire. However, as noted previously, it often is the case that better prediction can be obtained by combining multiple sources of information. By using

Table 5.1. *Correlations among three predictors and job performance for biomedical research company example*

1. Miller Analogies Test	1.0			
2. College grades	0.5	1.0		
3. Letters of recommendation	0.3	0.3	1.0	
4. Job performance	0.4	0.3	0.3	1.0
	1.	2.	3.	4.

multiple regression, we learn that the correlation between a combination of verbal ability, college grades, and letters of recommendation and job performance is .45. Thus, the combined predictors account for 20% of the variability in job performance.

Of the combined predictive power of verbal ability, college grades, and letters of recommendation, how much is unique to verbal ability? One practical reason for wanting to know the unique predictive power of a test of verbal ability, or of any other test, is that tells us how much validity will increase when the test is added to an existing selection battery, and conversely, how much validity will decrease when a test is removed from a selection battery. To find out the unique predictive validity of verbal ability, we simply determine how much variance in job performance increases when verbal ability is added last (i.e., after college grades and letters of recommendation) to a multiple regression prediction equation.[1] These results are presented in Table 5.2. In a first step, college grades are used to predict job performance. The increase in variance in job performance accounted for by using college grades in selection is 9%. Because college grades are the sole predictor at this point, 9% also is the squared correlation between college grades and job performance (.3). The correlation between letters of recommendation and job performance also was .3, but when letters of recommendation is entered after college grades into the prediction equation, the increase in variance accounted for is not 9% but only 5 percent. It is true that letters of recommendation account for 9% of job performance, but only 5% is unique to letters of recommendation. The remaining 4% of variance accounted for is shared with college grades. In a final step, verbal ability is added as a predictor. The increase in variance accounted for is 6%, which represents the unique predictive validity of verbal ability. Adding 6% to variance accounted for in job performance is a substantial improvement in predictive power, but less than 16% gotten by squaring the validity coefficient for verbal ability (.4).

In summary, validity coefficients typically reported for measures of general cognitive ability overestimate their unique predictive power when used in a battery of correlated tests and other sources of information, as they invariably are. Note that this same logic applies to other predictors such as college grades and letters of recom-

Table 5.2.   Incremental validity of college grades, letters of recommendation, and general cognitive ability for biomedical research company example

Variable Added	Percentage increase in job performance, variance accounted for
Step 1. College grades	9
Step 2. Letters of recommendation	5
Step 3. General cognitive ability	6
Total percentage accounted for	20

mendation. In the present example, the unique predictive power of college grades (1%) and letters of recommendation (3%) are less than their squared validity coefficients.

If the unique predictive validity of general cognitive-ability measures is less than is suggested by their validity coefficients, how much less is it? Perhaps the only serious attempt to answer this question was a study by Hunter and Hunter (1984). They carried out a "meta-meta-analysis" involving 23 meta-analyses that summarized results from thousands of individual validity studies. Meta-analysis is a collection of methods that enables one to do a quantitative synthesis of a research area. An important outcome of meta-analysis for correlational studies is an estimate of the average correlation between two variables or constructs across all studies included in the meta-analysis. (For experimental studies, the comparable outcome is an estimate of the average effect size associated with manipulation of some independent variables.) The relevant part of Hunter and Hunter's (1984) study for present purposes was their attempt to determine the validity of cognitive-ability tests when used in conjunction with alternative predictors such as grades and interviews. Astonishingly, despite the thousands of validity studies they included in their review, they were forced to drop this aspect of their research design for lack of data.[2] The few studies that had included multiple predictors did not even report the correlations among the multiple predictors necessary to determine their unique predictive validity. This is a particularly disappointing state of affairs because multiple measures probably could have been analyzed in the majority of primary studies: Even the minimum job application provides data concerning educational history, and applicants are required to provide recommendation letters for many jobs. Researchers appear to have been blinded by what we have termed the "*g*-eocentric" view (Sternberg & Wagner, 1993). Analogous to the pre-Keplarian geocentric view of the universe in which the earth was assumed to be at the center of the universe, and therefore the most important object in the heavens, the *g*-eocentric view holds that general cognitive ability is the center of measurement for job performance. Other constructs are assumed to be proxies for general cognitive ability or to represent effects of the primary causal agent of general cognitive ability. With this world view, why attempt to incorporate other variables in one's studies?

2. Validity coefficients overestimate the magnitude of theoretical relations between general cognitive ability and job performance

Not only are validity coefficients poor estimates of the role of general cognitive ability measures in selection applications, they also overestimate the magnitude of theoretical relations between general cognitive ability and job performance, for a similar reason. A meaningful understanding of the theoretical relation between general cognitive ability and job performance requires a causal model that includes all causal influences on job performance. Such a model allows one to estimate direct, indirect, and spurious causal effects of cognitive ability and other causes of job performance.

A direct causal effect is a causal influence on job performance that is not mediated by some other influence. If, for example, there is a direct causal influence of general cognitive ability on job performance of .2, a one unit increase in general cognitive ability would result in a .2 unit increase in job performance. An indirect causal effect is a causal influence that is mediated by some other causal influence. For example, Hunter (1983) reported that general cognitive ability influenced job performance indirectly through its effect on job knowledge: Individuals who were high in general cognitive ability acquired more knowledge about their jobs, and this knowledge in turn improved their job performance. The indirect effect of general cognitive ability on job performance through job knowledge was about twice as large as its direct effect. Finally, a spurious effect is an apparent causal influence that can be accounted for by correlations with other predictors. For example, McClelland (1973) argued that supervisors, who tend to be higher in socioeconomic status, may give higher performance ratings to workers who share their socioeconomic status and lower performance ratings to workers who do not. Because lower socioeconomic status is associated with lower performance on IQ tests, McClelland argued that correlations between IQ test scores and job performance ratings may be spurious, in part, because of their joint association with socioeconomic status.

Unfortunately, due to the previously mentioned impoverished database of studies that include multiple potential causes of job performance, virtually nothing is known about the relative magnitudes of direct, indirect, and spurious effects of general cognitive ability and other potential causes of job performance. The few path-analytic studies that have been carried out have included only the bare minimum of variables in causal roles. For example, the exogenous causal variables in Hunter's (1983) path-analytic model were cognitive ability and job knowledge. A follow-up study added job experience to the model (Schmidt, Hunter, & Outerbridge, 1986). These important studies represent a critical direction for research on job performance, but their primitive character (i.e., few causes, simple relations) is surprising for a field of psychology that has played a major role in the origin of some of the most sophisticated and useful methodologies, such as item-response theory modeling and meta-analysis. But this state of affairs is consistent with the *g*-eocentric view described earlier: Interest has been confined to developing better cognitive-ability tests (item-response theory models) or in promoting their validity (meta-analysis), to the neglect of investigating other constructs that are likely to have joint causal influences on job performance.

3. Some adjustments of correlations that are appropriate for answering theoretically interesting questions can provide misleading answers to practical ones

In meta-analytic studies of relations between general cognitive ability and job performance, two kinds of adjustments commonly are done.

The first adjustment is to counteract restriction of range. Validity coefficients and all correlation coefficients are affected by the amount of variability in scores. Lots of variability results in larger validity coefficients, little variability results in smaller validity coefficients. What is desirable is to have the right amount of variability, which for selection purposes, is the amount of variability in the population of job applicants. Unfortunately, subjects in most studies are employees rather than job applicants, because only employees will have job performance data necessary to demonstrate the predictive validity of a test on job performance. If only high-scorers on the test being evaluated have been hired, then the range of employee test scores will be restricted relative to that of job applicants. If the test is a valid predictor of job performance, then range restriction will be observed for job performance as well. A formula, available from most measurement texts, can be used to estimate the correlation that would have been obtained had a given sample had more or less variability than it actually did. Use of this formula is how investigators correct for restriction of range.

Use of a formula to correct for restriction of range requires knowing the standard deviation of predictor scores for the population of job applicants. A sample-based estimate of this population parameter is the standard deviation of scores for all job applicants, including those who were not hired. Unfortunately, the vast majority of studies do not provide this required information. Although most companies retain the test scores of job applicants who were not hired, most studies only include scores of employees rather than of job applicants. The situation for dealing with restriction of range in the criterion measure of job performance is even more troubling. When poor scorers on the test are not hired, job-performance data obviously will be unavailable. And it is the standard deviation of job performance for all job applicants, hired and not hired, that is needed to correct for restriction of range in the criterion measure of job performance. The only way to obtain the necessary data would be to try out a test for a prolonged period of time without making the test scores available to either the individuals who make hiring decisions or to the individuals who generate job-performance data.

Because the required data are rarely available, the standard deviation needed to correct for restriction of range usually must be estimated from other sources. Although one might be tempted to use the standard deviation reported in the test manual, rarely is it appropriate to do so. The standard deviation reported in the test manual will be based on a stratified, random sample that represents the population of all adults. But for many jobs, the applicant population – those individuals who meet the qualifications required by the job and who would apply for it – represents only a narrow segment of the entire population of all adults. For example, candidates for managerial positions often are required to be college graduates, a population markedly less variable in cognitive ability than adults in general. Technical and professional jobs may require advanced training in addition to a college degree. Unless it is the case that the population of job applicants is literally adults in general, which includes individuals whose IQ test scores fall in the mentally retarded range, using the standard deviation found in the test manual will "over-correct" validity coefficients, making them spuriously large.

The second common adjustment of validity coefficients is for unreliability in the test and in the criterion measure of job performance. This practice makes sense for theoretical studies of relations between cognitive ability and job performance, but is questionable when the goal is to address the more practical question of what is the actual validity of test X when used to select individuals for a particular job in company Z. The effect of unreliability in the test and in the criterion measure of job performance is to reduce the magnitude of the validity coefficient. One might adjust validity coefficients upwards because of measurement error in a theoretical study that seeks the best estimate of the true magnitude of relations between the constructs of cognitive ability and job performance. Constructs ideally would be measured without error, so estimating the validity coefficient that would obtain had our measures of cognitive ability and job performance been perfectly reliable makes sense for a theoretical study. After all, we don't want to have to rewrite the textbooks every time that a more reliable measure is developed. But for the practical question of determining the actual validity of a particular test for selecting employees for a particular company, the practice of correcting validity coefficients for unreliability is questionable. The actual validity of a test used for real selection is affected by the reliability of the test and the criterion measure of job performance, and it is actual rather than ideal validity that justifies use of a test locally, and that determines the effectiveness of selection based on test results in terms of the actual measures of job performance that are available.

The utility of cognitive-ability tests for job selection

Whether or not one concludes that the validity of cognitive-ability tests is sufficient to make them valuable for individual selection decisions, the tests might be of considerable overall value to a company or even a nation as a whole. Recall that estimates of personnel savings that would result by using a cognitive ability test for selection ranged from $376 million over ten years for government computer programmers (Schmidt et al., 1979) to $80 billion per year for the economy as a whole were IQ testing to be used universally for job selection (Hunter & Schmidt, 1982). If these estimates are in the ballpark, perhaps the somewhat meager validity found at the level of individual selection would be tolerable.

A formula for calculating a test's utility was presented by Cronbach and Gleser (1957), but saw little use because it requires an estimate of the standard deviation of job performance in terms of dollars (Hunter & Schmidt, 1983). What is required is an estimate of the difference in money earned for the company by two individuals, one of whom is a standard deviation higher in job performance than the other. Hunter and Schmidt proposed several ways to estimate the standard deviation of job performance in dollars, and used the following formula to calculate utility:

$$U = (N)(T)(r_{xy})(SD_y)(X)$$

U is utility, which is the estimated savings in personnel costs (or alternatively, the estimated increase in productivity in terms of dollars). Utility is the product of five terms. The first term, N, is the number of individuals hired. If a test enables a company to hire more productive workers, then the more workers hired the greater the savings. The second term, T, is the average number of years worked by those hired. The longer the more productive workers stay with the company, the more the company saves. Note that the combined product $(N)(T)$ represents what we might call "worker years." The same product results from hiring 10 workers whose average duration of employment will be 1 year, or from hiring 1 worker whose average duration of employment will be 10 years. The third term, r_{xy}, is the estimated true correlation between test performance and job performance. Obviously, the more predictive the test is of job performance, the greater the utility of the test. The fourth term, SD_y, is the dollar amount associated with a standard deviation difference in job performance. What is needed there is an estimate, in dollars, of how much more money an above-average employee (i.e., 85th percentile in job performance) earns for the company than does an average employee (i.e., 50th percentile in job performance). The greater the relation between job performance and money earned by the company, the greater the utility of a test that predicts job performance. The final term, X, is the average predictor score of individuals actually selected, expressed in applicant population standard scores (Z-scores). Because the units for this variable are standard scores of the population of job applicants with a mean of 0 and a standard deviation of 1, this term will be positive when the average test scores of individuals hired are better than the average of all applicants. This term provides an indicator of how select the individuals that a company hires are relative to the population of job applicants. If the company is able to hire the top scorers on the test, utility will be higher than if the company has to settle for mid-level scorers. Identifying a top prospect is one thing; getting them to accept a job offer is another. Provided that a test does predict job performance, the more a company is able to hire top scorers the greater the actual utility of the test.

Although the previously cited examples of utility estimates ranged from millions to billions of dollars, these estimates are inflated because of some of the same problems noted for validity coefficients, and by several additional problems unique to utility estimation.

1. Utility estimates are inflated by assuming a baseline of random selection

Recall the previous utility estimate of $376 million saved by the federal government if cognitive ability tests were used to hire computer programmers. The figure of $376 million in savings by using a cognitive-ability test is in comparison with an alternative of random selection of computer programmers, even though random selection is rarely, if ever, done in practice (Hunter & Schmidt, 1983). Utility estimates that assume a baseline of random selection may be of theoretical interest, but they will overestimate the actual savings that would result if a test is added to the existing selection procedures, unless the existing selection procedures are to hire at random.[3]

The problem appears to arise because of the utility formula relies on the zero-order correlation between test scores and job performance. As noted previously in the discussion of the validity, the semipartial correlation is the coefficient that represents the unique contribution of any one test or selection procedure to the combined battery of selection procedures, and would seem to be the more appropriate coefficient to use in a utility formula.

2. Utility estimates are based on the erroneous assumption of an inexhaustible supply of top candidates

Claims that cognitive-ability tests are valid for all jobs suggests that universal use of the tests for selection would add billions of dollars to the economy of the United States. Hunter and Schmidt (1982) provide a figure of $80 billion per year for widespread use of cognitive-ability tests for selection. But paradoxically, as the prevalence of cognitive-ability testing for job selection approaches universality, utility approaches 0. The problem is that utility estimates assume that the supply of top scorers is inexhaustible, whereas in real life, the supply of top scorers in any given community, state, or even nation is exhaustible. Competition among organizations for top scorers means that utility cannot go up for everyone. With widespread use of cognitive ability tests for selection, gains in utility for one organization are wiped out by losses in utility for another.

An example of near-universal reliance on cognitive-ability testing is provided by the case of admission to colleges and universities. Nearly all colleges and universities use either SAT scores or ACT scores, in conjunction with other information such as high school grades, personal statements, interviews, and letters of recommendation to make admissions decisions. However, there is competition among colleges and universities for the best students. Students the admissions committee offers admission to at Harvard may elect to go to Yale or MIT. Students offered admission to Florida State may elect to go to Duke or the University of Florida. In the end, the more highly prized colleges and universities have more success recruiting top-scoring students than the less highly prized colleges and universities. Competition for students affects utility. The relevant term in the formula is X, the mean test score of selected individuals expressed in applicant population standard scores. If we convert the SAT and ACT scores of all applicants to a standard score with a mean of 0 and a standard deviation of 1, the term X for highly prized schools such as Harvard and Yale will be positive, perhaps as high as 3. This means that these schools are able to recruit students whose average test scores are 3 standard deviations above the mean. The value of X for less highly prized schools such as Florida State will be less, perhaps about 1. Consequently, the utility of scholastic aptitude test scores for Florida State is reduced due to losing out in a competition for top scoring students to more highly prized schools. Note that for schools whose entering class has an average test score that is less than the overall applicant average, X becomes negative (recall it as a Z-score with a mean of 0), as does the utility estimate. Thus the utility estimates reflect the fact that gains in utility for one organization are offset by losses in utility for another. As cognitive-ability testing becomes universal, the average value of X approaches its own mean of 0, which results in zero overall utility.

3. Estimating the standard deviation of job performance in dollars remains largely a subjective and difficult problem

Utility analysis has not played much of a role in social science research because of difficulty in estimating SD_y, the standard deviation of performance in dollars. How many dollars is an above-average performer worth compared to an average performer? Consider the example of an academic department. My psychology department engages in an annual exercise of ordering its members in terms of their yearly contributions in the areas of scholarship, teaching, and service, for the purpose of dispensing what, in the best of years, amount to meager merit raises. Having participated in the process for several years, I know who tends to be rated average and who tends to be rated above average, but I have no confidence that I could come within an order of magnitude of a correct figure for what this difference in performance translates to in dollars. Lest one think that the problem is confined to weird jobs such as that of academic psychologist, I have had occasion to carry out test validations in different organizations. I repeatedly have found that knowledgeable insiders place much less confidence in an organization's performance-appraisal system, compared with outside researchers who eagerly seek criterion-related validity data to validate their tests. Evaluating performance is hard; attaching a dollar amount to it is even harder.

Hunter and Schmidt (1983) have made progress in developing approaches to improve estimation of the standard deviation of performance in dollars. For example, one of their approaches is to give superiors a standard set of questions to answer, and then to average responses across superiors. Approaches such as this one may reduce subjectivity in this kind of estimation task, but will not eliminate it, and estimation error directly affects utility estimates: An estimated standard deviation of performance in dollars of $2000 results in a utility estimate that is double that based on an estimated standard deviation of $1000.

4. Utility estimates ignore the economic and social costs of adverse impact

In the present context, adverse impact refers to a selection procedure than unfairly affects a group of individuals. Test fairness and bias in testing are controversial subjects for which many basic questions remain unresolved. However, it is illustrative to consider the case of a test that would appear to be unbiased using rather stringent psychometric criteria, yet which nevertheless will have adverse impact. Consider a cognitive-ability test that is unbiased according to the following criterion: for any given test score, the predicted level of job performance is identical for majority- and minority-group members. A more technical way of saying this is that the minority and majority groups share the same regression line when cognitive ability is used to predict job performance. All this means is that if you earned a test score of, say, 105, which we will consider to be just a few points above the actual mean of the test, your predicted level of job performance will be just above the mean level of job performance, and this predicted level of job performance will be the same whether you belong to the majority or minority group. Taking a concrete example, let's assume that test performance favors the majority group by one standard deviation, which it typically does, and also that the validity coefficient for our test of cognitive ability is .5, which is generous. This situation is portrayed in Figure 5.1.

The key result presented in Figure 5.1 is that the majority and minority groups differ more in terms of test performance than in predicted job performance: The distance between means on the horizontal (test score) axis is greater than the distance between means on the vertical (job performance) axis. This will be the case, even for apparently unbiased tests, when the majority group outperforms the minority group on the test, and the validity coefficient for the test is less than 1.0. Now consider a cut-off that would select the top half of majority-group members. This cut-off would select only 16% of minority-group members, even though 31% of the minority-group members are predicted to perform at or above the majority-group mean on job performance itself (Hunter & Hunter, 1984; Thorndike, 1971). If everything stays the same except that we use the more realistic validity coefficient of .25, we will still

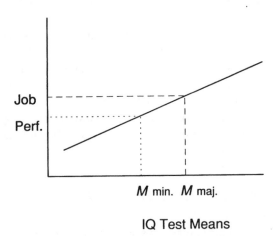

IQ Test Means

Figure 5.1. Difference between majority–minority differences in test performance and in predicted job performance with a validity coefficient of .50.

select only 16% of minority-group members, even though fully 40% should perform at or above the majority mean on job performance. Adverse impact, represented here by the discrepancy between the percentages of minority-group members who meet the test cut-off and who would meet the selection criterion on job performance, increases as validity decreases (see Seymour, 1988, for an extended discussion of adverse impact).

The economic costs of adverse impact are difficult to quantify, but are real and substantial. At a minimum, they would include (a) the lost productivity of minority-group members who were not hired because of their test scores, yet who would have outperformed majority-group members who were hired; (b) lost taxes and lost spending as a consequence of minority-group unemployment; and (c) the cost of social programs that are necessitated by the considerable rate of minority-group unemployment, among other causes. With the ever-increasing proportion of minority-group members in the United States, the economic costs of adverse impact are likely to increase, and would increase even more were cognitive-ability testing to become universal.

Improving validity and utility through common sense

As the earlier discussion shows, there is considerable disagreement about the validity and utility of cognitive-ability testing for job selection. Fortunately, there is considerable agreement about how to increase validity and utility on the one hand, and decrease adverse impact on the other, of selection procedures: "If we could find predictors . . . other than ability to add to the prediction supplied by ability tests, then we could simultaneously increase validity and decrease adverse impact" (Hunter & Hunter, 1984, p. 74).

An example of a promising new construct that may improve the validity and utility of selection procedures is the construct of practical intelligence or common sense (Sternberg & Wagner, 1986). Neisser (1976) was one of the first modern psychologists to make a distinction between the "academic intelligence" type tasks found in the classroom and on IQ tests, and the type of tasks found in the everyday world that require a more practical kind of intelligence. If academic intelligence can be conceptualized as the facility with which formal knowledge is acquired in schooling, practical intelligence can be conceptualized as the facility with which tacit knowledge is acquired from one's daily experience. Tacit knowledge refers to practical know-how that usually is not openly expressed or stated (*Oxford English Dictionary,* 1933; Polanyi, 1976). In organizations, it is acquired informally from "on-the-job" experience or passed on from mentor to protégé.

In the past decade, practical intelligence has been the focus of a growing number of studies carried out in a wide range of settings and cultures. Summaries of various parts of this literature have been provided by Ceci (1990), Rogoff and Lave (1984), Scribner and Cole (1981), Sternberg (1985), Sternberg and Frensch (1991), Sternberg and Wagner (1986, 1993), Sternberg, Wagner, and Okagaki (1991), and Voss, Perkins, and Segal (1991). Consider several findings that support the distinction between academic and practical intelligence.

1. Lay persons' and experts' conceptions of intelligence

Although they should not be accepted uncritically, the conceptions of intelligence held by lay persons and by experts provide evidence of the usefulness of the distinction between academic and practical intelligence for carrying out everyday affairs (lay persons) or research on intelligence (experts). Everyday parlance includes a number of expressions that appear to represent the presence or absence of practical competence, including "street smart," "savvy," having "learned the ropes" or "gotten one's feet wet," and being "wet behind the ears." Practical competence also figured in definitions of intelligence offered by leading researchers who participated in the 1921 symposium sponsored by the editors of *The Journal of Educational Psychology*, and in the definitions of leading researchers who were asked to define intelligence 65 years later (Sternberg & Detterman, 1986). More formal studies of the implicit theories of intelligence held by lay persons and experts also support a distinction between practical and academic kinds of intelligence (Sternberg, Conway, Ketron, & Bernstein, 1981).

2. Life-span development of academic and practical competence

Elderly adults commonly report growth over their lifespan in perceived ability to solve practical problems despite evidence of a decline in their ability to solve traditional academic-type problems (Williams, Denney, & Schladler, 1983). Empirical studies in which adults of differing ages are given academic and practical tests indicate that the asymtote of practical competence occurs several decades after that of academic competence (Cornelius & Caspi, 1987; Denney & Palmer, 1981). This difference in life-span developmental functions for academic and practical competence is mirrored by a number of social conventions and institutions. For example, one must be 35 or older to be elected President of the United States, and members of the boards of major corporations are nearly always in their 50s and early 60s, despite the fact that academic competence begins to decline soon after completion of formal schooling.

3. Correlational studies of academic and practical tasks

Investigators have reported little or no relations between performance on academic and practical tasks given to individuals in a variety of domains, including nonskilled jobs in a milk-processing plant (Scribner, 1984, 1986), racetrack handicapping (Ceci & Liker, 1986, 1988), grocery shopping (Lave, Murtaugh, & de la Roche, 1984; Murtaugh, 1985), management (Dorner & Kreuzig, 1983; Dorner, Kreuzig, Reither,

& Staudel, 1983; Wagner, 1987, 1991; Wagner & Sternberg, 1985, 1990), and sales (Wagner, Rashotte, Sternberg, & Okagaki, 1993).

Earlier, in the discussion of the validity of cognitive-ability tests for job selection, I argued that the zero-order correlation between a single test and job performance provides an inflated estimate of the unique predictive power of that test when the test is only one source of information used in selection. The more appropriate statistic is the squared semipartial correlation, which is the same as the increase in R^2 or variance accounted for when a predictor is added last to a multiple regression equation in which all predictors are used to predict job performance. An empirical demonstration of this kind of validation study is provided by a study of business managers who were participants in the Leadership Development Program at the Center for Creative Leadership (Wagner & Sternberg, 1990).

Participants in the Leadership Development Program complete a battery of tests including the Shipley, an IQ test; 17 subtest scores from the California Psychological Inventory, a self-report personality inventory; 6 subtest scores from the Fundamental Interpersonal Relations Orientation–Behavior (FIRO–B), a measure of desired ways of relating to others; the Hidden Figures Test, a measure of field independence; four subtest scores from the Myers–Briggs Type Indicator, a measure of cognitive style, the Kirton Adaptation Innovation Inventory, a measure of preference for innovation; and five subtest scores from the Managerial Job Satisfaction Questionnaire, a measure of job satisfaction. By adding a measure of practical intelligence, the Tacit Knowledge Inventory for Managers (TKIM) (Wagner & Sternberg, 1991), we were able to determine the unique predictive power of practical intelligence in the form of tacit knowledge, in the context of other common measures used in managerial selection. The criterion measure of managerial performance was a work sample, consisting of Behavioral Assessment Data ratings of performance in two small-group managerial simulations called Earth II and Energy International. The work sample required managers to work in groups of 5 to solve realistic business problems. Trained observers rated the performance of the managers in eight categories: activity level, discussion leading, influencing others, problem analysis, task orientation, motivating others, verbal effectiveness, and interpersonal skills. It was necessary to average the ratings and sum them across the two simulations to yield a criterion measure with sufficient reliability. The Spearman–Brown corrected split-half reliability of this total score was .59.

The best predictors of the criterion score of managerial performance were tacit knowledge ($r = -.61, p < .001$) and IQ ($r = .38, p < .001$). (The negative correlation for tacit knowledge is expected because of the deviation scoring system used in which better performance corresponds to less deviation from the expert prototype and thus to lower scores.) There was little correlation between tacit knowledge and IQ ($r = -.14, p > .05$). To determine the unique predictability of tacit knowledge in the context of IQ and the other predictors of work-sample performance, we carried out a series of hierarchical regressions. For each hierarchical regression analysis, the unique predictability of the Tacit Knowledge Inventory for Managers was presented by the change in R^2 from a restricted model that contained various measures as predictors, to a full model that had the same predictors plus tacit knowledge. These results are presented in Table 5.3.

In this table, the measures listed in the column titled "Measures in restricted model" were the predictors that already had been entered in the regression prior to entering the tacit-knowledge score. In the first example, the sole predictor used in the restricted model was IQ. The values reported in the column titled "R^2 change when tacit knowledge is added" are the increases in variance accounted for in the criterion when tacit knowledge was added to the prediction equations. For the first example, tacit knowledge accounted for an additional 32% of criterion variance that was not accounted for by IQ. The values reported in the final column titled "R^2 for full model" indicate the proportion of variance in the criterion that is accounted by tacit knowledge and the other measures when used in conjunction.

The results were straightforward: for every hierarchical regression, adding tacit knowledge increased variance in work-sample performance accounted for significantly and substantially. When tacit knowledge, IQ, and selected subtests from the personality inventories were combined as predictors, nearly all of the reliable variance in work-sample performance was accounted for. These results support the strategy of enhancing validity and utility by supplementing existing selection procedures with additional ones. They also suggest that the construct of tacit knowledge cannot readily be subsumed by the existing constructs of cognitive ability and personality, as least as they were represented by the measures used in the study.

Conclusions

A review of claims made by proponents of cognitive-ability tests for job selection suggests that estimates of the validity of the tests derived from meta-analysis, and of

Table 5.3. Hierarchical regression results from the Center for Creative Leadership Study

Measures in restricted model	R^2 change when tacit knowledge is added	R^2 for full model
1. IQ	.32***	.46***
2. 17 CPI subtests, IQ	.22**	.66*
3. 6 FIRO-B subtests, IQ	.32***	.65***
4. Field Independence, IQ	.28***	.47***
5. Kirton innovation, IQ	.33***	.50***
6. 4 Myers–Briggs subtests, IQ	.35***	.56***
7. 5 Job-Satisfaction subtests, IQ	.32***	.57***

*$p < .05$; **$p < .01$; ***$p < .001$

the estimated savings in personnel costs derived from utility analysis, exaggerate the unique validity and utility of cognitive-ability tests for real selection.

Validity coefficients, whether corrected or not, ignore redundancy in prediction with other sources of information that are used in selection, and thus overestimate the unique predictive role of any single source of information. Unfortunately, despite the existence of literally thousands of validation studies, a *g*-eocentric view apparently has blinded researchers to the need to collect and report the required data to estimate the unique predictive validity of cognitive ability tests for job selection. Validity coefficients also overestimate the magnitude of theoretical relations between cognitive ability and job performance because they do not take into account other plausible causes of job performance that should be included in a completely specified causal model. Finally, corrections to validity coefficient that make sense for answering theoretical questions can lead to inflated answers to practical ones.

Utility estimates suffer from similar problems noted for validity coefficients, which is not surprising when one realizes that utility estimates are based on validity coefficients. Reported estimates of millions and billions of dollars that could be saved by widespread use of cognitive-ability tests for job selection are inflated by (a) assuming a baseline of random selection; (b) assuming an inexhaustible supply of high-scorers; (c) subjectivity in estimating critical parameters, especially the standard deviation of job performance in dollars; and (d) ignoring the economic as well as social costs of adverse impact.

Acknowledging the differences between academic and practical contexts provides a key to improving the validity and utility of selection procedures. Measures of practical intelligence or common sense appear to predict job performance, yet are relatively uncorrelated with existing cognitive ability tests and other common selection tools. Consequently, they contribute incrementally and substantially to prediction of job performance.

Don't count context out.

Notes

1 The unique contribution to prediction of a variable in the presence of other predictors is given by the squared semipartial correlation between the variable and the criterion holding constant the other predictors, which is identical to the increase in R^2 (i.e., R^2 change or ΔR^2) obtained when the variable is added last to the regression equation. The squared semipartial correlation will be less than the squared zero-order correlation, unless the cognitive-ability test is completely uncorrelated with the other selection procedures, or the other selection procedures are completely uncorrelated with the criterion. Neither circumstance is likely to obtain in practice. Other less interesting situations can occur in which the squared semipartial correlation coefficient will not be less than the squared validity coefficient. For example, if the cognitive-ability test is completed unrelated to the criterion, both coefficients will equal 0.

2 See Reilly and Chao (1982) for a summary of the meager literature on alternative selection procedures.

3 When comparing the relative utility of two (or more) selection practices such as cognitive tests versus work samples, the relative difference in estimated utility between the selection practices is not inflated by the random baseline problem, even though the individual absolute-utility estimates are inflated.

References

Barrett, G. V., & Depinet, R. L. (1991). A reconsideration of testing for competence rather than for intelligence. *American Psychologist, 46,* 1012–1024.

Ceci, S. J. (1990). *On intelligence . . . more or less: A bio-ecological treatise on intellectual development.* Englewood Cliffs, NJ: Prentice Hall.

Ceci, S. J., & Liker, J. (1986). Academic and nonacademic intelligence: an experimental separation. In R. J. Sternberg & R. K. Wagner (Eds.), *Practical intelligence: Nature and origins of competence in the everyday world* (pp. 119–142). New York: Cambridge University Press.

Ceci, S. J., & Liker, J. (1988). Stalking the IQ-expertise relationship: When the critics go fishing. *Journal of Experimental Psychology: General, 117,* 96–100.

Cornelius, S. W., & Caspi, A. (1987). Everyday problem solving in adulthood and old age. *Psychology and Aging, 2,* 144–153.

Cronbach, L. J. & Gleser, G. (1957). *Psychological tests and personnel decisions.* Urbana: University of Illinois Press.

Denney, N. W., & Palmer, A. M. (1981). Adult age differences on traditional and practical problem-solving measures. *Journal of Gerontology, 36,* 323–328.

Dorner, D., & Kreuzig, H. (1983). Problemlosefahigkeit und intelligenz. *Psychologische Rundschaus, 34,* 185–192.

Dorner, D., Kreuzig, H., Reither, F., & Staudel, T. (1983). *Lohhausen: Vom Umgang mit Unbestimmtheit und Komplexitat.* Bern: Huber.

Gottfredson, L. S. (1986). Societal consequences of the *g* factor. *Journal of Vocational Behavior, 29,* 379–410.

Hawk, J. (1986). Real world implications of g. *Journal of Vocational Behavior, 29,* 411–414.

Hunter, J. E. (1983). A causal analysis of cognitive ability, job knowledge, job performance, and supervisory ratings. In F. Landy, S. Zedeck, & J. Cleveland (Eds.), *Performance measurement and theory* (pp. 257–266). Hillsdale, NJ: Erlbaum.

Hunter, J. E., & Hunter, R. F. (1984). Validity and utility of alterntive predictors of job performance. *Psychological Bulletin, 96,* 72–98.

Hunter, J. E., & Schmidt, F. L. (1982). The economic benefits of personnel selection using psychological ability tests. *Industrial Relations, 21,* 293–308.

Hunter, J. E., & Schmidt, F. L. (1983). Quantifying the effects of psychological interventions on employee job performance and work-force productivity. *American Psychologist, 38,* 473–478.

Lave, J., Murtaugh, M., & de la Roche, O. (1984). The dialectic of arithmetic in grocery shopping. In B. Rogoff & J. Lave (Eds.), *Everyday cognition: Its development in social context* (pp. 67–94). Cambridge, MA: Harvard University Press.

McClelland, D. C. (1973). Testing for competence rather than for "intelligence." *American Psychologist, 28,* 1–14.

Murtaugh, M. (1985). The practice of arithmetic by American grocery shoppers. *Anthropology and Education Quarterly,* Fall.

Neisser, U. (1976). General, academic, and artificial intelligence. In L. Resnick (Ed.), *Human intelligence: Perspectives on its theory and measurement* (pp. 179–189). Norwood, NJ: Ablex.

Oxford English Dictionary (1933). Oxford: Clarendon Press.

Polanyi, M. (1976). Tacit knowing. In M. Marx & F. Goodson (Eds.), *Theories in contemporary psychology* (pp. 330–344). New York: Macmillan.

Ree, M. J., & Earles, J. A. (1992). Intelligence is the best predictor of job performance. *Current Directions, 1,* 86–89.

Reilly, R. R., & Chao, G. T. (1982). Validity and fairness of some alternative employee selection procedures. *Personnel Psychology, 35,* 1–62.

Rogoff, B., & Lave, J. (Eds.) (1984). *Everyday cognition: Its developmental and social context.* Cambridge, MA: Cambridge University Press.

Schmidt, F. L., & Hunter, J. E. (1981). Employment testing: Old theories and new research findings. *American Psychologist, 36,* 1128–1137.

Schmidt, F. L., Hunter, J. E., McKenzie, R. C., & Muldrow, T. (1979). The impact of valid selection procedures on work force productivity. *Journal of Applied Psychology, 64,* 609–626.

Schmidt, F. L., Hunter, J. E., & Outerbridge, A. N. (1986). Impact of job experience and ability on job knowledge, work sample performance, and supervisory ratings of job performance. *Journal of Applied Psychology, 71,* 432–439.

Schmidt, F. L., & Hunter, J. E. (1992). Development of a causal model of processes determining job performance. *Current Directions in Psychological Science, 1,* 89–92.

Scribner, S. (1984). Studying working intelligence. In B. Rogoff & J. Lave (Eds.), *Everyday cognition: Its development in social context* (pp. 9–40). Cambridge, MA: Harvard University Press.

Scribner, S. (1986). Thinking in action: Some characteristics of practical thought. In Sternberg, R. J., & Wagner, R. K. (Eds.), *Practical Intelligence: Nature and origins of competence in the everyday world* (pp. 13–30). New York: Cambridge University Press.

Scribner, S., & Cole, M. (1981). *The psychology of literacy.* Cambridge, MA: Harvard University Press.

Seymour, R. T. (1988). Why plaintiffs' counsel challenge tests, and how they can successfully challenge the theory of "validity generalization." *Journal of Vocational Behavior, 33,* 331–364.

Sternberg, R. J. (1985). *Beyond IQ: A triarchic theory of human intelligence.* New York: Cambridge University Press.

Sternberg, R. J., Conway, B. E., Ketron, J. L., & Bernstein, M. (1981). People's conceptions of intelligence. *Journal of Personality and Social Psychology, 41,* 37–55.

Sternberg, R. J., & Detterman, D. K. (Eds.) (1986). *What is intelligence?* Norwood, NJ: Ablex.

Sternberg, R. J., & Frensch, P. (Eds.) (1991). *Complex problem solving: principles and mechanisms.* Hillsdale, NJ: Erlbaum.

Sternberg, R. J., & Wagner, R. K. (Eds.) (1986). *Practical Intelligence: Nature and origins of competence in the everyday world.* New York: Cambridge University Press.

Sternberg, R. J., & Wagner, R. K. (Eds.) (1993). *The mind in context.* New York: Cambridge University Press.

Sternberg, R. J., & Wagner, R. K. (1993). *The g-ocentric view of intelligence and job performance is wrong. Current Directions in Psychological Science, 2,* 1–5.

Sternberg, R. J., Wagner, R. K., & Okagaki, L. (1991). Practical intelligence: The nature and role of tacit knowledge in work and at school. In H. Reese & J. Puckett (Eds.), *Advances in lifespan development.* Hillsdale, NJ: Erlbaum.

Thorndike, R. L. (1971). Concepts of culture-fairness. *Journal of Educational Measurement, 8,* 63–70.

Voss, J. F., Perkins, D. N., & Segal, J. W. (Eds.) (1991). *Informal reasoning and education.* Hillsdale, NJ: Erlbaum.

Wagner, R. K. (1987). Tacit knowledge in everyday intelligent behavior. *Journal of Personality and Social Psychology, 52,* 1236–1247.

Wagner, R. K. (1991). Managerial problem-solving. In R. J. Sternberg & P. Frensch (Eds.), *Complex problem solving: principles and mechanisms* (pp. 159–183). Hillsdale, NJ: Erlbaum.

Wagner, R. K., Rashotte, C. A., Sternberg, R. J., & Okagaki, L. (1993). *Tacit knowledge in sales.* Manuscript in preparation.

Wagner, R. K., & Sternberg, R. J. (1985). Practical intelligence in real-world pursuits: the role of tacit knowledge. *Journal of Personality and Social Psychology, 48,* 436–458.

Wagner, R. K., & Sternberg, R. J. (1990). Street smarts. In K. Clark & M. Clark (Eds.), *Measures of leadership* (pp. 493–504). Greensboro, NC: Center for Creative Leadership.

Wagner, R. K., & Sternberg, R. J. (1991). *The Tacit Knowledge Inventory for Managers (TKIM).* San Antonio, TX: The Psychological Corporation.

Wigdor, A. K., & Garner, W. R. (1982). Ability testing: Uses, consequences and controversies: Pt. 1. Report of the committee. Washington, DC: National Academy Press.

Williams, S. A., Denney, N. W., & Schadler, M. (1983). Elderly adults' perception of their own cognitive development during the adult years. *International Journal of Aging and Human Development, 16,* 147–158.

6　Leader intelligence, interpersonal stress, and task performance

Fred E. Fiedler and Thomas G. Link

Cognitive-ability tests have been notoriously poor predictors of leadership performance. Considering that leadership requires such intellectual functions as planning, decision making, coordination and evaluation of work performance, the poor relationship between leader intelligence and performance is highly counterintuitive. Several reviews of the literature have extensively summarized relations between a wide variety of intellectual abilities ("intelligence") and leadership and managerial performance. These reviews have been very consistent in reporting median correlations of between .20 to .30, thus accounting for less than 10% of the variance (see, for example, Bass, 1990; Ghiselli, 1963b; Mann, 1959; Stogdill, 1948). Given the strong editorial bias against publishing nonsignificant results, even these low correlations are likely to be overestimates of the true relationship. In our research on various military samples, for instance, the median correlations between various leader intelligence scores and performance scores was .10 (see Table 6.1).

These low correlations present an interesting dilemma for leadership theory. On the one hand, they suggest that good leaders need not have strong intellectual abilities. On the other hand, these findings fly directly in the face of institutional wisdom and long-standing organizational practice to look for bright, rather than dull, managers. Moreover, as already noted, such leadership functions of searching for and analyzing information, developing plans and actions strategies, and making decisions clearly are intellectual in nature. And even more puzzling, as we shall see, are the consistent findings that leader intelligence, under certain conditions, correlates negatively with performance. Cognitive Resource Theory (CRT) (Fiedler & Garcia, 1987) attempts to reconcile and explain these conflicting findings.

The role of stress as moderator

The major task of CRT is to elucidate the role of such cognitive resources as intellectual abilities, technical competence, and experience, and the conditions under which they contribute to group and organizational performance. As this chapter demonstrates, the degree to which intellectual abilities can contribute to task performance depends largely on the nature of the leadership environment. We shall follow

Table 6.1. Correlations between leaders' intelligence and performance

Sample (military leaders)	Correlation	N
Squad leaders[a]	−.04	158
Coast Guard officers[b]	−.02	130
Platoon sergeants[c]	−.05	120
Platoon leaders[c]	.23*	95
Battalion staff officers[c]	.42*	27
Company commanders[c]	.26	39
First sergeants[c]	.16	41
Battalion staff officers[d]	−.15	36
Company commanders[d]	−.07	43
Battalion staff officers[b]	−.25	47
Company commanders[b]	.35*	45
Executive officers[b]	.35	28
ROTC[e]	.10	34
Fire lieutenants[f]	−.11	31
Fire captains[f]	.42	18
Median	.10	

*p < .05.
[a]Bons (1979)
[b]Fiedler, Potter, Zais & Knowlton (1979)
[c]Borden (1980)
[d]Bettin (1982)
[e]McGuire (1987)
[f]Frost (1983)

Berry's (1986) definition of intelligence as "the end-product of individual development in the cognitive–psychological domain, but not motor, emotional and social functioning" (p. 32).

The underlying rationale of our research, first proposed by Blades (1976), is that the leader's intellectual abilities can contribute to performance only if there is an unbroken chain that links the leader's abilities to the behavior of group members who perform the task (Blades & Fiedler, 1976). We begin with the assumption that more intelligent leaders are better able to plan, make decisions, and develop action strategies than those with lower intelligence. These plans, decisions, and action strategies in turn can affect the performance of the task only if (a) the leader is able to focus his or her intellectual abilities on the task; (b) these plans, decisions, and strategies are communicated to group members, and (c) the group members are motivated and equipped to carry them out. We shall focus on the first of these steps, namely the leader's ability to formulate action plans and make decisions. We must then ask what major obstacles might block the leader's ability to apply his or her intellect to the process of planning and decision making. Personality theory points to stress and anxiety as the primary candidates.

Job stress and stress with the boss

Stress is an ubiquitous phenomenon in organizational life and plays an important part in the way in which organizations behave and function. This point has been well documented in the organizational literature (e.g., Beehr, 1985; Buck, 1972; McGrath, 1976). It is important to distinguish between two types of organizational stress, namely job stress and interpersonal stress. Most of the literature up to now has focused on the former – stress caused by difficult and complex tasks and noxious environmental conditions such as noise, time pressure, physical danger, role ambiguity, and conflict.

A high level of job stress has been associated with low job satisfaction, poor performance, absenteeism, attrition, and psychosomatic illness (Chemers, Hayes, Rhodewalt & Wysocki, 1985). It also results in generally lowered levels of performance (Barnes, Potter & Fiedler, 1983). However, mild job stress of the type more typically found in organizations focuses the individual's attention on the task and may, therefore, increase the performance of more intelligent individuals.

In contrast, the effects of interpersonal stress have been largely ignored in organizational literature, although they are equally pervasive in organizations. This type of stress is generated by personality clashes and conflict with key subordinates and superiors ("boss stress"). The latter is particularly important since the boss' evaluation so strongly affects feelings of self-esteem and self-efficacy. One less-than-outstanding evaluation by an immediate superior in the military services can ruin an entire career. Concern about one's evaluation by the boss, therefore, tends to create a great deal of anxiety (Borden, 1980) and evaluation apprehension (Sarason, 1984).

Interestingly enough, correlations between reported boss stress and the boss' performance ratings are generally small and not significant. In fact, most bosses are quite unaware of the effect they have on their subordinates, and many find it hard to believe that they are not seen as warm, patient, and ever ready to listen to their employees' criticisms.

The effects of boss stress, and the evaluation apprehension that usually accompanies it, are quite substantial. One effect is that evaluation apprehension distracts the individual's attention from the task. Instead of concentrating on the job, individuals tend to ruminate on their own shortcomings, the possibility of failure and its consequences, etc. (Sarason 1984; Spielberger & Katzenmeyer, 1959). Since the employees' intellectual abilities are not focused on the task, they cannot contribute effectively to such intellectually demanding aspects of the job as planning and decision making. Not surprisingly, then, we should find that the leader's intellectual abilities correlate more highly when boss stress is low than when boss stress is high. As our research has shown, and stated here in somewhat oversimplified terms, leaders are able to apply their intellectual abilities to the task only when stress is low. Several of our studies illustrate this very consistent and intriguing finding.

Army leaders

A series of studies was conducted on Army squad leaders (Bons & Fiedler, 1976), and Army company commanders and battalion staff officers (Fiedler, Potter, Zais & Knowlton, 1979). The squad-leader study measured intelligence with the Army's General Classification Test, the predecessor of the Armed Forces Qualification Test (AFQT). In other studies the measure of intelligence was the Wonderlic Personnel Test (1977).

Job stress was measured on a graphic scale in the case of the squad-leader study, which asked to what extent the job, or the relationship with the boss (the immediate superior) was very tense and stressful, or relaxed and not stressful at all. Other studies used several items measuring job stress and boss stress. Performance was evaluated by two superiors in the squad-leader study and the battalion commander and executive officer in the study of company commanders and staff officers. Performance was measured on a 16-item scale developed specifically for research with military personnel (Bons & Fiedler, 1976). This scale, also used in other military studies which are reported here, asks superiors to rate subjects on job duties, such as organizing the group, carrying out administrative duties, and handling periods of heavy demand. Split-half reliability on this scale was .92 in the squad-leader study, and similar levels of agreement have been found in other studies.

Each of these three samples was divided as closely as possible at the median of the stress scales, and correlations were then computed between leader intelligence and performance. Note that leader performance and stress were not highly correlated in all of these studies. Table 6.2 shows the results. As can be seen, in each of the samples, the correlation between leader intelligence and performance is higher in the low-stress than the high-stress condition. Also note that the difference in correlations is higher when the samples are divided on boss stress than on job stress.

Infantry division leaders

A validation study was conducted by Borden (1980) on 160 officers and 167 non-commissioned officers (NCOs) in various leadership positions in a combat infantry

Table 6.2. Correlations between intelligence and performance under conditions of low and high stress with boss

	Boss stress	
	Low	High
Squad leaders[a]	.51[b]	.09
Company commanders	.56	−.86[b]
Battalion staff officers	.17	−.13

[a]Stress above or below 1 SD. [b]$p < .05$

division. Performance evaluations were obtained from 2 to 5 superiors, again using the Bons (Bons & Fiedler, 1976) scale. Stress was measured on 11-point scales which asked to what extent the job and the relationship with the boss were "very stressful" or "not stressful at all." The Wonderlic Personnel Test measured intelligence. The subjects in each job category were divided into thirds on the job-stress and boss-stress scales. Figure 6.1 shows the average of the standardized means of performance by leaders with higher and lower intelligence scores. As can be seen, the predictive power of intelligence was considerably greater for leaders who reported low stress than for those who reported moderate or high stress. In fact, among those in each job category who reported high stress, the less-intelligent leaders performed substantially better than the more-intelligent leaders. Again, the moderator effect of boss stress was considerably greater than the effect of job stress.

The Fiedler et al. (1979) and the Borden (1980) studies raised several important questions.

1. To what extent can we generalize from the findings of the two sets of studies which have been described here?
2. Does boss stress affect all aspects of the leader's functions to roughly the same extent, or are certain intellectual functions more strongly affected than others?
3. Are certain components of intelligence more vulnerable to boss stress?
4. What is the reason for the negative correlations between leader intelligence and performance under stress?

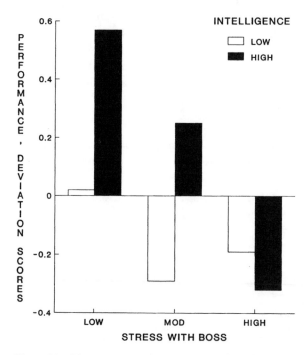

Figure 6.1.   IQ, stress and performance (Borden, 1980)

1. Generalizability of the findings. The first question concerns the degree to which stress and the interaction between stress and intelligence contribute to performance. Table 6.3 shows the results of 18 multiple regressions from 13 different samples of leaders for whom intelligence scores, stress ratings, and performance ratings by superiors were available. Most of the samples are from military populations (i.e., company commanders, executive officers, platoon leaders, first sergeants, platoon and squad leaders, and officer candidates), and fire-department officers. In all but the sample of the squad leaders, the measure of intelligence was the Wonderlic Personnel Test (1977). In the squad-leader sample, we relied on the Armed Forces Qualification Test. Level of stress was based on subjects' ratings, and performance was rated by

Table 6.3. Variance in performance explained by intelligence, stress, and intelligence:stress interaction

Study	Intelligence[a]	Stress[b]	Intelligence: Stress interaction	Total	N
Infantry division					
Executive officer	.18**	.00	.14**	.32**	26
Platoon leader	.06**[c]	.03*	.13***	.22***	98
First sergeant	.03	.13**	.06*	.22**	41
Platoon sergeant	.00	.06***	.03*	.09**	117
Company commander	.11**	.11**	.00	.22**	36
Fire department					
Captains					
Fire perf[d]	.00	.04	.01	.06	18
Administrative perf[d]	.05	.05	.15	.26	18
Lieutenants					
Fire	.05	.02	.10*	.17	28
Administrative	.01	.07	.21**	.29**	28
Other					
ROTC students	.01	.02	.29***	.32***	34
Staff officers	.06*	.05	.08**	.19**	47
Line officers	.12**	.03	.03	.18**	45
Squad leaders (Pretraining)	.06***	.00	.01	.07	127
Squad leaders (Posttraining)	.06***	.01	.05***	.12***	125
National guard officer					
Candidates (rated perf)	.03	.12*	.04	.20**	43
Bettin					
Company commanders	.00	.03	.01	.05	43
Battalion staff off	.02	.01	.01	.04	36

Note: Intelligence is entered into the equation first, stress second, and the interaction third.
[a]Intelligence is either general intelligence or fluid intelligence.
[b]Stress is stress with boss, two or three categories.
[c]Numbers in table are increase in r^2 in performance due to that variable.
[d]Performance is total in-basket score.
*$p < .10$; **$p < .05$; ***$p < .01$.

superiors using the Bons scale for military personnel and a sc ιwhat modified scale for fire-department officers.

In the regression analyses shown in Table 6.3, intelligence was entered first to show the predictive ability of intelligence alone. Following Pedhazur (1982) and Cohen and Cohen (1975), stress was entered next, followed by the stress:intelligence interaction, which is the product of stress and intelligence scores.

As can be seen, the predictions of performance were significant in 11 of the 16 samples of leaders. A substantial amount of variance was contributed to the interaction in five of the samples. Here again, the intelligence:stress interaction accounts for a major portion of the variance in performance. It is therefore clear that stress plays a major role in predicting performance.

2. *Leader functions most vulnerable to stress.* The second question is whether interpersonal stress affects all or only certain leadership functions. This question could be addressed in a study of Coast Guard personnel assigned to a large headquarters organization.

The subjects of this study were 130 officers and petty officers assigned to a U.S. Coast Guard headquarters (Potter & Fiedler, 1981). Most of these men headed staff sections or departments. All subjects took the Wonderlic (1977) Personnel Test, and filled out various questionnaires, including one indicating perceived job and boss stress. Performance was rated by superior officers on a slightly modified Bons scale.

The sample was divided into those above and below the median of the boss-stress scale. We then correlated intelligence and performance for subgroups which reported low and high stress. As in previous studies, intelligence and performance correlated in the predicted direction when boss stress was low, i.e., .16 ($n = 60$, n.s.). In the high-stress group, intelligence and performance correlated $-.27$ ($n = 61$, $p < .05$; difference between r's significant at .05).

In addition to testing again whether intelligence scores correlate more highly in nonstressful than stressful situations, this study indicated which specific aspects of the leadership process were most vulnerable to stress. Officers and petty officers estimated the amount of time and effort which they devoted to each of 10 staff functions. Those whose level of effort in a particular job function was relatively high were then divided into those with low or high scores on the stress scales, and their intelligence was correlated with performance (see Table 6.4).

As Table 6.4 shows, the use of intelligence was most strongly affected by stress in jobs involving such intellectually more demanding functions as "advising on policies" and "making decisions." Stress has considerably less effect on jobs involving routine paper work or supervising personnel. The next question was which factors or components of intellectual ability were most vulnerable to boss stress, and which aspects of performance would be most strongly affected.

3. *Components of intelligence most affected by stress: the in-basket study.* In a study by McGuire (1987; cited in Fiedler, McGuire & Richardson, 1989), 34 army cadets

Table 6.4. Correlations between intelligence and performance in decision and supervisory functions of Coast Guard personnel under low and high stress

	Intelligence and performance			
	Boss stress		Job stress	
	Low	High	Low	High
Decision making				
Making decisions	.11 (21)	−.47 (13)†	.15 (25)	−.53* (14)
Policy advising	.27 (30)	−.46* (22)†	.06 (29)	−.24 (23)
Communicating and executing orders				
Supervising subs.	.07 (29)	.04 (18)	.15 (23)	−.01 (24)
Training	.11 (26)	−.17 (21)	.03 (16)	−.12 (24)
Administration				
Paperwork	−.01 (25)	−.25 (21)	−.03 (25)	−.16 (21)

$*p < .05$
†Difference between correlations is significant.

were given a short version of the Horn tests of crystallized and fluid intelligence. Crystallized intelligence measures the ability to acquire knowledge from school, the environment, etc. Fluid intelligence is the ability to apply previously acquired knowledge to new problems (Horn, 1986). This study also permitted us to replicate the finding that decision-making functions were most vulnerable to stress.

Cadets were randomly assigned either to a low- or a high-stress condition. In the low-stress condition the cadets came in civilian clothes, and the task was monitored by an undergraduate who looked uninterested. Cadets in the high-stress group came in full uniform and were monitored by two uniformed officers. They were also told that they might have to explain or justify their responses to the commander of their ROTC unit.

We had hoped that the experimental manipulation of stress would clearly differentiate those who did and did not feel stress. And the experimental manipulation did, indeed, differentiate the stress ratings in the high- and low-stress groups at a statistically significant level. However, as in other studies, the results indicating effect of experimentally induced stress on correlations between intelligence and performance were considerably weaker than when the cadets were divided on the basis of perceived stress. It was clear from this and other studies that some cadets appeared not to react to the stress manipulation in the expected manner, or did not acknowledge it. For this reason the sample was divided at the median into those who reported relatively low and relatively high stress in a post-task questionnaire. The reported analyses are based on this measure.

The cadets were given the Army's 21 item in-basket exercise (Rogers, Lilley,

Wellins, Fischl & Burke, 1982). The responses to this in-basket are classified into various behaviors, for example, decisiveness, sensitivity, etc. They were then scored by two trained raters on the basis of their appropriateness. Table 6.5 shows the behavior categories tapped by the Army In-Basket Exercise as well as the correlations between each of the categories and fluid intelligence. The correlations with crystallized intelligence were low and nonsignificant. However, stress had a marked effect on the contribution of fluid intelligence on behaviors related to decision-making functions. The effect of stress on cadets with high and low fluid intelligence under low and high reported stress is best illustrated by Figure 6.2.

The most striking finding is the decrement of performance of leaders with relatively high fluid intelligence who reported high evaluation stress. Interpersonal stress most strongly affected the relationship between fluid intelligence and performance. As in the Coast Guard study, decision making and other intellectually demanding tasks were most affected by stress. Stress seemed to have considerably less effect on correlations between crystallized intelligence and performance. Again we are faced with the question of why the more intelligent leaders performed so poorly when they experienced interpersonal stress.

4. *Underlying causes for negative correlations between intelligence and performance.* It is relatively easy to explain the finding that leader intelligence does not

Table 6.5. Army Inbasket dimensions and their correlation with fluid intelligence across levels of perceived stress

	Perceived stress condition	
	Low	High
Decision making		
Problem analysis	.54***	−.13[a]
Judgment	.12	−.56**[a]
Decisiveness	.43**	−.58**[b]
Administrative behaviors		
Planning & organizing	.48**	−.33[a]
Delegation	.40**	−.33[a]
Administrative control	−.20	−.37
Motivational behavior		
Initiative	.35	−.07
Interpersonal behavior		
Sensitivity	.22	−.28
Communication skills		
Written communication	.22	.24

Note. Sample size: low stress = 19, high stress = 15.
[a]Correlations between low and high stress significantly different, $p < .05$.
[b]Correlations between low and high stress significantly different, $p < .01$.
*$p < .05$; **$p < .01$.

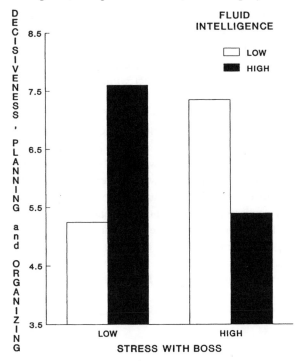

Figure 6.2. Mean performance on decision making by ROTC cadets with relatively high or low fluid intelligence and high or low boss stress (McGuire, 1987).

correlate with performance under certain conditions. These include (a) the presence of interpersonal stress which distracts the leader from attending to the task, (b) nondirective leader behavior that impedes or prevents the leader's plans and decisions from reaching group members, and (c) subordinates who are not capable of or motivated to perform the task.

It is considerably more difficult to account for the counterintuitive findings that intellectual abilities correlate negatively with performance under conditions of boss stress. We tentatively offer two partially overlapping hypotheses that may help us to understand the reasons for these negative correlations. The first hypothesis compares the use of intelligence and experience across levels of stress. The second hypothesis focuses on leader behavior under stress.

One important clue comes from the consistent findings that the correlations of performance with leader intelligence and with leader experience are virtually mirror images of each other. At this point, a brief digression about the role and function of leadership experience is necessary.

Webster's Dictionary defines work-related experience as " ... anything observed or lived through, as well as time spent in a job or an organization, or the period of such activity as teaching experience" (p. 645). The time an individual has spent in a job or an organization is, in fact, the most commonly used operationalization of experience. (For a discussion of problems as well as advantages of these measures, see Fiedler, 1992). The implication in all definitions is that experience provides the opportunity to learn and practice behaviors that are effective in coping with job-related problems. This will allow the leader to react without much deliberation to familiar recurrent problems.

Our studies have shown that leader experience and performance correlate in the direction opposite from the correlations between intelligence and performance (Fiedler & Garcia, 1987). When the one is positive, the other is negative. This is well illustrated when we plot the mean correlation between intelligence and performance on the same graph as the mean correlations between experience and performance (Figure 6.3). Similar results are obtained in other studies (see Fiedler & Garcia, 1987). These findings suggest that intellectual abilities and experience are incompatible and interfere with each other. Thus, leader experience contributes to performance only when the individual is highly uncertain of what to do, or must act quickly under emergency-like conditions.

Experimental psychology, personality theory (Barker, Dembo & Lewin, 1941), and social facilitation theory (Zajonc, 1965) tell us that conditions of stress evoke

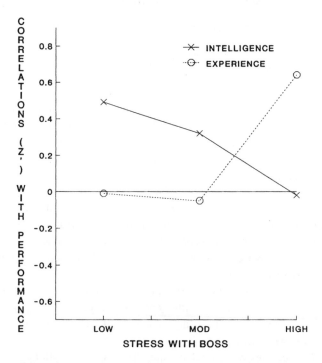

Figure 6.3. Average correlations (z-transforms) between intelligence scores, experience (time in service) and performance ratings of army leaders at various levels who reported low, moderate, or high stress with their boss.

overlearned or dominant behavior. Moreover, the behavior that emerges under stress is typically automatic. The reaction is quick and not performed with deliberation. In contrast, intellectual effort implies thoughtful deliberation and careful weighing of alternatives. It is obvious that we cannot behave in an automatic and unthinking manner in response to a stressful situation while simultaneously deliberating and weighing alternative plans and action strategies.

At the same time, we need to consider that highly intelligent people are more likely to rely on intellectual effort in solving problems than are those who have relatively low intelligence (Fiedler, 1992). Conversely, highly experienced people tend to rely on their experience; that is, they capitalize on the tools they have. Hence, the higher the leader's intelligence, the more the likelihood that he or she will lean towards deliberating and weighing alternatives, or working toward a creative solution. We also know, however, that certain tasks should be performed by rote, following a previously learned drill or routine. Firefighters, while rushing to a burning building, should not try to develop new methods of combating a fire.

Two consequences are likely in a stressful situation, and especially one in which there is interpersonal stress: (a) the highly intelligent leader will attempt to tackle the problem by intellectual power, and (b) interpersonal stress diverts the leader's focus from the task; therefore, the leader's intellectual effort is not likely to solve the problem.

Since the stressful situation requires quick and preferably automatic responses, careful deliberation and weighing of alternatives will impede rather than assist with solution of the problem. The higher the leader's intelligence, the more likely he or she will be to find intellectual solutions which will interfere with overlearned responses. Thus, intelligence will correlate negatively with performance.

Support for this argument comes from a study of 58 junior Army officers and senior noncommissioned officers who were given the task of ranking five military training schedules on the basis of 35 information items under various conditions of stress (Locklear, 1989). The information items, typed on 3 × 5" cards, were mounted on hooks on an "information board" (Payne, 1976) which permits the investigator to observe how much information different subjects seek to obtain, and what, if any, method, they use in searching for the information. Subjects were given 10 minutes to inspect and reinspect as many items as they wished, and they were then required to rank the five training schedules.

Performance was defined as agreement with the ranking of the schedules by a panel of military training experts. The rankings of present concern were made under two conditions of stress: low stress, and time stress (subjects were told that they had to perform the task in half the time ordinarily required, although they were actually given the same amount of time as they had in the other condition).

The use of the information board allowed us to count the number of cards each person inspected and reinspected, and this activity can be defined as indicative of intellectual effort. By comparison, a person who only casually glances at a few information items and makes the ranking on the basis of intuition can be assumed to have put forth very little intellectual effort. Although this had not been intended, the task turned out to be very difficult. Only 2 of 58 leaders obtained a perfect score in the "job-stress" condition, and only 3 did so under low stress. This was, therefore, not a highly suitable task for intellectual problem solving.

The data confirmed that the more-intelligent leaders made more intellectual effort than did those of less intelligence (correlation between intellectual effort and intelligence was .46 – all n's = 58, $p < .01$). As mentioned earlier, the task was not readily amenable to intellectual solutions. This is shown by the correlation of −.38 ($p = < .05$) between intelligence and performance. On the other hand, experience (time in military service) correlated positively with performance (.29, $p < .05$). Thus, the greater the leader's experience, the lower the intellectual effort, and the better the performance (Table 6.6).

These findings strongly suggest that experience interfered with intellectual effort. The latter conclusion fits our everyday observations. Trying to concentrate on our feet makes it difficult to dance. Trying to think of how we hold our tennis racket makes it difficult to play well. Thus, the brighter the individual is, the more his or her intelligence and intellectual effort will interfere with jobs that require experience-based behavior.

Looking at leader behavior directly, evidence from Gibson, Fiedler, and Barrett (1993) indicates that highly intelligent leaders talk more under stress but contribute less. This study looked at 54 3-person groups who were performing creative tasks. Typed transcripts of the group-member interactions were content analyzed to determine the amount of talking by leaders and by group members, and the number of substantive ideas contributed by leaders and group members. A "babble" index was then defined as the ratio of talking to substantive ideas.

While the less intelligent leaders babbled more in the nonstressful conditions, the more intelligent leaders babbled more in the stressful conditions. Not only did they talk more while producing fewer substantive ideas, but they also caused their group

Table 6.6. Correlations between intelligence measures and time in service with total searches and performance

	Inspections		Performance	
	Base rate	1/2 Time	Base rate	1/2 Time
Fluid intelligence	.31*	.33**	−.20	−.30*
Crystallized intelligence	.41***	.41***	−.15	−.38**
Time in service	−.42***	−.41**	−.14	.29*
Inspections significance[a]	−.25	.32*		

Note. Sample size = 58.
[a]Inspection and performance data from the same condition.
*$p < .05$; ** $p < .01$; ***$p < .001$.

members to babble more than the groups led by less intelligent leaders. In addition, amount of babble was negatively related to effective performance.

Discussion

This chapter has presented a series of studies that show that a relatively stress-free leadership environment enables leaders to make substantially more effective use of their intellectual abilities. Interpersonal stress sharply attenuates the relationship between leader intelligence and performance. In fact, under conditions of boss stress, leader intelligence can interfere with effective performance as indicated by the fairly consistent negative correlations.

The basic findings described here show that leader intelligence correlates highly with performance only when there is low interpersonal stress; it correlates negatively under certain limited conditions, that is, high boss stress. These are potentially important conclusions when we consider that leaders are often selected and assigned because of their intellectual abilities. Moreover, those who appear most able are typically asked for advice and assistance in making major decisions. If these individuals are considerably less effective under certain conditions than those who are less intelligent, it is clear that the organization will experience major difficulties. By identifying the conditions and mechanisms under which these more-able leaders are effective, we can design more powerful selection and assignment policies and methods.

Traditionally, our selection and classification methods have sought to identify the most intellectually able individuals on the assumption that there is a linear relationship between intellectual ability and performance. Meta-analyses reported by Hunter, Schmidt, and Jackson (1982) suggest that predictions of leadership performance from intelligence tests are higher if certain assumptions and corrections are made. However, the fact remains that the zero-order correlations between leader intelligence and performance remain too small to be of practical use.

Our research shows that the identification by means of currently available ability tests must be seen as only the first step in the prediction and selection process. Having identified those who have the capacity to perform a given set of tasks, we must now also find methods for assuring that these talented individuals are placed into leadership situations in which they can make effective use of their abilities, or that they and their superiors are taught to "engineer" their leadership situations so as to capitalize on the cognitive resources for which they were originally hired.

Acknowledgments

The research reported in this paper was supported by Army Research Institute Contract #MDA903-89-K-0193 (Fred E. Fiedler, Principal Investigator). The authors wish to thank Judith Fiedler and Dennis Hrebec for their help in the preparation of this manuscript.

References

Barker, R., Dembo, T., & Lewin, K. (1941). Frustration and regression: an experiment with young children. Vol. XVIII, No. 1. *University of Iowa studies: Studies in child welfare.* Iowa City, IA: University of Iowa Press.

Barnes, V. E., Potter, E. H., III, & Fiedler, F. E. (1983). The effect of interpersonal stress on the prediction of academic performance. *Journal of Applied Psychology, 68*(4), 686–697.

Bass, B. M. (1990). *Bass & Stogdill's handbook of leadership: Theory, research and managerial application* (3rd ed.). New York: The Free Press.

Beehr, T. A. (1985). Organizational stress and employee effectiveness: A job characteristics approach. In T. A. Beehr & R. S. Bhagat (Eds.), *Human stress and cognition in organizations* (pp. 57–81). New York: Wiley Interscience.

Berry, J. W. (1986). A cross-cultural view of intelligence. In R. J. Sternberg & D. K. Detterman (Eds.), *What is intelligence?* Norwood, NJ: Ablex.

Bettin, P. J. (1982). Leadership Experience: The contribution of relevance & diversity to leadership performance. Unpublished master's thesis, University of Washington, Seattle.

Blades, J. W. (1976). *The influence of intelligence, task ability and motivation on group performance.* Unpublished doctoral dissertation, University of Washington, Seattle.

Blades, J. W., & Fiedler, F. E. (1976). *The influence of intelligence, task ability, and motivation on group performance* (Tech. Rep. No. 76–78). Seattle: University of Washington, Organizational Research.

Bons, P. M., & Fiedler, F. E. (1976). Changes in organizational leadership and the behavior of relationship- and task-motivated leaders. *Administrative Science Quarterly, 21*, 453–473.

Borden, D. E. (1980). *Leader-boss stress, personality, job satisfaction and performance: Another look at the inter-relationship of some old constructs in the modern large bureaucracy.* Unpublished doctoral dissertation, University of Washington, Seattle.

Buck, V. E. (1972). *Working under pressure.* New York: Crane.

Chemers, M. M., Hayes, R. B., Rhodewalt, F., & Wysocki, J. (1985). A person environment of job stress: a contingency model explanation. *Journal of Personality & Social Psychology, 3*, 628–635.

Cohen, J., & Cohen, P. (1975). *Applied multiple regression/correlation analysis for the behavioral sciences.* Hillsdale, NJ: Erlbaum.

Fiedler, F. E. (1992). The role and meaning of leadership experience. In K. E. Clark, M. B. Clark, & D. P. Campbell (Eds.) *Impact of leadership.* Greensboro, NC: Center for Creative Leadership.

Fiedler, F. E. (1992). Time-based measures of leadership experience and organizational performance: A review of research and a preliminary model. *Leadership Quarterly, 3*(1) (pp. 5–23).

Fiedler, F. E., & Garcia, J. E. (1987). *New approaches to effectiveness leadership: Cognitive resources and organizational performance.* New York: Wiley.

Fiedler, F. E., McGuire, M. A., & Richardson, M. (1989). The role of intelligence and experience in successful group performance. *Journal of Applied Sport Psychology, 1*(2), 132–149.

Fiedler, F. E., Potter, E. H., III, Zais, M. M., & Knowlton, W., Jr. (1979). Organizational stress and the use and misuse of managerial intelligence and experience. *Journal of Applied Psychology, 64*(6), 635–647.

Frost, D. E. (1983). Role perceptions and behavior of the immediate supervisor: Moderating effects on the prediction of leadership effectiveness. *Organizational Behavior and Human Performance, 31*, 123–142.

Ghiselli, E. E. (1963b). Intelligence and managerial success. *Psychological Reports, 12*, 898.

Gibson, F. W., Fiedler, F. E., & Barrett, K. (1993). *Stress, babble, and utilization of leader intellectual abilities (Leadership Quarterly,* in press).

Horn, J. (1986). Intellectual ability concepts. In R. J. Sternberg (Ed.), *Advances in human intelligence* (Vol. 3). Hillsdale, NJ: Erlbaum.

Hunter, J. E., Schmidt, F. L., & Jackson, G. B. (1982). *Meta-analysis formulating research findings across studies.* Beverly Hills, CA: Sage.

Locklear, J. C. (1989). *The effects of individual intelligence and organizational experience on pre-decisional information acquisition.* Unpublished master's thesis, University of Washington, Seattle.

Mann, R. D. (1959). A review of the relationships between performance in small groups. *Psychological Bulletin, 56*, 241–270.

McGrath, J. E. (1976). Stress and behavior in organizations. In M. D. Dunnette (Ed.), *Handbook of industrial and organizational psychology*. Chicago: Rand McNally.

McGuire, M. A. (1987). *The contribution of intelligence to leadership performance on an in-basket test*. Unpublished master's thesis, University of Washington, Seattle.

Payne, J. W. (1976). Task complexity and contingent processing in decision making: An information search and protocol analysis. *Organizational Behavior and Human Performance, 16*, 366–387.

Pedhazur, E. J. (1982). *Multiple regression in behavioral research* (2nd ed). San Francisco: Holt, Rinehart & Winston.

Potter, E. H., & Fiedler, F. E. (1981). The utilization of staff member intelligence and experience under high and low stress. *Academy of Management Journal, 24*(2), 361–376.

Rogers, R. W., Lilley, L. W., Wellins, R. S., Fischl, M. A., & Burke, W. P. (1982). *Development of the precommissioning leadership assessment program*. Army Research Institute Technical Report 560.

Sarason, I. (1984). Stress, anxiety and cognitive interference: Reactions to tests. *Journal of Personality and Social Psychology, 46*, 929–938.

Spielberger, C. D., & Katzenmeyer, W. G. (1959). Manifest anxiety, intelligence, and college grades. *Journal of Consulting Psychology, 22*, 278.

Stogdill, R. M. (1948). Personal factors associated with leadership: A survey of the literature. *Journal of Psychology, 25*, 35–71.

Webster's new 20th century dictionary of the English language. Cleveland, OH: World Publishing Company.

Wonderlic, E. F. (1977). *Wonderlic personnel test*. Northfield, IL: Wonderlic.

Zajonc, R. R. (1965). Social facilitation. *Science, 149*, 269–274.

Part III

General perspectives

7 When minds meet: interactions, coincidence, and development in domains of ability

Nira Granott and Howard Gardner

At the age of six, Billy Devlin's score on the mathematical portion of the SAT was on par with that of high school students, about eleven years older than he. Randy McDaniel wrote stories, plays, essays, and novels from the age of three. Like other child prodigies, Billy and Randy showed a developmental trajectory that was extremely rapid in the domain of their special ability (Feldman, 1986). How can such a developmental profile be explained?

Consider three other examples. Mexican children, born to pottery-making families, performed significantly higher on Piaget's task of substance conservation than do their peers of similar age, schooling, and socioeconomic class (Price-Williams, Gordon, & Remirez, 1969). Aboriginal children in Australia exhibited consistently higher performance in spatial tasks related to terrain exploration than in logical–mathematical tasks, although the opposite was true for their European peers (Dasen, 1974). By the age of six, many Japanese children, who learned to play violin using the Suzuki method, could play a Vivaldi concerto (Gardner, 1983). Were all these children prodigies?

At the other end of the spectrum, adult teachers, highly competent in their profession, explored unfamiliar robots. The robots reacted in different ways to light, sound, and touch, sometimes responded to nonobvious stimuli, and moved in puzzling patterns. The subjects did not know what stimuli were involved nor how the stimuli affected the robots. Microanalysis of the adults' understanding revealed initial knowledge structures very similar to children in their first years of life (Granott, 1991b). How can this microdevelopmental profile be explained?

In this chapter we introduce a framework within which we can discuss these developmental processes and phenomena, as well as the populations that exhibit them. After a brief theoretical background we develop a framework that focuses on domain-specific intelligences and their development. We maintain that interactions with diverse environments affect the development of intelligence in the domains related to those interactions. When such interactions are available to the individual over time, domain-specific intelligence develops even when not expected (as the examples of child prodigies and cultural "whiz kids" indicate). On the other hand, when opportunities for such interactions are not available to the individual, domain-specific intelligence does not develop even when it is expected according to other

171

theories (as the example of adults' exploration of an unfamiliar domain demonstrates). We will show that specificity of intelligences and the effects of interactions with environments prevail across cultures, domains, and levels of inquiry. The interplay of these factors affects the developmental sequence in general, and has an impact on special phenomena in particular – such phenomena as child prodigies, "whiz kids" of different cultures, and adults' reasoning in unfamiliar domains.

Theoretical background

In the last decades, researchers have critiqued Piaget's theory of development, and shown that the picture of child development is less universal and not as determined a priori as claimed by Piaget. Three of the aspects critiqued were Piaget's narrow definition of intelligence, the assumption of evenness of development across domains, and the focus on interaction with objects and things in the physical environment, to the neglect of the child's social environment.

The capacities assessed by Piaget refer mainly to logical–rational thinking, and relate particularly to physical sciences. Piaget did not consider the child's other capacities that relate to understanding social relations, to emotional realm, to art, music, dance, movement, and creativity (Gardner, 1979). By the same token, Piaget's assessment of logic-oriented capacities relied mostly on verbal reports (Donaldson, 1978; Gelman, 1972). Piaget's assessment ignored the effect on the child's performance of different physical materials (like clay, building blocks, or beakers of water), different symbol systems (like language, pictures, or numbers), and diverse modes of responses (like language, gesture, or drawing) (Gardner, 1979).

Similarly, researchers challenged Piaget's claim for evenness of development across domains. In contrast to Piaget's views, other researchers claimed that cognitive development was neither unitary across domains nor derived from growth of unitary cognitive structures (Gelman & Spelke, 1981). Instead, these researchers suggested that young children have principled understanding in domains of knowledge, through a skeletal set of principles that support selective attention and guide further learning in a given domain (Gelman & Greeno, 1989). According to this view, the young child's competences are domain-specific and domain-linked.

Another line of critique questioned Piaget's focus on the isolated child, with little regard to the child's social environment. Following Vygotsky (1962, 1978) and the Soviet school, many researchers viewed cognitive change as an interpersonal process rather than a process related to the individual in isolation. Furthermore, Piaget's discussion of social interaction, limited as it was, suggested an explanation that contradicted other theories, such as those suggested by Vygotsky (1962, 1978) and Bandura (1977, 1986).

In the Piagetian view, when children interact with adults, they usually comply with adults' authority. Such compliance in turn prevents cognitive restructuring. When considering social interaction, the Piagetian school emphasizes cognitive conflict resulting from interaction among peers (Doise & Mugny, 1984; Doise & Palmonari,

1984; Murray, 1972, 1983; Perret-Clermont, 1980; Piaget, 1926). Cognitive conflict generates disequilibrium; as a result of assimilating the other's point of view, equilibrium and cognitive restructuring take place.

In contrast, according to Vygotsky, cognitive processes are initiated by adult–child interaction, and are later internalized by the child (Vygotsky, 1978) in the same way that external speech becomes egocentric and then turns to inner speech (Vygotsky, 1962). Studies in the Vygotskian approach focus on adult–child interaction (Rogoff, Malkin, & Gilbride, 1984; Saxe, Guberman, & Gearheart, 1987; Wertsch, 1979; Wertsch, McNamee, McLane, & Budwig, 1980; Wertsch, Minick, & Arns, 1984). Unlike Piaget's indication of cognitive conflict, these studies analyze the intersubjectivity and shared meaning that evolve between the child and a more capable partner. Studies that analyze cooperation among peers (Forman, 1987; Forman & Cazden, 1985) also underscore the importance of collaboration, shared meaning, mutual support, and exchange of guidance.

Piaget's explanation, indicating the benefits of peer interaction over interaction with adults, contradicts still another approach suggested by social learning theory (Bandura, 1977). In this view, human behavior is learned observationally, through modeling. What children observe in others guides their own actions. A model reinforces certain behaviors, and the way the individual thinks of herself in specific environments affects her interaction and cognitive development (Bandura, 1986).

As we see, both the Vygotskian approach and social learning theory highlight the role of social interaction in development, unlike Piaget's focus on interaction with the physical world. These approaches explain the function of social interaction in ways that do not conform with the Piagetian explanation.

The examples presented in the beginning of this chapter are related to these critiques of Piaget's theory. Piagetian theory holds that knowledge structures are unitary across domains. According to this theory, we would expect Billy and Randy to have similarly advanced knowledge structures in all domains of knowledge. We would also expect that adults, who are at their formal-operation stage, will perform consistently across domains; it is difficult, then, to explain the emergence of childlike knowledge structures in adults who explore an unfamiliar domain. Piagetian theory focuses on interaction with objects as a principal determinant of children's development; yet examples like the Aboriginal child-navigators and the Japanese young violinists indicate the importance of interactions with the social environment.

The theoretical framework suggested in this paper addresses these limitations of the Piagetian theory. First we confront Piaget's narrow definition of intelligence and the assumption of evenness across domains, suggesting instead a pluralistic view of intelligence (Gardner, 1983). Then we propose a "second-order Multiple Intelligences effect" that takes into account the effect of interaction with the diverse environments of the individual. We further suggest that "social interaction" encompasses multiple phenomena, only part of which are described and explained by the theories mentioned above. The specific types of interactions of individuals within a given domain may affect their abilities in that domain in different ways. Our domain-specific, contextual, and environment-dependent approach to the individual's evolving capacities sheds light on extraordinary phenomena such as child prodigies, cultural-specific abilities, and lagging abilities within specific domains.

The multiple intelligences approach

Gardner's (1983) Multiple Intelligences theory, or MI, for short, posits a small set of human intellectual potentials that typically relate to different cultural domains: linguistic, musical, logical–mathematical, spatial, bodily–kinesthetic, intrapersonal, and interpersonal. Linguistic intelligence entails sensitivity to different spoken and written languages, to shades of meanings, and to interactions among linguistic connotations. Musical intelligence relates to sensitivity to pitch, rhythm, and timbre. Logical–mathematical intelligence concerns numerate capacities, negotiation with hypothetical statements, and exploration of relationships obtaining among those statements. This intelligence deals with abstract formal systems and their interconnections. Spatial intelligence entails an ability to recognize different instances of a given visual–spatial element and to transform – or recognize transformations of – one element into another. This intelligence enables us to conjure up mental imagery, make mental transformations of that imagery, and graphically represent spatial information. Bodily–kinesthetic intelligence is responsible for mastery over actions of one's body. Intrapersonal intelligence gives us accurate, full knowledge about ourselves, our strengths, and our feelings, and allows us to make informed decisions about ourselves. Interpersonal intelligence involves capacity to read intentions and desires of other individuals and to influence them in desired ways.

According to MI theory, each intelligence has core processing abilities that are unique to that particular intelligence. For example, linguistic intelligence has phonological and grammatical processors and musical intelligence has tonal and rhythmic processors (Gardner, 1983). There are differences among the intelligences in their computational cores (e.g., the information-processing mechanisms that process tones and patterns of rhythms). The individual's sensitivity to information also varies across intelligences (for example, her sensitivity to sounds, pitch, and timbre). Similarly, the individual's access to diverse symbol systems (like musical notation or mathematical formulations) varies across intelligences. All these differences contribute to the relative development of a specific intelligence over other intelligences.

According to MI theory, cognitive strengths and weaknesses are domain-specific and cannot be predicted from one intelligence to another (Gardner & Hatch, 1989). Preliminary assessments at Harvard Project Zero show that performance of young children in each domain is largely independent of their performance in other domains. Examination across domains can identify areas of relative strength and relative weakness for each child. Within-group comparisons indicate that most children demonstrate strength or weakness in certain domains in relation to other children (Hatch & Gardner, 1990; Krechevsky & Gardner, 1990). The developmental level of a child in one domain, therefore, does not predict her level of development in other domains. Instead, each domain exhibits a different developmental trajectory (Korn-haber, Krechevsky, & Gardner, 1990). While progressing through the developmental sequence, children's achievements prove specific within each of the symbolic do-mains (Gardner & Wolf, 1983).

In the following discussion, we introduce a distinction between "MI-generic" and "MI-special" abilities. Many people have a proclivity toward certain domains. A per-son can be "musically talented," or may be gifted in verbal expressiveness. Often, these abilities do not fall beyond the normal range, though they may be above the average in the population. An intelligence that is stronger than the other intelligences of an individual, yet falls within the normal range, will be referred to as "MI-generic" ability. Every person has a potential for developing each intelligence to some extent. MI-generic abilities vary across individuals (one person can have higher linguistic intelligence than another person) as well as within individuals (a person can have higher linguistic intelligence than musical intelligence). In contrast, the term "MI-special" refers to extraordinary intelligence, such as characterizing the child prodigies we have encountered before. Billy and Randy had MI-special abilities relative to other children their age. The development of many domains was advanced by the contribu-tion of outstanding figures who had extraordinary abilities in that domain, like Ein-stein, Mozart, and Picasso (Gardner, 1993). We will relate to such extraordinary MI as "MI-special," to be distinguished from "MI-generic," species-wide abilities.

The view presented in this chapter suggests that, in addition to innate proclivities, differences in human abilities across domains – both MI-generic and in MI-special – continue to evolve from an early age and throughout ontogenesis due to the individ-ual–environment interactions. We turn now to these processes, which we call a sec-ond-order MI effect.

MI through interaction – A second-order MI effect

A second-order Multiple Intelligences effect refers to an interaction with the en-vironment, which selectively promotes certain intelligences and not others. First-order MI entail innate intelligences, the intellectual promise with which an individual is born. In contrast, second-order MI refer to the continuous evolution of a person's intelligences, resulting from interplay between his first-order MI and his ongoing interactive experiences throughout life with his diverse environments. While first-order MI refer to a state and label a potential, the second order address a process and relate to the dynamic development of an individual's MI.

The distinction between first- and second-order MI is somewhat similar to Hebb's (1949) distinction between intelligence A (indicating innate potential) and intelli-gence B (the functioning of a brain after development has occurred), but three exceptions should be noted. First, unlike Hebb, who discusses the assessment of intelligence A and claims that only intelligence B is affected by experience, we claim that one cannot separate the two factors – innate potential and environmental influence (Anastasi, 1958). As we will show, from early childhood, the individual's intelligences undergo a process of change as a result of interactions. The individual intelligences, at any point of time, represent the end result of first- and second-order MI. Another distinction is that second-order MI refer specifically to the effect of interactions with the environments. Though Hebb discusses the effect of experience, his reference to development may also include the effect of maturity. Third, unlike Hebb, we focus on the differences among the various intelligences in different domains of abilities. Putting all intelligences in one parcel and treating them all as one entity, in the psychometric tradition of some decades ago, obscures the underlying processes and hinders the understanding of cognitive abilities.

What is the mechanism through which second-order MI develop? Several processes generate the second-order MI. Some are elicited by the child, affected by his first-order MI, and reinforced through interaction; others are elicited by the environment, and reinforced by the child's response; yet others evolve through an interaction of the two factors.

The child's first-order MI affect what she attends to in her environment. A heightened sensitivity to certain stimuli can engage "selective attention" (Kahneman, 1973). In such cases, the child actually accesses only a selected part of the information potentially available to her in her environment. The environment's response, in turn, may reinforce this predisposition: positive feedback (like admiration of a child's navigation ability or pottery-making skills) reinforces the child's sensitivity to certain stimuli (like navigational cues in the environment, or different structures of pottery products). The child's first-order MI also affect her response to the environment. This aspect is similar to the claim that genotype (genetic constitution) affects a person's responsiveness to environmental opportunities (Plomin, DeFries, & Loehlin, 1977; Scarr & McCartney, 1983).

Conversely, too, genotype affects the environment's responsiveness to the individual. For example, active, smiling babies receive more social stimulation than sober, passive infants; cooperative, attentive preschoolers get more pleasant instructional interactions with adults than noncooperative, distractible children (Scarr & McCartney, 1983). We encounter here what Plomin et al. (1977) call "reactive genotype–environment correlation," and Scarr and McCartney (1983) term "evocative effect" of genotype–environment, referring to different responses that different genotypes evoke from their environments. Environments' responses, in turn, influence children's development: social stimulation and pleasant instructional interactions promote the development of smiling babies and cooperative preschoolers, respectively. The reactive or evocative effect is one of the ways in which environments influence second-order MI. In certain environments and socioeconomic strata, when a child is attentive, interested, and initiating interactions in a certain domain, such as music, language, or science, the environment will be more likely to respond with enriching interactions in that domain. The example of Randy McDaniel, the child-prodigy writer mentioned earlier, can demonstrate this point. Randy has a MI-special proclivity for language, exhibited early in life. Since infancy he has been interested in words and their tonal qualities. Randy's parents are sensitive to his ability and respond to it with special nurturing and fostering: they value his writing and promote it. Both parents have encouraged Randy, instructed, and guided him. Randy's father, a professional writer, has dedicated his time to teach Randy and coach him from a very early age (Feldman, 1986).

A second-order MI effect may be actually induced by the child's environment. Society's culture, tradition, and value systems infiltrate to influence the child through his interactions with his environment. In this way, the environment serves as a "cultural amplifier" (Bruner, 1966), amplifying cultural practices (like written language) and values (like appreciation of art). This effect is amplified when the child attends to the cultural cues, when he actually uses tools supplied by culture (Cole & Griffin, 1980; Newman, Griffin, & Cole, 1989). Such experiences can evoke "resonance" (Kornhaber, Krechevsky, & Gardner, 1990) in the child, reinforcing his emerging abilities.

Consider this example. The Aborigines' traditional culture, which is based on a hunting economy, values navigation skills. When travelling for long distances in barren land, nomadic Aborigines depend for their survival on finding their way from one waterhole to another. Aboriginal children have ample opportunities to practice navigation skill: they travel with their families often. Some travel frequently to other settlements; others still live for about four months each year in a "walkabout," travelling through their ancestral grounds. Spatial skills, related to terrain exploration, then, are amplified by the children's social environment and way of life, and are realized when the children practice them. In contrast, traditional culture experiences of Aboriginal children do not promote numerate skills. An Aboriginal hunter hunts one kangaroo at a time; an Aboriginal craftsman estimates his product's size and weight by sight and feeling. The Aborigine language has words only for one, two, and many, and does not have terms for sizes and measurement. Therefore, cultural experiences of the Aboriginal children, and their verbal interactions, promote their spatial skills much more than their mathematical skills (Dasen, 1974).

As we have seen, second-order MI can be generated in several ways: by the individual's selective attention; by her evocative effect on her environment, an effect which originates in her first-order MI; by her response to the environment's response; and by cultural amplification, which elicits "resonance" in the individual. These processes occur throughout an evolving relationship between the individual and the environment.

A pluralistic view of the individual–environment relationship

Like the individual's first-order MI, second-order MI may develop selectively in different domains. To understand the way second-order MI evolve, finer distinctions have to be made about the individual's interactions with the environment. Both terms, "environment" and "interaction," encompass a multitude of settings and processes that may have different and even opposing effects on the individual's abilities within different domains.

Diversity of environments

People operate within the context of various environments. These environments constitute a set of nested structures, each subsumed by another (Bronfenbrenner, 1979), like concentric circles surrounding the individual. For a child, the first and most intimate circle is his home and parents. Larger circles include friends, teachers, classmates, school, and so on. The closer the circle to the individual, the more intensive are the interactions of the individual with that environmental setting.

In each of these settings the individual encounters different kinds of environments: a physical environment, a symbolic one, and a social environment (see Figure 7.1). These are not necessarily similar across environmental settings. For example, children often use and play more with different objects at home than at school (including games, toys, educational tools, and everyday objects). Similarly, the symbolic environment at home or at school is often different – including the kind of books that are read, television programs that are watched, spoken language, and written language (i.e., Heath, 1983). By the same token, in each environmental setting, the child has different kinds of interactions with different people (parents, teachers, and classmates), and a different context for these interactions (living skills, emotional support, teaching, and playful activities).

Each of the environmental settings, through its social, symbolic, and physical

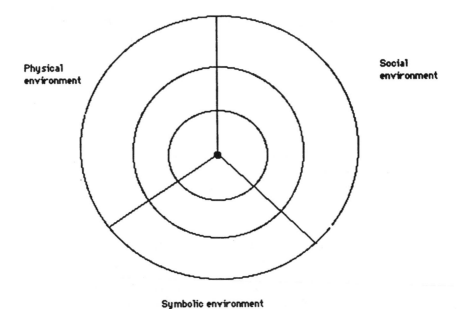

Figure 7.1. The individual's environment. The individual (in the center) has different environmental settings. Each setting includes a physical, social, and symbolic environment.

aspects, generates a second-order MI effect on the individual. The case of Billy Devlin can illustrate such an effect in its extreme. Billy's parents, his most proximate environmental setting, made a special effort to enrich Billy's social environment in his domain of special ability. To satisfy Billy's (MI-special) interests in mathematics and natural sciences, his parents arranged for him to have a range of tutors. They also made contacts with physicists, chemists, astronomers, geneticists, and biologists, whom he met and corresponded with. Not only did Billy's parents enrich his interactions with the social environment in the domain; they also enriched his symbolic and the physical environments. At the age of six, Billy was studying a junior high school mathematics book and reading at his leisure a college physics book. Billy's parents arranged visits to museums, universities, and laboratories, where he had access to specialized equipment (such as an electron microscope), tools, and materials (Feldman, 1986).

When examining the second-order MI effect of the individual–environment relationships, specific attention should be given to the different environments of the individual, the role they play in regard to different domains of ability, and the diverse relationships that evolve in the interaction between the individual and these environments.

Diversity of interactions

Environments affect the individual through the individual's interactions with them. Throughout these interactions, second-order MI continuously evolve. Yet, just as the concept of environment is general and covers diverse environments, so is the concept of interaction. The term "interaction" refers to a conglomerate of processes with different and sometimes opposing effects on the individual's development in different domains of ability.

The second-order MI effect is complex: with a given environmental setting (e.g., the close family), and within a given domain (e.g., linguistic expression) a person can have different types of interactions. With one and the same environmental setting, a person can also have different types of interactions in different domains (e.g., different types of interaction within the close family in the domains of verbal expression, music, sports, and mathematics). Moreover, with different environmental settings (e.g., family, school, and community), a person can have different types of interactions related to a given domain (such as different interactions in the linguistic domain with one's parents, siblings, teachers, other students at school, or the librarian in a community library).

As mentioned before, different theorists do not see eye to eye on the effect of interaction on cognitive change. With few exceptions, supporters of the Piagetian, Vygotskian, and social-learning theories do not agree on the types of interactions that promote cognitive change, or on the nature of the process. While it is possible to analyze interactions within each theory, the theories lack common ground. The view suggested below maintains that these theories are not mutually exclusive; moreover, they may portray only part of the interactive picture, and thus undermine the complexity and multiplicity of the phenomenon.

A more inclusive interaction model (Granott, 1993) suggests a wider range of interactions that are related to cognitive change. This model can assist in ferreting out the different effects of interactions on second-order MI. The model uses two dimensions: degree of collaboration and relative knowledge and expertise (see Figure 7.2). The horizontal dimension, degree of collaboration, extends for positive values of collaboration from the intersection of the two axes (indicating no collaboration, or independent activity), through increasing degree of collaboration, to high collaboration (indicating a united effort with continuous sharing). For negative values on the collaborative dimension, activities get less independent and increase in interchange of disruptive interaction toward the far-left end of the dimension, culminating in highly interlocked interdisruptive activities. The vertical dimension represents the expertise of the participants in relation to each other in the domain of the interaction. For example, take an interaction between a Mexican child, born to potter parents, who is a conserver, and a child of nonpotters, who is a nonconserver (children who are at a different developmental stage, according to Piaget). When the two collaborate on a conservation task, they have different knowledge related to the context of the interaction. There is even higher asymmetry of expertise when an Aboriginal child takes part in a navigation task with his father, a skilled navigator: the two have highly asymmetric expertise in the context of their interaction.

The model applies to interactions in different contexts and domains, to participants of different ages, and to different levels of expertise (since it only considers the

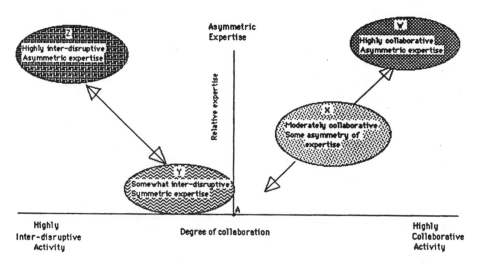

Figure 7.2. A framework for analyzing interactions according to degree of collaboration and relative expertise. Point A, in the intersection of the dimensions, represents symmetric expertise and independent activity.

relative expertise between the participants). Additional factors, other than degree of collaboration and asymmetry of expertise in the relevant domain, also affect interactions. These factors and their effect on interactions are discussed later.

Many types of interactions map onto the span delineated by these two dimensions. The intersection of the axes is characterized by a situation in which participants with symmetric expertise are each involved in an independent activity. The top-right area (marked W in figure 2) indicates highly collaborative interactions between participants with asymmetric knowledge and expertise. Adult–child interaction, with evolving shared meaning and highly collaborative support in the Vygotskian-school vein, corresponds to this area. In area X, interactions are characterized by moderate collaboration between partners of some asymmetric expertise. The Piagetian-school examples of a child conserver and a nonconserver, when each of them tries to explain his already formed view to the other, can demonstrate such an interaction. As we will see later, other types of interactions also map to different areas between these two dimensions.

The area to the left of the intersection of the axes, indicating negative (disruptive) interactions, has a similar structure. For example, if two peers who have equal expertise work mostly independently but disturb each other's actions occasionally, their interaction corresponds to the area marked by Y. The top left area (Z), on the other hand, indicates an interaction between partners of asymmetric expertise (expert–novice, or adult–child), which is highly interlocked in a disruptive manner.

Interactions that correspond to different values on the two dimensions have different attributes. In order to understand the way second-order MI evolve with the individual's interactive experiences, we have to examine the specific interactions within each domain of ability, since different kinds of interactions affect the individual's development in the corresponding domain differently. Collaborative interactions of diverse types can promote the participant's cognitive processes in different ways; disruptive interactions can hamper the participants' cognitive progresses.

Collaborative interactions

Conceptually, the dimensions for analysis are continuous. But in order to characterize the attributes of diverse interactions, three ordinal levels – high, medium, and low – have been set for each dimension (see Figure 7.3). Between participants with a given relative expertise in a domain (whether symmetric, moderately asymmetric, or highly asymmetric), the evolving interactions can be highly collaborative, moderately collaborative, or bear a high degree of independence. Each of these types of interaction has different attributes and differs in its second-order MI effect, as is briefly described below (see Granott, 1993, for further details).

Mutual Collaboration, Asymmetric Collaboration, and *Scaffolding,* have a high value on the collaborative dimension. This manifests in a common shared activity with a common operative goal. The participants negotiate the same situation, use

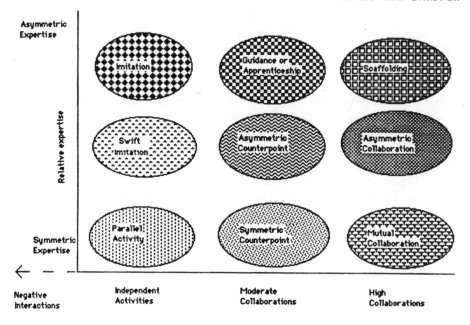

Figure 7.3. Collaborative interactions.

common materials, and operate on the same task. Yet these three types of interactions differ in the symmetry of the process of sharing knowledge and expertise, in the dominance on the activity, and in the attributes of the coconstruction of knowledge (see Table 7.1). The symmetric sharing in Mutual Collaboration sometimes generates simultaneous talk and abbreviated speech (Vygotsky, 1962). Scaffolding is characterized by asymmetric sharing and guidance, though throughout the interaction dominance often shifts to the less-expert partner, the child, or the novice (Wertsch & Stone, 1978). Asymmetric Collaboration is marked by some asymmetry of expertise, as in the case of a Japanese mother, who has already taken lessons in violin, and her son, who started to take violin lessons. The mother's expertise exceeds that of her child, yet the two may play together in a supportive and pleasant way that promotes the child's (and probably the mother's) violin mastery.

Parallel Activity, Swift Imitation, and *Imitation,* are mostly independent activities, with little degree of collaboration. The participants are each involved in their own activities, immersed in separate subsituations, with separate foci of attention. Their simultaneous and parallel activities are interspersed with temporary shifts to interaction. The interaction can be explicit and verbal, or implicit (Rogoff, 1990), manifested in looking at the other partners and their activities. During Parallel Activity, for example, peers of similar pottery expertise may each work with clay and create their own pottery, yet from time to time they look at each other's work and they may occasionally share comments on their activities. Similarly, young children's parallel

Table 7.1. Attributes of types of interactions

Imitation	Guidance or apprenticeship	Scaffolding
Separate activities imitating a more capable partner	Common goal embedded in short periods of guidance interspersed throughout independent activities	Common activity with complementing goals
Partial or no sharing	Periods of unidirectional sharing of knowledge	Sharing the situation, materials, observations; asymmetric sharing of knowledge and hypotheses
Unguided activity and observation	Partially guided activity, observations, and analysis	Guided activity, observations, and analysis
	Alternating shifts of unequal dominance; possible trend in the shift of dominance during the entire interaction	Throughout the interaction, a trend of shift of dominance from the scaffolding to the scaffold partner
Asymmetric flow of information, verbal or visual	Asymmetric flow of information	Asymmetric communication
		Guiding (by the scaffolding) vs. task-solving (by the scaffold) information and action
	Mostly complete sentences	Mostly complete sentences, based on shared understanding
Unsynchronized, separate, and highly unbalanced processes of knowledge construction	Unsynchronized, separate, and highly unbalanced processes of knowledge construction	Unidirectional guidance of the construction of knowledge

Swift imitation	Asymmetric counterpoint	Asymmetric collaboration
Separate activities with temporary shifts to imitating a more capable partner	Common goal embedded in individually initiated activity that is unequally alternating among the participants	Common operative goals and activities
Partial or no sharing	Sharing the situation, materials, and feedback; possible partial and mostly unidirectional sharing of knowledge structures	Sharing the situation, materials, products, previous knowledge, observations, and hypotheses
	Partly guided or directed sequence of activity, based on one partner's previous knowledge	Evolving sequence of activity, based on the shared activity of the participants and one partner's previous knowledge
	Alternating shifts of unequal dominance	Unequal dominance
Asymmetric flow of information, verbal or visual	Asymmetric flow of information and action	Asymmetric flow of information and action
		Talking spontaneously
		Incomplete sentences, accommodating to the different activity of the other

(continued)

Table 7.1. (*continued*)

Swift imitation	Asymmetric counterpoint	Asymmetric collaboration
Unsynchronized, separate, and unbalanced processes of knowledge construction; possible partial comparison or confrontation of knowledge structures	Unsynchronized, separate, and unbalanced processes of knowledge construction; possible partial comparison or confrontation of cognitive structures	Co-construction of knowledge through the interaction, in unbalanced processes

Parallel activity	Symmetric counterpoint	Mutual collaboration
Separate activities with temporary shifts to periods of interaction	Common goal shared in individually initiated activity that equally alternates between the participants	Common operative goals and activity
Partial or no sharing during the interaction	Sharing the situation, materials, and feedback; possible partial sharing of knowledge structures	Sharing the situation, materials, products, observations, and hypotheses
Separate activities, partial or no continuous common sequence of activity	Evolving sequence of activity, based on previous activity of all partners and on the corresponding feedback	Evolving sequence of activity, based on the shared evolving activity of all participants
	Alternating shifts of equal dominance for chunks of the activity	Equal dominance with quick shifts from one partner to the other
Symmetric or asymmetric flow of information, verbal or visual	Symmetric flow of information and action	Symmetric flow of information and action
	Little information sharing during independent construction of knowledge	Talking spontaneously and simultaneously
		Abbreviated speech
Unsynchronized separate processes of knowledge construction; partial comparison or confrontation of cognitive structures	Unsynchronized processes of knowledge construction, but similar during the entire activity; comparison or confrontation of cognitive structures	Coconstruction of knowledge through the interaction, in balanced symmetric processes

play is a form of Parallel Activity. Imitation refers to limited interaction based mainly on independent activities between partners of unequal expertise (adult–child, or expert–novice), when the novice (or the child) imitates the expert (or adult) (see Bandura, 1977). Swift Imitation occurs between peers of moderate asymmetry of expertise. The less expert partner imitates the other's performance smoothly and easily, by briefly glancing at her partner. For example, when Sherry and a group of other adult robot-explorers were discussing how to start their explorations, light flashed on Sherry from a flashlight used by Lynn, a more experienced peer who was exploring the robot's reaction to light. Glancing at Lynn, Sherry said: "Oh, look at that! Let's see, the forward behavior is with the light, right?" as she started exploring the robot the way Lynn was (Granott, 1993). Abundant similar examples are found in children's painting, block building, and other activities in kindergarten and elementary school.

In interactions with moderate collaboration – *Symmetric Counterpoint, Asymmetric Counterpoint,* and *Guidance or Apprenticeship* – the collaboration manifests itself in a common operative goal, common focus of attention, common materials, and a common task. The participants watch each other's activity and listen to each other. Yet, to a large degree, their activities are independent, and they alternate dominance on the activity. In Symmetric Counterpoint, as in musical counterpoint, the participants retain some independent activities, which are woven together. Each of the peers, in his turn, performs an activity – or talks – without coordinating it with his partners beforehand. By sharing a focus of attention, watching the other's activity or listening to the other, the participants learn from one another throughout the interaction. For example, when trying to solve a problem in the functioning of one of the robots, Sam and Dorothy alternate turns. While Sam explores the robot, Dorothy watches. Apparently, she learns from his experimentation, for later, when her turn comes, Dorothy succeeds in solving the problem on her first try, although she could not have done it previously (Granott, 1993). Guiding or Apprenticeship are asymmetric moderate collaborations. Such interactions evolve, for example, when a violin teacher demonstrates specific performance to his young student, gives directions and guides the child's performance, and then watches the child perform. Asymmetric Counterpoint has moderate asymmetry of expertise. In a Suzuki group lesson, for example, children of different ages and levels of expertise take turns performing. One plays a piece and the others listen and watch (Gardner, 1983). Similarly, during the music group discussion, participants of some asymmetric expertise take turns: while one talks, the others listen.

Each of the collaborative interactions can contribute to the participant's knowledge in the related domain, generating a second-order MI effect. However, each type of collaborative interaction affects the development of domain-related knowledge differently and influences differently the individual's attitude toward the domain. Highly collaborative interactions may promote cognitive growth to a greater extent than do less collaborative interactions with the same partners, and therefore may have a stronger second-order MI effect. A highly collaborative interaction with a more expert partner can accelerate cognitive growth in a way that is more in tune with one's needs and level of understanding, and therefore may have a particularly strong second-order MI effect. Highly collaborative interactions with peers who have a similar expertise may generate similar cognitive change – and a similar second-order MI effect – for both. The more diverse and intensive the types of collaborative interactions that an individual has, the more his knowledge in the domain may develop. In contrast, negative or disruptive interactions in the domain will have an opposite second-order effect on the development of his intelligence in that domain.

Disruptive interactions

Disruptive interactions can be viewed as a mirror image of the collaborative interactions: they have a similar structure but with negative connotations. Such interactions disrupt an activity in which one of the participants, some of the participants, or all of them are involved. Disruptive interactions interfere with participants' discussion, destroy a product, or stop an exploration; they can impede achievement of a goal, prevent completion of a task, and hinder the related processes of knowledge construction.

Disruptive interactions can evolve between peers of equal expertise (e.g., two children of similar age and ability in the domain of the interaction), partners with some different expertise, or partners with highly asymmetric expertise (expert–novice or adult–child).

The least interdisruptive interactions, like their low-collaborative parallels on the positive side of the dimension, consist of mostly independent activities. In these interactions, the participants are each engaged in their own activities. However, the activities are interspersed with short periods of interaction, characterized by a disruptive interchange.

Highly interdisruptive interactions are characterized by extremely interlocked and interfering activities. In such interactions, for example, the participants talk simultaneously so that neither of them can express and develop his views or hear what the other is saying. In other interdisruptive interactions the participants interfere with each other's activity when simultaneously trying to use the same materials and dominate the activity.

In between the least interdisruptive and the highly interdisruptive interactions, interactions are characterized by moderately interlocked activities. In these interactions, as in their moderately collaborative parallels on the positive side of the dimension, there is a counterpoint between the participants' activities. During the counterpoint, the activities of at least one participant are disruptive.

Negative interactions cannot be ignored: the world is not always benign and the child not always willing to learn (Goodnow, 1990). Mothers sometimes restrict their children's learning to prevent a mess or to hurry a process (Valsiner, 1984), because of their ideas of what children should and should not do (Glick, 1985), or due to restricted communication codes and family control patterns (Hess & Shipman, 1965). Later in life, other people can intervene, for protecting a person or for other reasons, and negative relationships can form (Shweder, 1990). The environments' value systems can induce negative interactions when strong proclivities of a child are not valued. For example, a child's scribbling can be considered a waste of time, her doodling a waste of paper; she may be reproached for daydreaming and being useless. Not only are her abilities unacknowledged, but agents in the environment may also attempt to inhibit their expression while demanding the development of abilities in other domains. When an expert (or adult) undermines the novice's (or child's) ability, prevents access to materials, stops certain activities, or deprives the other's ability to pursue certain directions of inquiry, the interaction can have a severe effect, hindering the development of the novice (or child) in the domain of the interaction. Such disruptive interactions can have a powerful negative effect on the novice's (or child's) knowledge construction. Disruptive interactions with a more expert partner may have a stronger effect than those with peers of equal expertise, to whom the individual can ascribe less authority.

When, in a given domain, an individual has disruptive interactions, these inter-actions may negatively affect his intellectual development in that domain. This negative second-order MI effect will be stronger if these disruptive interactions are not compensated for by positive collaborative interactions in that domain.

The analysis of the different types of interactions, according to this model, is based on examination of two dimensions – degree of collaboration and relative expertise in the domain of the interaction. However, other factors often affect the interaction as well. In order to understand the second-order MI effect, these other factors also have to be taken into account.

Other factors affecting interactions

Factors other than relative expertise and degree of collaboration may also affect interactions. One of these factors is knowledge and expertise in other (unrelated) domains, which may affect the participants' expectations of each other's expertise. An expert–novice pattern of relationship, in such a case, may transpose to a different domain in which the "expert" is no more knowledgeable than his partner.

Another factor influencing the patterns of interaction is social role. For example, an authority–submission relationship between two persons at work may affect the interaction between them in other unrelated contexts. Similarly, a child may comply to an adult's authority and defer his own point of view (Piaget, 1965). Gender-related patterns may affect boy–girl and man–woman interactions, giving more dominance on the interaction to the male. Race and class can have a similar effect.

Previous patterns of interaction between the same participants, molded through common experiences in the past, can also affect their present interactions. Finally, personality traits (such as leadership, initiative, or passivity) and self image will also affect interactions.

It seems that when the aforementioned factors do not correspond to the partici-pants' relative knowledge and expertise in the context of the interaction, these factors may divert the interaction to less productive directions, and may diminish its effect on cognitive growth.

The model analyzing the different types of interactions can contribute to under-standing the second-order MI effect, which is generated through interactions in different domains. In different environmental settings, different types of interactions may develop in different domains. In evaluating the second-order MI effect in a given domain, therefore, we have to examine each environmental setting, and take into account the different types of interactions that evolve with that setting in the domain under scrutiny. The complexity of the second-order MI effect, induced by the diversity of the environments and of the interactions with them, is caused by the domain-specific focus that environments and interactions often have.

Domain-specific foci of environments and interactions

A second-order MI effect develops differently across domains. Earlier we discussed factors that affect the development of second-order MI; now we want to highlight the domain-specificity of the process.

Environments can give children selective exposure to different domains. The Mexican children born to potter families, for example, have substantial exposure to clay and related activities. By the same token, the Suzuki method focuses on exposing the child to the musical domain. From an early age, the child listens daily to musical recordings. Toward the end of the first year, the music he listens to converges on twenty short songs that will later constitute his core curriculum. Even before the child starts his violin lessons, his mother plays violin every day, arousing his curiosity and excitement until he is allowed to touch the violin himself (Gardner, 1983).

Similarly, through their social, symbolic, and physical environments, various settings offer the individual opportunities for interactions that differ across domains. Take the case of Randy, for example. Randy's interactions with his parents, and especially with his father, the writer, were highly focused on writing and on related activities (like reading or watching the "Nova" series that supplied a context for his writing). Physical and symbolic environments supported Randy's writing – from a typewriter he started to write with at the age of three, through a library and museums Randy visited with his parents, to posters, models, comic books, and educational television programs in his areas of interest (Feldman, 1986). Randy's interactions with his parents focused on the linguistic domain – his MI-special ability – and interactions with other domains were subordinate to his interest in writing.

Not only does the intensity of interactions differ across domains, but so do the environment's approaches towards different domains and their value systems. People acquire interpretive frameworks from their environments and categorize areas of knowledge as "better" or "poorer" accordingly (Goodnow, 1990). In this way, environments affect the individual's motivation toward different domains. Various environments devise ways to encourage children and acknowledge their accomplishments – by grades and honor rolls at school, competitions and prizes in sports, exhibits in arts, shows in drama, and concerts in music. The domains preferred at different environmental settings differ, and so do the environment's enticements and rewards. Each environmental setting, in its interactions with the individual, tries to promote the individual's ability in its preferred domain. By contrast, environmental settings can also shape the individuals' concepts and attitudes in an active controlling way (Goodnow, 1990) through negative interactions.

Value systems and foci of interaction in one environment do not necessarily match those of another. At school, children have more activities focused on reading and writing than on sports, but the opposite is true at a sports club. Obviously, an art center offers more intense interactions in arts than in other domains, and a music school in music.

These differences among environments in their value systems and foci of interaction affect second-order MI differently across domains. The individual–environment interactions that relate to a given domain do not affect intelligence across the board. Rather, they have a specific effect on the individual's mental abilities, an effect that relates mainly to the domain of the interactions. Availability of interactions in other domains may induce similar cognitive effects in the other domains as well; however, transfer of abilities that were developed in one context and one domain to other contexts and domains is problematic (e.g., Brown, Kane, & Echols, 1986; Salomon & Perkins, 1989) and often does not occur.

The example of the adult "robot explorers" illustrates the problem of transfer across domains. This example presents an extreme case of an unfamiliar domain and a context within which the subjects did not have any previous experience. All the same, different theories would expect high-level functioning from these subjects. According to the Piagetian theory, being at a formal-operation stage, these adults are expected to reason in an abstract way even in this domain. According to computational approaches, being intelligent and highly competent in their profession as well as in other familiar domains, these adults are expected to solve problems in an advanced way (Newell & Simon, 1972). However, this is not the case.

The study, which followed and analyzed the explorations of 35 adults (Granott, 1991a,b) indicated that when dealing with a highly unfamiliar context and domain, the subjects' actions and explanations of the robots' functioning evolved through qualitatively different phases. Analysis of the microdevelopment of the underlying knowledge structures, using developmental theory (Fischer, 1980), revealed that knowledge structures in the new context had to be laboriously reconstructed from initial low-level development phases.

The subjects' initial knowledge structures, related to the specific domain and context, without regard to their general abilities and knowledge structures in other domains, were at first based on sensorimotor structures (parallel to initial sensorimotor levels in Fischer's skill theory) and continued to be so for a considerable amount of time. At first, the subjects did not differentiate between properties of a robot and its response to their actions. Before differentiation started, the robot's patterns of movement seemed random, as the subjects reported: "I happened to be standing in front of it and I didn't realize it. But when I moved away I noticed my shadow was gone . . . ." Or: "At first it seemed pretty random, and then it became clear it was not random at all. . . . Somebody would make a sound, it would change direction . . . ."

With initial differentiation, subjects started to form causal mappings between their actions and the robot's movement. For example: "I thought, gee, that's just programmed to go the same distance every time, that's going to be boring, and I was starting to turn toward those things that were sort of loud and calling attention to themselves when Jennifer walked by and it changed, when she'd just gotten near it, it started to change its distance that it was going, and I was like, Oh! ... "

Through elaborate experimentation, both the subjects' actions and the robot's movements underwent further differentiation. The subjects' repeated explorations resembled young children's circular reactions, and were similarly targeted to establishing causal relations between variations in their actions and variations in the robot's movement.

Only after much experimentation did the first representations form in the context of the robots. In contrast to the earlier phases, in which concrete variability in the robot's movement could not be understood independently of one's actions on it, subjects started to represent the robot's pattern of movement independently of their actions. At the representational levels, the subjects' modes of exploration changed, as well as their explanations.

Two sessions (2 hours each) of intensive interactions with remarkable interest, curiosity, and motivation, did not suffice for the formation of knowledge in the highly unfamiliar domain beyond early representational structures. Only a few subjects, who asked for additional sessions of exploration, started to understand the robots on more advanced levels. These subjects may have had higher motivation, interest, and probably higher MI-generic inclination to the domain of scientific thinking. Only in the additional sessions did more advanced representations appear and abstract structures start to emerge, again through laborious explorations.

These examples form an extreme manifestation of the domain-specificity of intelligent abilities and second-order MI. While the subjects were developing sensorimotor knowledge structures, and before they could form representations and abstractions in the domain-specific context, they clearly had representational and abstract structures in other areas and domains. Obviously, the subjects could talk about the task and articulate their thoughts in abstract manners. Yet, at the same time, they could not form representations within the task content; they could not represent specific phenomena or grasp abstract processes within that specific domain. While the subjects used representations and reasoned in an abstract way in other contexts and domains, these knowledge structures and cognitive abilities could not easily transfer to the new context. Rather, these structures had to be reconstructed with much effort, through intensive interactions with the new materials (their physical environment) and with their partners (the social environment).

These examples indicate that knowledge structures may be domain- and context-specific to a larger extent than usually assumed. These results strongly suggest that knowledge structures cannot be "transferred" to a new and different context and domain, but rather have to be reconstructed within each domain. The amount of effort needed for this reconstruction may correlate with the unfamiliarity of the context and the domain.

Previous interactions with the environments, then, have domain-specific effects and influence the development of second-order MI differently across domains. Part of the subtlety of analyzing the second-order MI is caused by the need to consider the domain-specific foci of the diverse interactions with the different environments.

Another subtlety in the analysis of second-order MI derives from their dynamic nature. Throughout life, there is a continuous change in the individual's environments and in the interactions with these environments.

Dynamic nature of environments and interactions

Second-order MI unfold over time. The process is neither homogeneous nor uniform in nature. Rather, it is composed of manifold subprocesses that change throughout the individual's lifetime.

First, the individual's environments change over time. Throughout development, the child interacts with ever-widening environmental settings (White & Siegel, 1984). In his early years, home is the predominant setting. As the child grows up and moves out into the community, the settings become larger and range across increasing physical distances (from the closer family and the intimate kindergarten of the young child, through the larger schools of the adolescent, to the social circles, work, community, and cultural circles of the adult).

When people pass through these settings and their different social environments, their symbolic environments change as well. By reading, writing, listening to and watching media, children get access to events and people remote not only in space, but also in time (White & Siegel, 1984). Symbolic environments increasingly become more complex and more specialized. High school students learn foreign languages, advanced mathematical notations, and programming. Their vocabulary changes, as do the mastery and the content of their reading and writing. In college and graduate school, their symbolic environment becomes even more specialized, whether in musical notation, physics formulas, scientific theories, literature readings, or arts.

Similarly, physical environments change. Many preschoolers encounter similar generic materials (paints and clay) and objects (toys and educational games) in several environmental settings (home, kindergarten, and friends). However, throughout elementary school, high school, college, and graduate school, students get increasing access to more domain-specific tools, equipment, and materials, whether in arts, science laboratories, or programming classes. In a similar vein, physical environments at work, for adults, often include materials, objects, tools, and equipment not used at home or in other environmental settings.

For Japanese youngsters, the Suzuki method deliberately creates continuous links between different environmental settings (home and music school). As part of the program, musical activities (listening to musical recordings, watching the mother play violin) take place at home (Gardner, 1983). Later, the program devises a link between the settings in the form of a group lesson in which the mother participates, as well as other children of different ages, their mothers, and the teacher. In this way, the child is gradually introduced to the new environmental setting, its activities (exercises and performances), physical environment (musical tools), and social environment (teacher and other students). However, as we will discuss later, rarely are such deliberate links made between environmental settings. The change in environments, therefore, may cause discontinuities in interactions across domains, and in this way may often have implications for the individual's second-order MI.

A second factor in the dynamic nature of individual–environment relationships refers to the interactions themselves. A person can have different interactions with different people. As social constellations change, the individual's social interactions may change as well. This holds at the macro level – with a change in the person's social environments – as well as at the micro level – during an interactive event, with reconfigurations of the social group. When people join in or drop out of an interacting group, the nature of the interaction often changes. By the same token, whether on a professional level or among children, when the individual's relative expertise or status changes, for better or for worse, her interactions with the environment often change too.

With the ongoing change in environments over time, and the increasing domain-specificity of these environments, the nature of the individual's interactions in regard to different domains necessarily changes as well. As the example of the young violinists indicates, the interrelations among the environments and their interactions with the individual play a major role in the development of the individual's abilities in different domains.

We attribute considerable importance to convergence – or, when lacking, to incongruence – of the effects of the individual–environment relationship on the individual's development. There are diverse aspects in the individual–environment relationship: types of interactions with the environments, environments' value systems, domains in which interactions with the different environments evolve, and the way all these match with children's MI-generic and MI-special proclivities. Convergence, or coincidence, of these aspects can be of extreme importance for understanding the nature of the individual's abilities in different domains.

Coincidence between first- and second-order MI

Feldman uses the term "coincidence" to indicate "the melding of many sets of forces that interact in the development and expression of human potential" (Feldman, 1986, p. 11). Similarly, we highlight the importance of coincidence of factors influencing the development of any individual within particular domains of ability. Specifically, we focus on compatibility between the individual's initial proclivities – her first-order MI – and the combined second-order MI effect of her interactions with her environments.

Coincidence between first- and second-order MI creates favorable conditions that accelerate the child's progress in the corresponding domains. Such was the case with Billy and with Randy, whose home environments cherished and promoted their MI-special abilities. For young violinists, the Suzuki method laboriously devises "planned coincidence": music is introduced to their home environment from an early age. The mother plays violin to arouse the child's interest, and when the child starts taking violin lessons, his mother practices and plays violin with him at home during the week (Gardner, 1983). This example illustrates that not only MI-special but also MI-generic abilities may be accelerated through coincidence.

Coincidence between an individual's more potent MI and the individual–environments positive interactions in the corresponding domain can encourage and reinforce the individual's development in that domain. However, due to the diversity of the environments and of their positive and negative interactions with the individual, such a coincidence cannot be taken for granted. Furthermore, because of the dynamic and changing character of the environments and the interactions, even if coincidence occurs at a certain time in the individual's life, it cannot be assumed to prevail throughout his lifetime.

We have seen the effect of coincidence on the development of children's abilities in specific domains. A second-order MI effect contributed to the substance-conservation ability of the Mexican children, born to potter families. This occurred owing to a coincidence between their interactions with the physical environment – having easy access to playing with clay – and with their social environment – their families, the pottery makers. Similarly, the second-order MI effect contributed to higher development of spatial ability (as compared to logical–mathematical ability) of the Aboriginal children. Coincidence has promoted their spatial ability: their experiences in travelling (and related interactions with the physical environment) converged with their social environment's tradition (attributing higher importance to navigation than to measurement, size, and quantity), and coincided with their interactions with the social environment (using a language with no number and measurement concepts).

Coincidence can be reinforced by diversity of collaborative interactions, as the example of the young Japanese violinists demonstrates. Not only did these youngsters have "planned coincidence" with their MI-generic musical ability, but the Suzuki method also arranged for them to have various types of collaborative interactions with partners of different levels of expertise. The mother had to develop expertise in the domain, to play (or even learn to play) violin (Gardner, 1983). The child could watch the mother listening to music or playing violin, and later imitate her. The child participated in a group, again receiving a model – his mother's participation, or other children's performances (interactions that are mostly based on Imitation). Later, the interactions became more collaborative: at home, the child was practicing daily together with his mother, though the focus was gradually shifting to him, in a way characteristic of Scaffolding. In class, he was guided or scaffolded by his teacher; during the group lessons he participated in performances of musical pieces in counter-point interactions with peers of different levels of expertise. All these diverse types of collaborations (with partners of various degrees of expertise) combined to enrich and promote the child's development in the music domain.

Just as coincidence of favorable conditions can promote the development of various abilities, coincidence of unfavorable conditions can inhibit or repress children's growth and development. Goldman Segall (1990, 1991), for example, reports on Andrew, a fourth-grade student. Andrew grew up in a low socioeconomic inner-city neighborhood. He lived with his mother, who was very young and had difficulty raising him. Andrew had a talent for creative narrative. Like Randy, his linguistic skills were developed. He had a feeling for drama, good diction, and could use literary sources as a starting point for his creations. Andrew was craving for recognition, which he created in his imaginary stories but did not get from his environments. Andrew rarely had positive interactions in his domain of ability with his mother, teacher, or classmates. He was thought of by his mother as not being credible because he tended to make up stories. He was often punished for long periods, kept away from his friends and from other activities. Andrew's ability was not appreciated at school either: his narrative was considered as telling lies rather than inventing stories. Though his teacher admitted that he was talented, the teacher said his writing skills and his behavior did not fit the norm. Andrew saw himself as bad, even believed it was good to be bad. A different environment might have encouraged Andrew's abilities and funnelled it to creative writing or story telling, helping him distinguish between reality and imagination, and valuing his abilities in the latter. However, Andrew's actual environment reproached and rejected him and his talent. His mother could not handle him; he moved to a foster home. Ultimately he was suspended from school.

Randy and Andrew both had strong creative narrative and linguistic abilities. Yet while for Randy his abilities coincided with positive interactions with his environment, for Andrew there was no such coincidence. While Randy's environment was acknowledging, supporting, and promoting his skill, Andrew's environments were reprimanding him for it. While Randy's parents supplied enriching physical and symbolic environments, Andrew's impoverished environment was further restricted by punishment. While Randy's self image was of being unique, Andrew's was of being bad. While Randy exhibited and developed his talent, Andrew tried to cover it up, pretending he was just telling the truth.

Even when the initial environmental setting of a child acknowledges and promotes his stronger ability, such a coincidence may wither when his environments change, as Randy's case demonstrates. With his parents' feedback, appreciation, and support, Randy developed a deep feeling of uniqueness and specialty. However, at school, it became harder for him to maintain this feeling. A friend of his wrote a poem, an event that shocked Randy; his teachers did not consider him unique, since his mathematical and scientific abilities were not extraordinary. Moreover, as we have seen, the patterns of interaction available to Randy did not satisfy him as he was growing up; by then he was looking for collaborative interactions with his friends. The domain of writing, though, did not lend itself easily to such interactions, as other domains might have done. At the age of eight, Randy started developing interest in music, a domain that gave him intensive opportunities for collaboration with his peers. The new interest pulled Randy away from writing, from his uniqueness, and – at least temporarily – toward the ordinary (Feldman, 1986).

Coincidence includes the types of interactions sought by a person. Randy was seeking collaborative interactions with his peers; yet, this is not always the case. Some of the subjects who participated in the exploration of the robots expressed their feelings that interactions with their peers were not enough. These subjects would have liked to have scaffolding or guiding interactions with partners more expert than themselves. The types of interactions that an individual prefers form part of the coincidence between his first- and second-order MI. These preferences may reflect an individual profile, with different varieties of interpersonal intelligence. Preferred types of interaction may also differ across domains, depending on the individual's level of expertise in a domain, the partners for interaction in the domain, type of activities, materials, and so on.

Coincidence between a child's first- and the second-order MI effects in all of her environments means a convergence of many conditions: support and encouragement of the home environment, school environment, peers, and other environmental settings; access to enriched positive interactions with the physical and symbolic aspects of the domain; and dedication of time, effort, and energy by the child in that domain. When coincidence occurs, the child's abilities can develop and flourish. But a lack of such coincidence can have a critical effect on the child's abilities, pulling them toward the unremarkable.

Lack of coincidence and pull toward the average

We have highlighted the importance of the environments in affecting the development of the individual's intelligences. Scarr and McCartney (1983) review supportive findings, indicating that extreme environments, which provide unusual enrichments or deprivations, alter the developmental level of children. These findings show that adopted children profit from their enriched environments and score higher on IQ tests than their biological parents, even though their scores still correlate with those of their biological parents. Conversely, deprived environments have adverse effects on many aspects of development. These environments, according to Scarr and McCartney, are very extreme and outside of the normal range of rearing environments.

However, we suggest that the effect of environments may be more pronounced and occur in less extreme cases with reference to abilities in a specific domain (special MI-generic talents) rather than conventional IQ scores and general intellectual abilities. Almost no environment, within the normal range, deprives children of education and opportunities across the board. Yet, certain special abilities of children in specific domains remain unrecognized all too often. For example, Project Spectrum of Harvard Project Zero identified eight students (out of seventeen) who had outstanding abilities in various domains, though these strengths were recognized neither by their parents nor by their teachers (Krechevsky & Gardner, 1990). Although not deprived of general education, these children had specific abilities that did not get environmental support and encouragement. At the Key School in Indianapolis (Gardner, 1991), where children are deliberately exposed to a "diet" of experiences for each of the intelligences, parents and teachers are often surprised by the range of gifts that surfaces. If these findings are representative of the larger population (and there is no apparent reason to assume otherwise), it seems that normal environments may often fail to recognize children's special abilities.

What happens after childhood? Scarr and McCartney, for example, maintain that throughout development the effect of the environment weakens, and the influence of genetic proclivities becomes more prominent. A young child is passive in the choice of her environments – these are chosen by her caregivers. But as years go by and the child becomes an active chooser of her environments, she matches these environments to her proclivities. However, we suggest that when abilities are examined within domains this may not be the case. The range of possibilities at a later age is already limited by previous experiences. By the age a person can choose his environments, it may be too late to cultivate dormant abilities in undeveloped domains. For example, when his parents cannot afford a musical instrument or music lessons, that choice is not available for the young child. Even in the rare cases when school offers such instruction and has musical instruments available for practice, the child may have to compete with other skilled and proficient students. He may be intimidated by the competence of others, discouraged from taking the first hard steps to develop competence in the domain, or not be chosen for the activity altogether. As an adult, when he might be able to afford the expenditure, he may be an amateur or a fan listener. Development of many skills, like dance, sports, writing, or sciences, rarely can start at an advanced age. While the environments are chosen by the adult himself and not by others, as Scarr and McCartney claim, this choice may come too late in life to change the individual's development in domains of ability.

We suggest that in a focus on the individual's multiple intelligences and on each domain separately, the coincidence of the influencing factors is crucial. When coincidence is lacking, and favorable conditions for developing innate abilities do not prevail, strong intelligences may be hampered, drawing individuals' intelligences toward the average. Even in the case of a child prodigy like Randy, the changing environments could divert his focus away from his domain of MI-special ability. When coincidence is lacking, and favorable conditions for developing innate abilities do not prevail, strong intelligences may be hampered, drawing individuals' intelligences toward the average. The individual's abilities do not develop in domains to which the individual didn't have access in his interactions with his environments, as the example of the robot-explorers demonstrates. Moreover, rarely can individuals overcome unfavorable conditions and develop high innate potential when not even a single person, in any of their environments, supports and encourages them, as was the case for Andrew. On the other hand, when the effect of interactions within several environmental settings coincide, as the cases of the Mexican, Aboriginal, and Japanese children indicate, many youngsters within that environment exhibit higher abilities in the related domain than their peers who lack that coincidence. The more the environmental settings converge in supporting specific abilities, the greater the chances of these abilities to grow, flourish, and bear exceptional fruits.

Summary and conclusions

The nature of human abilities and the ways they develop has stimulated informed discussions for generations, and probably will continue to do so. In this chapter, we adduce arguments in favor of a multiple view of human abilities and of the forces that join for promoting them. We maintain that the individual has diverse intelligences that are not necessarily equal across domains. MI-generic or MI-specific abilities of a person, her innate first-order multiple intelligences, continue to develop through interactions with her environments, interactions that form a second-order MI effect. Our multiple view applies also to the ongoing process of development. In our view, both the individual's environments and the interactions with these environments are diverse and dynamic, and affect the individual in a way that is domain-specific. We highlight the importance of coincidence, or convergence, among these environmental and interactional attributes, which affect first- and second-order MI of the individual. This coincidence, or the lack of it, can explain the individual's pattern of development in different domains of abilities.

Paraphrasing Boring (1923), who said intelligence is what intelligence tests measure, we say: intelligence is what the individual's environments promote through interactions which engage the individual's potential abilities, her first-order MI. Throughout the chapter, various examples reviewed prodigies' high MI-specific abilities, strong MI-generic abilities of children within the normal range, and, in contrast, adults' abilities in unfamiliar contexts with which and within which they had no previous interactions. We have demonstrated that in the children's cases, when their abilities in a certain domain are promoted by their environments, their abilities in that domain develop at an accelerated pace relative to other children who lack that environmental support. On the other hand, even highly competent adults who lacked previous interactions and environmental support within a specific domain did not develop (in that domain) knowledge structures that would have been expected according to other theories. All these examples indicate the importance of interactions with the environments in specific domains for the evolution of knowledge structures across ages.

The meager results obtained so often in our educational systems provoke a question: when we say that the individual's abilities are promoted by interaction with the environment, what do we mean by "promote"? Is this not what conventional educational systems attempt to do? The previous discussion sheds some light on the quality of a successful "promotion." In the examples we have reviewed of child prodigies and the cultural "whiz kid," domain-related interactions in various environmental settings coincide, and, above all, coincide with the children's home environments. Their environmental settings are interrelated, and a meaningful context in one environmental setting is also valued in the other. Moreover, the Mexican children, born to pottery-making families, Aboriginal children who travel with their families often, and Japanese violinists who get lessons in groups that include their mothers and other children of different ages and levels of expertise, all have diverse interactions in domains in which their special abilities develop. They all interact with expert adults, as well as with other children and other adults of different levels of expertise. They all have different kinds of interactions, as real life, in contrast to school, usually affords. All these enable the development of remarkable domain-specific abilities. On the other hand, a lack of coincidence, as the example of the adult robot-explorers indicates, can have a detrimental effect on the development of the corresponding domain-specific abilities.

In this respect, to what extent do the experiences our children get at school coincide with their home experiences? How rich are the interactive opportunities provided by the classroom environment? Children at school are usually isolated in groups of similar ages, their interactive opportunities are constrained and limited, and, in some domains, their experiences are extremely shallow. We have cited findings indicating that children's abilities often remain unidentified by their parents and their teachers. Our schools focus on logical–mathematical and linguistic abilities, and may well miss other abilities of children. On the other hand, even the interactions offered by school to children whose strength is in the logical–mathematical or linguistic domains are often not enough to fully promote these abilities – not enough in their intensity, richness, diversity, flexibility, and relations to other aspects in the children's lives.

After the industrial revolution, a hidden curriculum of school systems fostered discipline – punctuality, obedience, and rote, repetitive work (Toffler, 1980). What should be the hidden curriculum of our educational systems today? We propose a focus that yields creative and self-fulfilled individuals. To raise such individuals, society has to be more attentive to their special abilities in different domains, and to give them opportunities for interactions that promote these abilities. Perhaps the examples of Mexican pottery makers, nomadic Aborigines, Suzuki-educated violinists, and several child prodigies, compared with examples of competent adults who did not have previous relevant opportunities, can give us clues about how to reform education in order to achieve this goal.

References

Anastasi, A. (1958). Heredity, environment, and the question "how"? *Psychological Review, 65*(4), 197–208.

Bandura, A. (1977). *Social learning theory.* Englewood Cliffs, NJ: Prentice Hall.

Bandura, A. (1986). *Social foundations of thought and action: A social cognitive theory.* Englewood Cliffs, NJ: Prentice Hall.

Boring, E. G. (1923). Intelligence as the tests test it. *The New Republic, 6,* June, 35–37.

Bronfenbrenner, U. (1979). *The ecology of human development.* Cambridge, MA: Harvard University Press.

Brown, A. L., Kane, M. J., & Echols, C. H. (1986). Young children's mental models determine analogical transfer across problems with a common goal structure. *Cognitive Development, 1,* 103–121.

Bruner, J. S. (1966). On cognitive growth, In J. S. Bruner, R. R. Oliver, & P. M. Greenfield (Eds.), *Studies in cognitive growth.* New York: Wiley.

Cole, M. & Griffin, P. (1980). Cultural amplifiers reconsidered. In D. Olson (Ed.), *Social foundations of language and thought.* New York: W. W. Norton.

Dasen, P. R. (1974). The influence of ecology, culture, and European contact on cognitive development in Australian Aborigines, In J. W. Berry & P. R. Dasen, *Culture and cognition: Readings in cross-cultural psychology.* London: Methuen.

Doise, W. & Mugny, G. (1984). *The social development of the intellect.* Oxford: Pergamon Press.

Doise, W. & Palmonari, A. (Eds.) (1984). *Social interaction in individual development.* Cambridge: Cambridge University Press.

Donaldson, M. (1978). *Children's minds.* New York: Norton.

Feldman, D. H. (1986). *Nature's gambit: Child prodigies and the development of human potential.* New York: Basic Books.

Fischer, K. W. (1980). A theory of cognitive development: The control and construction of hierarchies of skills. *Psychological Review, 87*(6), 477–531.

Forman, E. A. (1987). Learning through peer instruction: A Vygotskian perspective. *The Genetic Epistemologist, XV*(2), 6–15.

Forman, E. A. & Cazden, C. B. (1985). Exploring Vygorskian perspectives in education: The cognitive value of peer interaction. In J. V. Wertsch (Ed.), *Culture, communication and cognition: Vygotskian perspective.* Cambridge: Cambridge University Press.

Gardner, H. (1979). Developmental psychology after Piaget: An approach in terms of symbolization. *Human Development, 22,* 73–88.

Gardner, H. (1983). *Frames of mind: The theory of Multiple Intelligences.* New York: Basic Books.

Gardner, H. (1991). *The unschooled mind.* New York: Basic Books.

Gardner, H. (1993). *Creating Minds.* New York: Basic Books.

Gardner, H. & Hatch, T. (1989). Multiple intelligences go to school. *Educational Researcher, 18*(8), 4–10.

Gardner, H. & Wolf, D. (1983). Waves and streams of symbolization: Notes on the development of symbolic capacities in young children. In D. R. Rogers & J. A. Sloboda (Eds.), *The acquisition of symbolic skills.* London: Plenum Press.

Gelman, R. (1972). Logical capacity of very young children: Number invariance rules. *Child Development, 43,* 75–90.

Gelman, R. & Greeno, J. G. (1989). The nature of competence: Principles for understanding in a domain. In L. B. Resnick (Ed.), *Knowing, learning, and instruction: Essays in honor of Robert Glaser.* Hillsdale, NJ: Erlbaum.

Gelman, R. & Spelke, E. (1981). The development of thoughts about animate and inanimate objects: implications for research on social cognition. In J. H. Flavell & L. Ross (Eds.), *Social cognitive development: frontiers and possible futures.* Cambridge: Cambridge University Press.

Glick, J. (1985). Culture and cognition revisited. In E. D. Neimark, R. De Lisi, & J. L. Newman (Eds.), *Moderators of competence.* Hillsdale, NJ: Erlbaum.

Goldman Segall, R. (1990). *Learning Constellations: A multimedia ethnographic research environment using video technology for exploring children's thinking.* Unpublished doctoral dissertation, Massachusetts Institute of Technology, Cambridge, MA.

Goldman Segall, R. (1991). Three children, three styles: A call for opening the curriculum. In I. Harel & S. Papert (Eds.), *Constructionism.* Norwood, NJ: Ablex.

Goodnow, J. J. (1990). The socialization of cognition: What's involved? In J. W. Stigler, R. A. Shweder, & G. Herdt, *Cultural psychology: Essays on comparative human development.* Cambridge: Cambridge University Press.

Granott, N. (1991a). Puzzled minds and weird creatures: Phases in the spontaneous process of knowledge construction. In I. Harel & S. Papert (Eds.), *Constructionism.* Norwood, NJ: Ablex.

Granott, N. (1991b). *From macro to micro and back: On the analysis of microdevelopment.* Paper presented at the 21 Annual Symposium of the Jean Piaget Society, Philadelphia, PA.

Granott, N. (1993). Patterns of interaction in the co-construction of knowledge: Separate minds, joint effort, and weird creatures. In R. Wozniak & K. W. Fischer (Eds.), *Development in context: Acting and thinking in specific environment.* The Jean Piaget Society Developmental Series, Vol. 2. Hillsdale, NJ: Erlbaum.

Hatch, T. & Gardner, H. (1990). If Binet had looked beyond the classroom: The assessment of multiple intelligences. *International Journal of Educational Research, 14,* 415–430.

Heath, S. B. (1983). *Ways with words: Language, life, and work in communities and classrooms.* Cambridge: Cambridge University Press.

Hebb, D. O. (1949). *The organization of behavior: A neuropsychological theory.* New York: Wiley.

Hess, R. D. & Shipman, V. C. (1965). Early experience and the socialization of cognitive modes in children. *Child Development, 36,* 869–886.

Kahneman, D. (1973). *Attention and effort.* Englewood Cliffs, NJ: Prentice Hall.

Kornhaber, M., Krechevsky, M., & Gardner, H. (1990). Engaging intelligence. *Educational Psychologist, 25*(3&4), 177–199.

Krechevsky, M. & Gardner, H. (1990). The emergence and nurturance of multiple intelligences: The Project Spectrum approach. In M. J. A. Howe (Ed.), *Encouraging the development of exceptional skills and talents.* Leicester, England: The British Psychological Society.

Murray, F. B. (1972). Acquisition of conservation through social interaction. *Developmental Psychology, 6*(1), 1–6.

Murray, F. B. (1983). Learning and development through social interaction and conflict: A challenge to social learning theory. In L. S. Liben (Ed.), *Piaget and the foundations of knowledge.* Hillsdale, NJ: Erlbaum.

Newell, A. & Simon, H. A. (1972). *Human problem solving.* Englewood Cliffs, NJ: Prentice Hall.

Newman, D., Griffin, P., & Cole, M. (1989). *The construction zone: Working for cognitive change in school.* Cambridge: Cambridge University Press.

Perret-Clermont, A. N. (1980). *Social interaction and cognitive development in children.* London: Academic Press.

Piaget, J. (1926). *The language and thought of the child.* New York: Harcourt, Brace.

Piaget, J. (1965). *The moral judgment of the child.* New York: Free Press.

Plomin, R., DeFries, J. C., & Loehlin, J. C. (1977). Genotype–environment interaction and correlation in the analysis of human behavior. *Psychological Bulletin, 84*(2), 309–322.

Price-Williams, D., Gordon, W., & Ramirez, M. (1969). Skill and conservation: A study of pottery-making children. *Developmental Psychology, 1*(6), 769.

Rogoff, B. (1990). *Apprenticeship in thinking: Cognitive development in social context.* New York: Oxford University Press.

Rogoff, B., Malkin, C., & Gilbride, K. (1984). Interaction with babies as guidance in development. In B. Rogoff & J. V. Wertsch (Eds.), *Children's learning in the "zone of proximal development." New Directions For Child Development, 23.* San Francisco: Jossey-Bass.

Salomon, G. & Perkins, D. N. (1989). Rocky roads to transfer: Rethinking mechanisms of a neglected phenomenon. *Educational Psychologist, 24*(2), 113–142.

Saxe, G. B., Guberman, S. R., & Gearhart, M. (1987). Social Processes in early number development. *Monographs of the Society for Research in Child Development, 216,* vol. 52 (2).

Scarr, S. & McCartney, K. (1983). How people make their own environments: A theory of genotype-environment effects. *Child Development, 54,* 424–435.

Shweder, R. A. (1990). Culture psychology – what is it? In J. W. Stigler, R. A. Shweder, & G. Herdt, *Cultural psychology: Essays on comparative human development.* Cambridge: Cambridge University Press.

Toffler, A. (1980). *The third wave.* New York: Bantam Books.

Valsiner, J. (1984). Construction of the Zone of Proximal Development in adult–child joint action: The socialization of meals. In Rogoff, B. & Wertsch, J. V. (Eds.), *Children's learning in the "Zone of Proximal Development"* (pp. 65–76). San Francisco: Jossey-Bass.

Vygotsky, L. S. (1962). *Thought and language.* Cambridge, MA: The MIT Press.

Vygotsky, L. S. (1978). *Mind in society: The development of higher psychological processes.* Cambridge, MA: Harvard University Press.

Wertsch, J. V. (1979). From social interaction to higher psychological processes: A clarification and application of Vygotsky's theory. *Human Development, 22,* 1–22.

Wertsch, J. V., McNamee, G. D., McLane, J. B., & Budwig, N. A. (1980). The adult–child dyad as a problem-solving system. *Child Development, 51,* 1215–1221.

Wertsch, J. V., Minick, N. & Arns, F. J. (1984). The creation of context in joint problem-solving. In B. Rogoff & J. Lave *Everyday cognition: Its development in social context.* Cambridge, MA: Harvard University Press.

Wertsch, J. V. & Stone, C. A. (1978). Microgenesis as a tool for developmental analysis. *The Quarterly Newsletter of the Laboratory of Comparative Human Cognition, 1*(1).

White, S. H. & Siegel, A. W. (1984). Cognitive development in time and space. In B. Rogoff & J. Lave *Everyday cognition: Its development in social context.* Cambridge, MA: Harvard University Press.

8   From intelligence to knowledge construction: a sociogenetic process approach

Jaan Valsiner and Man-Chi Leung

Can we ever make sense of intelligence? That question reflects an inherent meta-theoretical focus that is appropriate to apply to the majority of concepts derived from common language and turned into psychologists' scientific terms. Many of them seem to have a long-lasting appeal to psychologists and to the lay public, yet the popularity of psychological terms does not clarify their meaning (oftentimes it makes those meanings even more fuzzy than before). Nor does that popularity help to discover novel facets of the phenomena – the repetition of the same empirical procedures may preconstruct a view of the phenomena that is consequently agreeable, and still only scratch the tip of the iceberg of the complexity of the real world.

No matter how viewed (except for the adamant application of denial mechanisms at this point), psychology in the 1990s continues to be in a conceptual crisis that has hampered it all through its independent existence. This crisis seems to be wrought by the dominance of an empiricist belief system without careful and constructive theoretical analysis proceeding interconnectedly with the empirical work. The concept of intelligence, and its uses in psychology, constitute the best illustration of the combination of the discipline's hyperactive empirical enterprise with limited theoretical elaborations. Research on intelligence has dutifully followed the common language meanings of the term in some languages rather than others (Keats, 1992; Keats & Fu-Xi, 1989), and theoretical efforts to conceptualize intelligence have at times accepted fully tautological arguments (e.g., "intelligence is what intelligence tests measure").

Fortunately, in recent decades, efforts to reconceptualize intelligence have been prominent. The reality of context-dependency of all psychological phenomena has become recognized (see Fry, 1984), the concept of intelligence has been put into a wider theoretical network (Sternberg, 1985), and there is increasing interest in the study of psychological phenomena as processes [rather than as static states, or traits (Csikszentmihalyi, 1985; Winegar, 1989)]. This complex change in psychology's rhetoric is largely due to the advent of the "cognitive revolution," which, irrespective of some theoretically detrimental "side effects" (Valsiner, 1991a), has released the thinking of psychologists from the previous constraints of behavioristic orthodoxy.

Our goal in the present chapter is to present a perspective on intelligence that

202

transcends the limitations of the common linguistic meanings of that term. In order to accomplish that goal, we will chart out the metatheoretical assumptions that have been taken for granted by most researchers of intelligence. We will then proceed to emphasize the perspective on intelligence that examines the process nature of a person's relating to his or her structured environmental context. This perspective turns our understanding of intelligence around in a way that mismatches the usual internal attribution of the trait, implied in most of the intelligence research of the past (Valsiner, 1984). Finally, we emphasize the sociogenetic nature of human intelligence – the relatedness of the person–environment relationship with the social suggestions emanating from "social others."

The puzzle of "intelligence": why is it a fuzzy concept

Intelligence, like many other concepts in psychology, is not well defined. Psychologists have not reached a consensus on what intelligence is. Most empirical studies of intelligence in psychology usually rely on common-sense meanings of the term in the background cultures of psychologists. The closeness of psychology's notion of intelligence to the common language meanings allows for interesting feedback from psychology to the thinking of the lay public. For instance, the IQ score (which is a highly technical concept) is widely accepted by the society as an indicator of how intelligent a person is, and as a predictor of how successful a person will be in school or in a job.

The closeness of the psychology of intelligence and laypersons' discourse about evaluative comparisons of people in a competitive way creates a complicated confounding between psychology and social life. Laypersons' discourse becomes encoded in psychologists' discourse (i.e., judgments about whether John is more intelligent than Ramses, become translated into the technical language of "what *is* John's IQ and *how much* does it differ from Ramses'?"). The latter technical discourse provides a legitimate-looking halo for the common-sense applications of the technology of psychometrics. In the history of psychometric testing, the practical needs of some strata of society have been framing the technical questions, discourse, and application efforts of the scientists (see Gigerenzer et al., 1989). Surely the relationship between society's socially constructed needs and psychologists' conceptualizations need not remain one of mutual complementarity (Valsiner, 1985, 1992).

Among different approaches to intelligence, the psychometric approach may be the one that is most well known and have the strongest influences on laypersons. Popular use of standard IQ tests may be one reason for the acceptance of this approach by the society. This use can be traced back to the appropriation of psychology as a discipline of applied value by social institutions during World War I, and in the decades following that. In this respect, the prominence of the psychometric approach to intelligence is a result of a social construction process, which has been noted to dominate psychology in many ways (see Danziger, 1990; Gigerenzer et al., 1989). An additional reason may be that the concept of intelligence in this approach is easy to understand. The emphasis upon quantitative evaluative comparisons in European and North American societies has guided the thinking of individual laypersons over recent centuries, as has the consensually validated belief in the exactness and solidity of quantified "facts" (Cohen, 1982; Swetz, 1987). It is therefore not very surprising that the psychometric world view that emerged from the "social physics" of Quetelet and eugenics of Galton and Pearson, has proliferated in the social sciences of the twentieth century.

However, neither the ease of understanding a concept at the level of common sense, nor the popularity of its social-institutional application, can serve as a valid criterion for the adequacy of a concept as a scientific tool. A careful investigation of the metatheoretical sphere of the concepts themselves, and their relations to the phenomena of targeted reality, is in order.

Metatheoretical issues of the psychometric approach

According to the psychometric standpoint, intelligence is considered a trait or a set of traits, just like other personality characteristics such as sociability or extroversion. The IQ score is the measure of the extent of this trait or set of traits in a person. This trait is usually considered as stable over time and across situations. Intelligence can be subdivided into two types of abilities: fluid and crystallized abilities (Cattell, 1963). Fluid intelligence refers to some basic cognitive capacities, such as the size of memory span and the ability of spatial perception, that are mainly biologically determined. Crystallized intelligence refers to abilities that are more dependent on cultural context and experience and are based in the domain of verbally encoded phenomena. Verbal comprehension and social skills are good examples of crystallized intelligence.

There are two main assumptions behind the psychometric concept of intelligence. First, intelligence is assumed to be context-free. This assumption carries over to psychologists' views of subjects' test-taking conduct. It allows the psychologists to set up specific settings for the purposes of the "measurement" of "intelligence." The context in which an IQ test is taken is very different from the contexts of solving many different problems in our daily life. A person who takes an IQ test is usually required to solve some problems as quickly as possible. For instance, he/she may be asked to arrange a set of blocks to form a specified pattern, or to translate a set of symbols into another set of symbols. Whatever the specific task, the assumption is being made that one is motivated to maximize one's performance. This assumption is evident in the specific tricks that are devised to verify that a particular subject might have deviated from the goal of maximization; but the phenomenon of how subjects relate to the testing situation (i.e., the issue of "metacontract" between subject and investigator; see Rommetveit, 1979) remains out of consideration. Scores on standard IQ tests could be used to predict intellectual performance in daily life only when the differences in contexts are ignored.

Second, the interindividual frame of reference (see Valsiner, 1987, 1989) is used in the psychometric approach, although the term "intelligence" itself would warrant the use of an intraindividual reference frame. The original (context-freed and commonsensical) notion of "intelligence" as a "property" of the individual person (i.e., set within an intraindividual reference frame) is almost automatically translated into a question of comparison with the measurements obtained from other persons (i.e., the interindividual reference frame). A child is considered as intelligent because he/she scores higher than most other children of the same age. This shift in frames of reference is of course endemic in psychology far beyond the issue of research on intelligence.

The implicit metalevel guidance of psychologists' thinking about intelligence by their social values is at its peak when discourse on "fairness" of tests is at stake. To make "fair comparisons" among people with similar collective-cultural backgrounds, the preferred content domains of the "mainstream" (or any other power-holding) substratum of the given society at the given historical period are used as the substance for intelligence-measurement devices. In this application, "fairness" of a test becomes defined from the point of view of the pre-encoded values of some dominant social power group (or ideology). In reality, the whole psychometric intelligence testing movement has been popular in the history of applied psychology because the test results explain inequalities between persons in scientific jargon. "Fairness" in testing is a good example of the social construction of the metacontract. As such, it is an insoluble problem, which can be discussed but not solved, since its solution is an issue of the sociocultural contexts of the test-makers, rather than the test-takers.

From psychometric to cognitive perspectives on intelligence

There is little new in the perspective of cognitive science if one looks carefully into the history of psychology (Valsiner, 1991). The stark contrast between the "cognitive" and "behavioristic" ideologies in contemporary psychology seems to be a social creation that overlooks the old solid traditions of mental psychology from Wilhelm Wundt to William Stern and Gestalt psychology. For instance, the Gestalt-psychological focus on the reasoning processes of human beings (Wertheimer, 1912; Wundt, 1916) and on problem solving (Duncker, 1945; Wertheimer, 1945) have constituted the foundation of much of contemporary cognitive psychology. Furthermore, the revitalization of the microgenetic approach, after its long history (see Draguns, 1984), demonstrates the historical connection.

The question of human intelligent conduct is no novelty in the history of psychology. The modern cognitive perspectives have a long prehistory in the mental-oriented psychology of late 19th-century Europe (Baldwin, 1906; Bergson, 1911; Janet, 1925; Wundt, 1916). However, the psychologist whose contributions to the understanding of intelligence are probably most important belongs to this century. The life and work of Jean Piaget were dedicated to creating a theory of intelligence along strictly mathematical (but not psychometric) lines.

The contributions of Jean Piaget

Piaget's work is undoubtedly the most mentioned, but least known in modern psychology. It is noteworthy that despite the widespread presentation of his contributions in introductory-level texts, serious investigations of his actual contributions are rare (see Chapman, 1988, Vuyk, 1981).

The main contribution by Piaget to the study of intelligence is the consistent emphasis upon the person–environment interaction in the process of constructing one's knowledge. This focus constitutes an approach within the individual–ecological frame of reference (see Valsiner, 1987, 1989), and is thus (a) incompatible with the psychometric approach, and (b) context-appreciative in its metatheoretical background. Both of these features make Piaget's contributions to the study of intelligence profound.

Piaget's theoretical constructions link the theorizing of his predecessors (Baldwin, Janet, and Bergson) with this century's increasingly empirical preoccupation of psychologists. He linked together very abstract theoretical (and logical–mathematical) concepts on the one hand, and very empirical, reality driven psychological phenomena on the other. This linkage was prominent from the very beginning of his scientific activities to their very end (see Beilin, 1992; Chapman, 1992).

The interactionist perspective Piaget created was well in line with the focus on organism–environment relatedness that was emphasized at the beginning of this century in many disciplines (Lewin, 1917; Stern, 1919; Uexküll, 1928). However, Piaget's main source of creativity was his informant Sébastien, who made him contemplate issues of a person's relations with the world, and to elaborate the notions of striving toward an ideal (but never obtainable) equilibrium (see Chapman, 1992, pp. 40–41). The functionalistic and structuralistic world view of Piaget was of relevance to the development of "cognitive science" in the 1970s (see Minsky, 1982) and continues to provide new insights in developmental psychology.

The information-processing perspective

The information-processing approach emerged in early 1970's and soon became the dominant theoretical perspective in research of human intellectual behavior. The appearance of the information-processing approach provides a new way of looking at human intelligence. It considers the human being as a general-purpose symbol processor that consists of a number of components. Each of them has a specific function. A person maintains his relationship with the external world by getting input from and producing output to the environment. The multistore model of Atkinson and Shiffrin (1971) is the best illustration of this concept.

Lachman, Lachman, and Butterfield (1979) list seven pretheoretical ideas that characterize the information-processing approach. The first one is viewing the person as a symbol manipulator. All human intellectual activities, including perception, memory, learning and using of language, problem solving, knowledge acquisition, imagination, and creation of knowledge, can be reduced to a few basic operations, such as encoding, storing, and retrieval of information. Second, the external world can be represented by symbols within the information-processing system. In the multistore model of Atkinson and Shiffrin (1971), objects and events of the environment are encoded into symbols by the sensory register, passed to other components, and at last decoded to become behavioral responses. Third, information-processing theorists take the systems approach. Different human activities and capacities are interrelated. Their interrelationship must be considered in the study of human intellectual behavior. Fourth, the human being is considered an active information-seeker. He is always searching for useful information from the environment in order to solve problems in a more effective and efficient way. Fifth, it is believed that human beings are endowed with some unique innate capacities, such as the ability to use language, that are important for some cognitive processes. It is believed that some aspects of cognitive functions are exclusive to human beings. Sixth, a stage model is employed. It is assumed that a cognitive process can be divided into a set of processing stages. Finally, the seventh metatheoretical idea of the information-processing approach is the limitation in generalization of theories based on laboratory experiments. The context of the laboratory is different from contexts in our daily life. There is a tendency to study human cognitive processes in their normal contexts. These contexts are "messy" (from the viewpoint of laboratory-oriented scientists – filled with social suggestions, subjects' resistances to research situations, and other real facts of life). Nevertheless, the discussion of intelligence is best fitted into the near-reality framework.

Two process-oriented approaches to "intelligence": from information processing to sociogenetic knowledge construction

It is important to demonstrate both the similarities and differences of our present approach, to the information-processing perspective. We will use the seven parameters which were used above to describe the information-processing approach, to delineate the boundaries of the present perspective.

First, the sociogenetic approach shares the conviction of the information-processing viewpoint that human beings are symbol manipulators. However, if the information-processing approach takes the symbols as givens (and proceeds to look at how these are manipulated), then our approach looks at symbols as constructed entities. Human beings are sign-constructing and sign-using (as well as symbol-abandoning) organisms. This semiotic constructivism is the center of our developmental approach. This fact leads to another relevant feature – the signs that are constructed by active human beings are bounded by the kinds of signs (symbols, icons, and indexes, to use Peirce's classification) that are afforded by the phylogenetic history of the species. This limitation leaves out a whole family of formal symbols (e.g., of the mathematical kind) that can be constructed by human beings, but which cannot be assumed to play a relevant role in the psychological functioning of the constructors themselves.

Second, the world that surrounds the active human being is coded culturally (semiotically), and that cultural structure of the world constitutes the input for symbol-analytic information processing. Here exists both an important similarity to (symbol encoding) and difference from (external semiotically organized world, rather than internal symbol-generating stimulation) the information-processing perspective.

Third, similar to the information-processing view, our approach is a systemic one. We are seeking to conceptualize the sociogenetic (social-developmental) system that leads to the emergence and further differentiation of the intramental psychological functions.

Fourth, not only do we view the person as an information-seeker (as the information-processing approach does), but we also believe that in the seeking process the person actively constructs information. This is an important difference – the information is not pregiven by the world (and searchable by active conduct in some pre-existing knowledge base), but the active organism constructs it in the process of relating to the world.

Fifth, the present approach fully diverges from the information processing perspective in the latter's positing of the existence of "unique innate capacities." The biologically guaranteed body, of course, is not denied. However, in the realm of psychological functions, our focus is on the process of emergence and constructive internalization of novel functions, not on disputes or proofs/disproofs of their ontological status at any recent time.

Sixth, the present perspective accepts the reasonableness of stage accounts (be they microgenetic, ontogenetic, or phylogenetic), but does not consider the description of stage sequences per se to be equal to the explanation of development. Stages merely constitute a period of relative stability (or "steady states") in between developmental progressions, and thus their ontological reality is relevant only as a set of relatively stable "anchor points" for the actual investigation of those progressions.

Finally, we do not want to denigrate the relevance of the laboratory as one version of the human socioecological niche (Valsiner and Benigni, 1986). Certainly, some psychological phenomena can be observed only under careful laboratory conditions, while others can never be triggered under such conditions. The controversy between proponents of "laboratory" and "real-world" cognitive studies constitutes a displacement of the issue of the generality of our theoretical constructs to the special question of differences in subjects' performance within different contexts. If our general theoretical systems were sufficiently rigorous (see Valsiner, 1991b for theory–data–phenomena relations), the very realistic differences in performance across different contexts would be explainable.

Towards a sociogenetic and teleophilic view of intelligence

As can be seen, the perspective outlined in this chapter differs both from the psychometric perspective and that of the "information-processing" approach. Intelligence is a process in which a person interacts with the environment with a future goal orientation, even if all the interaction with the environment takes place in the present. In this respect, our perspective could be called teleophilic, in contrast with the usually better known teleonomic viewpoint. The future goals are not real, as those goals can only be psychologically constructed prereflections of the future that belong to the present. The goals may make up an ill-defined multitude (or an undifferentiated structure) of possible future states, and yet they can provide direction for the person's actions in the here-and-now. In order to act, the person has to "flirt" with the constructed future goals – hence the appropriateness of the teleophilic label (over teleonomic). The teleophilic nature of human psychological functioning is at the same time teleogenetic – in constructing its goal orientations.

Intelligent conduct is context-bound. Our actions are constrained within a context, both by our goal-related selfconstraint and by the limits inherent in the structured context in which we live. Both these external contexts and the intrapsychological constraint systems share a sociogenetic origin, as their personal history is linked with past socially organized personal experiences. These personal experiences vary within a wide margin, which makes comparisons of intelligent conduct between different (extrinsically defined) "contexts" an almost futile enterprise. For example, if you are taking a test in the format of multiple-choice questions, your behavior is limited to choosing one of the N options. You are not allowed to write down the correct answer on the paper or to give a verbal response. Likewise, persons who take IQ tests are fully dependent on the constraints (item format, requirements for speedy responses, etc.) of the context, specified by the particular nature of the test. This structure of the specific context of "intelligence measurement" is surely but an extreme setting where we set our mental functions to work. When we face a problem in daily life, the context of that problem would put a different set of constraints on our behavior. Neither the "test setting" nor any "real-life" constraining condition is a "true" representation of the person's intellectual functioning; rather, it is the preadaptation by the person of a selfconstraining structure when moving from one situation to another that comes closer to the phenomena of intelligence that are worth further scrutiny. In human lives, problems are usually ill-defined (Simon, 1957) and affect-linked (Toda, 1980).

As active (and acting) persons, we also are involved in a constant selfconstraining process, utilizing our internally reconstructed and unique personal–cultural world to reduce the uncertainties inherent in our action contexts. The meaning/sense system that semiotically limits the range within which we try to construct solutions to our everyday life problems organizes our relationships with any context in which we may happen to be in a given moment.

The individual–socioecological frame of reference

In contrast with the use of an interindividual reference frame that is the dominant metatheoretical basis for the psychometric approach, and the mixture of intraindividual and individual–ecological perspectives (which are characteristic of the information-processing viewpoint), we base our reconceptualization of intelligence upon the individual–socioecological reference frame (see Valsiner, 1987, 1989). This frame of reference has been implicitly present in many sociogenetic viewpoints in developmental psychology (Valsiner & Van der Veer, 1988). It has become more widely (albeit implicitly) recognized recently in conjunction with interest in the work of Vygotsky (Van der Veer & Valsiner, 1991). In Vygotsky's theoretical framework, a psychological function (e.g., the set of processes subsumed under the label of "intelligence") of a person is best studied at the intersection of the intrapersonal (mental–affective) and interpersonal worlds of human beings. The former entails active and constructive internalization (internal reconstruction of novelty – Lawrence & Valsiner, 1993) based on the latter.

Vygotsky's sociogenetic perspective comes closest to the issues of intelligence in relation to his notion of the "zone of proximal development" (ZPD), which was introduced into his work in contrast to the traditional psychometric intelligence testing (see Van der Veer & Valsiner, 1991, chapter 13; Valsiner & Van der Veer, 1993). Through the concept of the ZPD, Vygotsky has introduced a developmental frame of reference to the study of intelligence. It is not, therefore, surprising that Vygotsky's contribution to general psychology is being first rediscovered by developmental psychologists (Rogoff & Wertsch, 1984), rather than by investigators of intelligence who follow a nondevelopmental tradition in their research.

The implementation of the individual–socioecological reference frame in the research practice of psychologists is complicated, since it implies a parallel look at the subjects' adaptation to study contexts, and a similar adaptation on behalf of the investigators. This difficulty is linked with person–environment interdependence.

Interdependence of person and environment

Another important theoretical axiom in our model is the relationship between the person and the environment. A person's actions always take place within some environmental context that is structured in some way. The structured nature of the environment of the acting person is conceptualized in terms of constraints on the person's acting and thinking. Both the physical nature of the environment and its cultural organization (as it is constructed by active human beings, including the individual person), codetermine the structure of constraints that the environment provides for the person. Thus the structure of constraints of the environment is not equivalent to the physical limits the environment prescribes. It is likewise, and simultaneously, organized by the cultural norms and meanings that human beings have constructed in their transaction with the environment. In this regard, all environments of human beings are cultural, since cultural norms and meanings regulate persons' transaction with every aspect of the physical environment. Intelligence is the process by which people actively adapt to, shape, and select the environment. The processes of adaptation to, shaping of, and selection of the environment are anchored within the structured nature of the environment. While adapting to the environment, the person accepts the environment in its present organization. While shaping the environment, he is trying to change the present organization into a new one. While selecting an environment, he is constrained by the availability of different environments for him to select, and by the conditions that limit the person's movement from one environment to another.

As we have shown, the traditional psychometric approach conceptualizes intelligence as a trait of a person (but measures it on the basis of interindividual contrasts). The interindividual frame of reference is used and intellectual behavior is considered as context free. Differently from that perspective, we conceptualize intelligence as a process. In this orientation we build upon Piaget's organizational theoretical perspective, adding to it the notion of social canalization of personal experiences. The individual–socioecological frame of reference is used and intellectual behavior is context-bound. It should be noted that our model shares some similar features with the information-processing approach in the sense that both models consider intelligence as a process rather than as a trait, but differs from it by the consistent use of the individual-socioecological perspective on knowledge construction.

The knowledge construction process

Let us try to make our structuralist and developmental perspective on knowledge construction explicit. The roots of this effort go back to the disequilibration/equilibration processes that Piaget tried to conceptualize from his structuralist and developmental point of view (see Piaget, 1971, pp. 147–185).

Table 8.1 constitutes a formal representation of our model of knowledge transformation. The main idea is that transformation of the knowledge structure is constrained, but not determined by the person–environment relationship. A number of features of this model should be emphasized. First, for any environmental input, there is always more than one possible change, dependent upon the state of the organism. Thus, transformation of knowledge is not determined by the environment. For instance, given that the environmental input is A, the knowledge may have no change, or change to X, or Y, or a novel state "?," which is unpredictable. If the environmental input is D, then the knowledge system either has no change or changes to something

Table 8.1. *A formal representation of the range of possible transformations of the knowledge structure, given the environment input*

Environmental input	Range of possible transformations
A	no change or X or Y or ?
B	no change or Y or ?
C	no change or X or Z or ?
D	no change or ?
E	no change or ?

unpredictable ("?"). Second, for each environmental input, there is only a limited set of possible transformations. Thus, knowledge transformation is constrained by the environment. For instance, given that the environmental input is B, possible transformations include no change, Y, or a novel state "?," but no X or Z. In another case, given that the environmental input is C, the knowledge structure may have no change, change to X, change to Z, or change to "?," but it may not change to Y. Third, knowledge transformation is open-ended. Given any environmental input, the knowledge structure always has the possibility of transforming to a novel state "?," which is unpredictable. Fourth, environmental input is also open-ended. This is indicated by the last row of Table 8.1. Unpredictable environmental inputs may come into the knowledge structure and their impact is also unpredictable.

It should be emphasized that this knowledge-transformation model does not explain why and how knowledge structures transform into particular states. The objective of this model is to depict the relationship between the state of knowledge structures and environmental input rather than making exact predictions of specific content-filled knowledge structures.

Structure of knowledge, and its transformation

We assume that knowledge is structured, and that this structure is open to transformations within a specifiable set of limits at any given time. The structure of knowledge ("knowledge base") may be unevenly differentiated, as different nodes within the knowledge hierarchy may be at any time ill-defined. Furthermore, the hierarchical knowledge structure can include intransitivities, which leads it to resemble a contradictory structure very much along the lines of the physically impossible figures that are the favorite subject matter for Escher's graphics.

In our elaboration here, it is assumed that our knowledge system is semistructured. It contains a huge number of subsystems; some of them are large some others are relatively small. Each subsystem is independent, that is, it is not linked with other subsystems, but it has a possibility of merging with other subsystems when knowledge transformation takes place. Each subsystem contains a number of elements, which form a hierarchical structure. These elements are concepts that represent objects and events in the external world. Figure 8.1 depicts the structure of a knowledge subsystem and its transformation.

In Figure 8.1a, P is a piece of knowledge at the highest level, Q and R are at the second level, and S and T are at the lowest level. P is directly linked with Q and R, and indirectly linked with S and T (through R). When an environmental input comes in, some possible transformations may occur, including addition, reorganization, splitting, merging, and their combinations. If an environmental input is added into this subsystem and becomes a part of it, this process is called addition. In Figure 8.1b, the environmental input A is linked with P and becomes a new element in the second level. Reorganization refers to the situation in which an environmental input makes the subsystem reorganize itself. There is no addition or loss of elements but the configuration of the subsystem is changed. For example, in Figure 8.1c, element T, which was formerly a third-level element under R, is now directly linked with P and becomes a second-level element. Splitting is another type of transformation whereby the subsystem divides into two or more subsystems. In Figure 8.1d, the original subsystem breaks up into two parts: one part containing P and Q, and another part containing R, S and T. The last type of transformation is one in which a subsystem may emerge with other subsystems to form a larger subsystem. In Figure 8.1e, the original subsystem merges with another subsystem and becomes a new four-level subsystem.

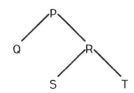

Figure 1a.

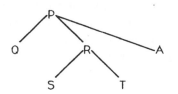

Figure 1b.

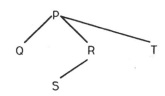

Figure 1c.

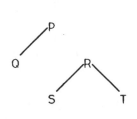

Figure 1d.

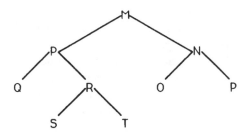

Figure 1e.

Figure 8.1.

Let us use examples to illustrate these types of knowledge transformation. Suppose that Figure 8.1a represents a 10-year-old boy's knowledge about fish. To make this example simple, we assume that in the knowledge subsystem of "fish" of this boy there are only four elements: sharks, whales, killer whales, and dolphins. This boy "knows" that sharks (represented by Q in Figure 8.1a) and whales (R) are two kinds of "fish," and that also killer whales (S) and dolphins (T) are two kinds of "whales." Notice that this boy's knowledge of fish is incorrect from an adult's point of view. One day he sees a swordfish in an aquarium and so he adds swordfish (represented by A in Figure 8.1b) as a new kind of fish. This is an example of addition because the incoming information itself, in this case the swordfish, is added in the knowledge subsystem of fish. Suppose that on another day his mother tells him that a dolphin is not a kind of whale, and this new information makes him reorganize his knowledge subsystem: dolphin (T in figure 8.1c) is moved from the third level (under whale) to the second level (under fish). Now this boy "knows" that sharks (Q), whales (R), and dolphins (T) are three different kinds of "fish." This is an example of reorganization since no element is added or lost but the connections among elements are changed.

Splitting can be illustrated by the following example: the father of the boy tells him that a whale is not a fish because whales use lungs instead of gills to breathe, and this new information makes the boy break the connection between fish (P in Figure 8.1d) and whale (R).

An example of merging is that the science teacher of the boy telling him that both fish and birds are vertebrates because they have backbones; with this information the boy merges fish (P in figure 8.1e) and bird (N) together and creates a new element – vertebrate (M) – which is now in the highest level in this new subsystem.

Social channeling of knowledge transformation

Thus far, our example of knowledge construction has remained within the Piagetian framework, emphasizing the set of possibilities for taking new information into the knowledge base, and changing the latter accordingly (i.e., the assimilation/accommodation process). The location of the sociogenetic functions in that scheme need to be elaborated.

At each stage of a knowledge structure, the social world with which the "carrier" of the knowledge structure interacts provides a heterogeneous field of social suggestions for the transformation of the structure into a novel form. The example worked out above (Figure 8.1) indicates the intricacies of this process – the "social others" of a person try to impact upon the knowledge structure to change it in its different loci, but the ways in which this input is utilized by the person follows the co-constructivist line. The person can actively block many of the social suggestions from altering the given knowledge structure, neutralize other impacts by not simply letting them link with the structure, and adjust the structure in ways that for the "social others" are unexpected (construction of novelty, or "?" conditions indicated in Table

8.1). In other words, knowledge construction takes place when the active knowledge constructor creates new knowledge by the assimilation/accommodation process, but under the constraining guidance of social suggestions from other persons.

Conclusions

In this chapter, we elaborated upon a sociogenetic process approach to knowledge construction. In so doing, the traditional discourse about "intelligence" – embedded heavily in the psychometric paradigm – was replaced by a focus on the process of person's construction of a knowledge structure, within limits set by the previous state of the structure and the social suggestions of others, which are targeted upon that structure. The knowledge-construction process is thus simultaneously personal and social, as it entails the interdependence of the active person with the socially organized world.

In replacing the notion of "intelligence" by a sociogenetic focus on knowledge construction we are transcending the realm of the common-sense know-how of laypersons. This is accomplished by using a metatheoretical perspective (individual–socioecological frame of reference) which replaces the usual (interindividual reference frame) view of "intelligence." Instead of trying to find out answers to the question "how intelligent is this person," we replace the question by reversing it into "hot *is* this person (being) intelligent" (i.e., in what ways does this person act in the process of knowledge construction). Admittedly, this amounts to an act of reorganization of psychology's knowledge structure, which is consistent with the ethos of the sociogenetic perspective.

References

Atkinson, R. C., & Shiffrin, R. M. (1971). The control of short-term memory. *Scientific American, 225,* 82–90.

Baldwin, J. M. (1906). *Thought and things.* Vol. 1. *Functional logic, or genetic theory of knowledge.* London: Swan Sonnenschein.

Beilin, H. (1992). Piaget's new theory. In H. Beilin & P. Pufall (Eds.), *Piaget's theory: Prospects and possibilities* (pp. 1–17). Hillsdale, NJ: Erlbaum.

Bergson, H. (1911). *Creative evolution.* New York: Holt.

Cattell, R. B. (1963). Theory of fluid and crystallized intelligence: A critical experiment. *Journal of Educational Psychology, 54,* 1–22.

Chapman, M. (1988). *Constructive evolution.* Cambridge: Cambridge University Press.

Chapman, M. (1992). Equilibration and the dialectics of organization. In H. Beilin & P. Pufall (Eds.), *Piaget's theory: Prospects and possibilities* (pp. 39–59). Hillsdale, NJ: Erlbaum.

Cohen, P. C. (1982). *A calculating people: The spread of numeracy in early America.* Chicago: University of Chicago Press.

Csikszentmihalyi, M. (1985). Emergent motivation and the evolution of the self. In D. Keiber & M. L. Maehr (Eds.), *Advances in Motivation and Achievement.* Vol. 4. (pp. 93–119). Greenwich, CT: JAI Press.

Danziger, K. (1990). *Constructing the subject: Historical origins of psychological research.* Cambridge: Cambridge University Press.

Draguns, J. (1984). Microgenesis by any other name .... In W. D. Froelich, G. Smith, J. Draguns, & U. Hentschel (Eds.), *Psychological processes in cognition and personality* (pp. 3–17). Washington, DC: Hemisphere.

Duncker, K. (1945). On problem solving. *Psychological Monographs, 58,* 1–113.

Fry, P. S. (Ed.) (1984). *Changing conceptions of intelligence and intellectual functioning.* Amsterdam: North-Holland.

Gigerenzer, G., Swijtink, Z., Porter, T., Daston, L., Beatty, J., & Krüger, L. (1989). *The empire of chance: How probability changed science and everyday life.* Cambridge: Cambridge University Press.

Janet, P. (1925). *Psychological healing.* Vols. 1–2. New York: MacMillan.

Keats, D. (1993). Cultural and environmental influences in the acquisition of concepts of intellectual competence. In J. Valsiner (Ed.), *Child development within culturally structured environments.* Vol. 3. *Comparative-cultural and constructivist perspectives.* Norwood, NJ: Ablex.

Keats, D., Fang Fu-Xi (1989). Cultural factors in concepts of intelligence. In Ç. Kagitçibasi (Ed.), *Growth and progress in cross-cultural psychology* (pp. 236–247). Lisse: Swets & Zeitlinger.

Lachman, R., Lachman, J. L., & Butterfield, E. C. (1979). *Cognitive Psychology and Information Processing.* Hillsdale, NJ: Erlbaum.

Lawrence, J. A., & Valsiner, J. (1993). Conceptual roots of internalization: from transmission to transformation. *Human development, 36,* 150–167.

Lewin, K. (1917). Kriegslandschaft. *Zeitschrift für angewandte Psychologie, 12,* 440–447.

Minsky, M. (1982). A framework for representing knowledge. In Y-H Pao & G. W. Ernst (Eds.), *Tutorial: context-directed pattern recognition and machine intelligence techniques for information processing* (pp. 339–419). Piscataway, NJ: IEEE Computer Society.

Piaget, J. (1971). *Biology and knowledge.* Chicago: University of Chicago Press.

Rogoff, B., & Wertsch, J. (Eds.) (1984). Children's learning in the "Zone of proximal development." *New Directions for Child Development, 23,* San Francisco: Jossey-Bass.

Rommetveit, R. (1979). Deep structure of messages versus message structure. In R. Rommetveit & R. Blakar (Eds.), *Studies of language, thought and verbal communication.* London: Academic Press.

Simon, H. (1957). *Models of man.* New York: Wiley.

Stern, W. (1919). *Die menschliche Persönlichkeit.* Leipzig: Barth.

Sternberg, R. (1985). *Beyond IQ: A triarchic theory of human intelligence.* Cambridge: Cambridge University Press.

Swetz, F. J. (1987). *Capitalism & arithmetic: The new math of the 15th century.* La Salle, Ill.: Open Court.

Toda, M. (1980). Emotion and decision making. *Acta Psychologica, 45,* 133–145.

Uexküll, J. (1928). *Theoretische Biologie.* Berlin: Verlag von Julius Springer.

Valsiner, J. (1984). Conceptualizing intelligence: From an internal static attribution to the study of the process structure of organism-environment relationships. *International Journal of Psychology, 19,* 363–389.

Valsiner, J. (1985). Common sense and psychological theories: The historical nature of logical necessity. *Scandinavian Journal of Psychology, 26,* 97–109.

Valsiner, J. (1987). *Culture and the development of children's action.* Chichester: Wiley.

Valsiner, J. (1989). *Human development and culture.* Lexington, MA: D.C. Heath

Valsiner, J. (1991a). Construction of the mental: From the "cognitive revolution" to the study of development. *Theory & Psychology, 1,* 4, 477–494.

Valsiner, J. (1991b). Theories and methods in the service of data construction in developmental psychology. In P. van Geert & L. P. Mos (Eds.), *Annals of theoretical psychology.* Vol. 7. (pp. 161–175). New York: Plenum.

Valsiner, J. (1992). In J. Siegfried (Ed.), *The role of common sense in psychology.* Norwood, NJ: Ablex Publishing Corporation.

Valsiner, J., & Benigni, L. (1986). Naturalistic research and ecological thinking in the study of child development. *Developmental Review, 6,* 203–223.

Valsiner, J., & Van der Veer, R. (1988). On the social nature of human cognition: An analysis of the shared intellectual roots of George Herbert Mead and Lev Vygotsky. *Journal for the Theory of Social Behavior, 18,* 117–135.

Valsiner, J., & Van der Veer, R. (1993). The encoding of distance: The concept of the "zone of proximal development" and its interpretations. In R. R. Cocking & K. A. Renninger (Eds.), *The development and meaning of psychological distance*. Hillsdale, NJ: Erlbaum.

Van der Veer, R., & Valsiner, J. (1991). *Understanding Vygotsky: A quest for synthesis*. Oxford: Basil Blackwell.

Vuyk, R. (1981). *Overview and critique of Piaget's genetic epistemology*. Vols. 1–2. London: Academic Press.

Wertheimer, M. (1912). Über das Denken der Naturvölker. *Zeitschrift für Psychologie, 60,* 321–378.

Wertheimer, M. (1945). *Productive thinking*. Chicago: University of Chicago Press.

Winegar, L. T. (Ed.) (1989). *Social interaction and the development of children's understanding*. Norwood, NJ: Ablex.

Wundt, W. (1916). *Elements of folk psychology*. London: Allen & Unwin.

9   PRSVL: an integrative framework for understanding mind in context

Robert J. Sternberg

I presented the PRSVL model of person–context interaction for the first time at HUMRRO (Human Resources Research Organization), a consulting organization. Upon entering the HUMRRO Building in Alexandria, Virginia, I encountered a challenging problem. I entered at the ground level, walked into an elevator, and pressed the number four in order to get to the fourth floor. The button didn't light, but the door closed. Instead of ascending, the elevator descended, and took me to the parking level. I re-entered the elevator, and again pressed the number four. The button didn't light. I pressed the "DO" button. The door opened. I tried to summon another elevator, but none of the others would come because one was already here. Clearly there was something wrong with this elevator.

I walked to the staircase and entered it. Upon entering, I tried the doorknob from the inside to make sure that I would later be able to get out of the staircase. I walked up to the fourth floor. The door from the staircase to the office was locked. I walked back down to the ground floor. I pressed the button to summon an elevator. A new elevator arrived. I entered the elevator and pressed the button for the fourth floor. The button did not light. The door closed and the elevator once again descended to the parking level. I then concluded that something was wrong with all of the elevators.

I walked up a flight of steps to the lobby, pondering if something was wrong with me. Upon arriving in the lobby, a woman approached me and asked me if I wanted to go to the HUMRRO suite. I nodded in the affirmative. We entered the elevator and she inserted a card into a slot in the wall. The elevator rose to the fourth floor. I had finally reached my destination.

It is always humbling to be confronted with an intelligence test shortly before one starts to speak about intelligence testing. But this particular intelligence test raised four points that I believe are critical to our understanding of human intelligence in particular, and our human potentialities more generally. First, defining problems narrowly (in this case, in terms of problems with the elevators or with myself) rendered the elevator problem insoluble: I could have gone on pressing buttons in various elevators forever without solving the problem. Second, in understanding and assessing human potentialities, we need to take into account the context in which people live and function. In the elevator example, the context was a set of security measures employed by HUMRRO to ensure that unauthorized people don't come up to their floor. In general, real-world problems could not be understood outside the context in which they occur. We need to take into account the interaction of the person with the context, not merely the person (in this case, myself) or the task that person faces (in this case, getting the elevators to work). Third, if we define our universe of assessment narrowly, we will always come back to *g*: Mental abilities of the kind measured by intelligence tests, whether psychometrically or cognitively analyzed, are simply not enough. They will always yield a *g,* but a limited one. Fourth, it's not enough even to look at other abilities, such as physical ones or personality. We need to look at the person–context interaction that goes beyond abilities as well as personality.

If our only goal is to obtain a rough-and-ready assessment of abilities, we may not want to be bothered by testing beyond that which gives us a measure of the traditional psychometric *g.* But if we're interested in broader questions, and perhaps more important ones, we need to expand our horizons. For example, why do so many CEOs drive their companies to ruin? Is it simply a lack of general intelligence? What is the difference between a good person and a good leader? What makes one person a natural lawyer, another a pilot, and another a scientist? Why do so many people with high IQs and GRE scores amount to so little? Why do people who do well in one organization not do as well in another? What's Donald Trump's problem? To answer questions such as these, we need to go well beyond the traditional universe of testing.

In this chapter, I will describe the PRSVL (which stands for Person-Roles-Situations-Values-Luck and is pronounced the same way as the name of the knight, Parsifal) model of person–context interaction in the study of human potentials. This model considers the person from a broad perspective, and also considers the multiple facets of context in which the person functions. Most importantly, though, it looks at the interaction between the person and his or her context. It considers jointly five variables: the person, the roles the person can take, the situations in which a person can find him or herself, the values of the person, and the luck that impinges upon the person's life. Figure 9.1 sketches the model as a whole.

In trying to learn about people in their contexts, we often ask the questions of who, what, where, when, why, and how? The PRSVL taxonomy deals with all five of these questions, precisely because it considers the person in his or her total context. All aspects of the taxonomy have been considered by the authors of chapters in this book. The question of *who* is addressed by the person category. The question of *what* is addressed by the roles category. The questions of *where* and *when* are addressed by the situations category. The questions of *why* and *how* are addressed by the values category. Finally, the *luck* category addresses an additional factor, which might be labeled the *whoops!* factor – the background variables and events in one's life over which one has no control.

The person

In order to consider fully the potentials of a person, we need to go beyond just looking at abilities. In particular, we need to look at five aspects of personhood: abilities,

1
PERSON
(who)
Abilities
  Mental
    Memory–Analytic
    Synthetic–Creative
    Practical–Contextual
  Physical

Knowledge
  Declarative
  Procedural

Styles
  Legislative–Executive–Judicial
  Monarchic–Hierarchic–Oligarchic–Anarchic
  Local–Global
  Internal–External

Personality
  Tolerance of Ambiguity
  Persistence in Overcoming Obstacles
  Willingness to Grow
  Willingness to Take Sensible Risks

Motivation
  Intrinsic
  Task-Focused

2
ROLES
(what)
Leader vs. Follower
Entrepreneur vs. Manager
Thinking vs. Doing
Staff vs. Line

3
SITUATIONS
(where, when)
High Stress vs. Low Stress
Close Supervision vs. Far Supervision
Short-Term Goals vs. Long-Term
    Goals
Physical Comfort vs. Physical
    Discomfort

4
VALUES
(why)
People vs. Productivity
Process vs. Product
Conformity vs. Independence
Individualism vs. Group Orientation
Altruism vs. Self-Interest
Innovation vs. Stability
Appearance vs. Reality

5
LUCK
(whoops!)
Status Variables
    SES of Family of Origin
    Race
    Gender
    Handicaps
    Nationality

Event Variables
    Hazards
    Opportunities

Figure 9.1. The PRSVL model of person–context interaction.

knowledge, thinking and learning styles, personality, and motivation. In considering abilities, I will consider only mental ones, although the physical abilities are important as well. Let's now consider each of these five aspects of the person in turn.

Abilities

I'll distinguish between three broad categories of abilities: memory–analytic, synthetic–creative, and practical–contextual. Each of these types of abilities is important to success in a variety of endeavors.

Memory–analytic abilities. In my triarchic theory of intelligence (Sternberg, 1985, 1988), I describe three kinds of information-processing components of *memory–analytic* abilities: *metacomponents,* which are higher-order thought processes involved in planning what one is going to do, monitoring it while one is doing it, and evaluating it after it is done; *performance components,* which are involved in executing the instructions of the metacomponents; and *knowledge-acquisition components,* which are involved in learning how to do something in the first place. I have written extensively about the functioning of these kinds of components, and won't repeat much of it here. I will let it suffice to give a few examples of each kind of component. Examples of metacomponents are recognizing that one has a problem in the first place, defining what the problem is, setting up a strategy to solve that problem, monitoring one's strategy as one is seeking to implement it, and evaluating the success of the strategy after one has completed implementing it. Examples of performance components are inferring relations between two concepts and applying what one has learned to a new context. Examples of knowledge-acquisition components are selectively encoding information so as to screen out what is relevant from what is irrelevant in a stream of input, and selective comparison, which involves bringing old information to bear on the solution of new problems.

Memory–analytic abilities are obviously important in intellectual functioning, and they are the focus of much cognitive research. Much of the research reviewed by Snow in Chapter 1 falls into this category. Ceci and Roazzi (Chapter 3) also discuss several such tasks. Equally, these abilities are the focus of the large majority of research projects that have been undertaken both by psychometrically oriented and cognitively oriented psychologists. But in the PRSVL framework, they are only a small portion of the factors that need to be taken into account in understanding and assessing human potential. From the present point of view, g is a very small g indeed. It may be general, but only within a narrow universe of discourse. I am not arguing against the importance of g in many tasks and in many situations. The very fact that it keeps recurring in a variety of different kinds of assessments attests to its importance. But one has only to go to a scientific convention or read a scientific journal in order to understand just how limited g can be. One can marvel at how well so many people can solve problems of little or no consequence as they pursue their scientific work. To me, the problem in science, as well as in so many other fields, is not that the professional practitioners are unable to solve problems (i.e., lack sufficient levels of g), but rather that the problems they choose to solve are often of such narrow scope or consequence in the first place.

I believe that it is somewhat unfortunate that the short-term rewards of many fields go to high-g people who are good problem solvers but not necessarily discriminating with respect to the problems they solve. For example, in order to have journal articles accepted or grant proposals funded, one needs to demonstrate convincingly the "tightness" of one's approach. But any research, including tightly conceived research, can be sterile, and much of what we read and hear about is just that. Fortunately, the long-term rewards of the field are won with more boldness, and with the imagination and creativity that is often not rewarded in the short-term.

Synthetic–creative abilities. Synthetic–creative abilities are of great importance in many pursuits. Gardner concentrates on synthetic abilities in Chapter 2. With the world changing at a pace that we have not seen in most of our lifetimes, the need to be flexible and to see old problems in new ways has never been greater. The military, for example, is now in a period of retrenchment and downsizing, making new perspectives all the more important.

The ability to think in a synthetic manner has been measured in a variety of ways (see, e.g., essays in Sternberg, 1988), as discussed by Gardner. In our own research, we have used both convergent and divergent measures. For example, among the convergent measures are nonentrenched-reasoning problems and conceptual-projection problems. Nonentrenched-reasoning problems (Sternberg & Gastel, 1989) involve seeing analogies, classifications, series, and the like, but with nonentrenched premises. For example, what would appear to be an ordinary analogy might be preceded by a statement such as "sparrows play hopscotch" or "villains are lovable." The examinee then has to solve the analogy as though the premise were true. Conceptual-projection problems require examinees to reason with unfamiliar concepts that are novel in kind, such as *grue,* meaning, "green until the year 2000 and blue thereafter" (Sternberg, 1982). The people who do well on these measures of novel ways of thinking are not necessarily the ones who do well on more conventional kinds of assessments.

We have also assessed synthetic abilities through the use of divergent measures (Sternberg & Lubart, 1991). For example, we have asked our examinees to write short stories, draw, generate advertising campaigns, and solve unusual scientific problems where there's no one correct answer. In this research, we have found the quality of the creative product to be moderately domain-specific: Although there is some correlation across domains, it is only moderate (about .4). Our research is based upon our "investment theory of creativity" (Sternberg & Lubart, 1991, 1992), according to which creative people are those who "buy low and sell high" in the world of ideas. In other words, they generate ideas that are not very popular among others, like stocks with low price–earning ratios. The ideas are often not well received, and may even be rejected outright. But creative people persist with these ideas, trying to persuade other people of their value. When they finally do, they "sell high" and move onto the next idea, again championing an unpopular cause.

This research has yielded some interesting findings. For example, our data support the notion that creative people do indeed buy low and sell high. Moreover, we have found relations between creativity and other aspects of our investment theory, including intelligence, knowledge, styles of thinking, personality, and motivation. We have also found what we refer to as a "cohort-matching." When we plotted the rated creativity of the works we received against the ages of our subjects, we found, as had many before us, that degree of creativity tends to decrease as people age. Generally, the decrease is found around the age of 40. But we also plotted the ages of our subjects against the ages of our raters, and found that raters tend to rate as more creative, at least in some domains (such as advertising and science), the works of subjects in their own age cohort. In other words, at least some of the decline observed in older people may be due to cohort-matching. As most raters are in the middle of the age distribution, one would expect creativity first to rise as the ages of the subjects match more closely the ages of the raters and then to fall as the ages become more discrepant. Thus, the often observed decline in creativity after the age of 40 or so may be due to rater effects rather than to loss of creativity itself.

Practical–contextual abilities. Practical–contextual abilities are the focus of the chapters by Berg and Calderone (Chapter 4) and by Wagner (Chapter 5). Ceci and Roazzi (Chapter 3) also consider such abilities. Although practical–contextual abilities involve more than adaptation to the environment, our research focus has been on adaptation, especially for managers in business. Much of this research has been in collaboration with Richard Wagner. We have also examined adaptation in salespeople, professors, and students. The qualitative patterns of data are the same across domains.

Our focus has been on the measurement of tacit knowledge, that is, the knowledge one needs to have in order to adapt to an environment that is not explicitly taught and that often isn't even verbalized. We have measured tacit knowledge via scenarios that stimulate the kinds of problems that people encounter in their jobs on an everyday basis (Sternberg, Wagner, & Okagaki, in press; Wagner & Sternberg, 1986). For example, in one exercise we might familiarize a business executive with the context and then give him a list of things he needs to get done in the next two months (not enough time to do them all). Given the list of activities, what are his priorities for getting each of them done? Or, in another exercise, the business executive might be asked to rate pieces of advice that a senior executive might give to a junior executive.

What have we found in such investigations? First, tacit knowledge increases, on the average, with experience. But experience is not sufficient for an increase in tacit knowledge. Rather, what seems to matter is how effectively one exploits the experience. In other words, the critical variable is not experience, per se, but learning from experience. Second, level of tacit knowledge does not correlate with *g*, at least not within the range of people who actually go into the occupations we have studied. In other words, with sufficient range of IQs, tacit knowledge would probably correlate with IQ, as would almost anything else. But the natural range to use is that for people who actually enter the occupation. People who are mentally retarded, for example, rarely become business executives, or even apply for those types of jobs. Thus, including the normal distribution of IQs in the population as a whole would be spurious in validating a test for business executives. Third, scores on the Inventory of Tacit Knowledge do not correlate with scores on the Armed Services Vocational Aptitude Battery, with measures of styles, or with personality variables. Thus, tacit knowledge is not just another name for a variable that is already measured by commonly used tests. Fourth, tacit knowledge predicts various measures of job success at about the .4 level of correlation, uncorrected for restriction of range, attenuation, or anything else. Fifth, when one computes subscores for tacit knowledge, such as tacit knowledge for managing oneself, managing others, and managing tasks, the various subscores are themselves correlated. Although the subscores yield a kind of "little *g*" for tacit knowledge, again this "little *g*" is not the same as psychometric *g*. Sixth, tacit knowledge correlates moderately across occupations (at about the .4 level). Seventh, the content of tacit knowledge differs across levels within an occupation. For instance, the tacit knowledge one needs to be a successful higher-level executive could be different from the tacit knowledge one needs to be a lower-level executive. Finally, tacit knowledge is teachable, although it is best taught through role-modeling and through mediated learning.

Our research with tacit knowledge suggests that there is more to success on the job than psychometric *g*. Other abilities, such as the ability to acquire tacit knowledge, matter as well. However, we are not claiming that tacit knowledge is all that is necessary for job success, or even that tacit knowledge is all of practical intelligence. Clearly, it is only part of what leads to success on the job. And with respect to practical intelligence, the abilities to select and shape environments are important as well, but are not measured by tests of tacit knowledge (Sternberg, 1985). Thus, tacit knowledge is just one element of many that leads to success on the job. Again, trying to identify a single thing, whether it's psychometric *g* or anything else, is not adequate for understanding the full range of variables that are important for job success.

Knowledge

Knowledge is important for success on the job and in other aspects in life. Snow deals to some extent with the role of knowledge in Chapter 1, as do Granott and Gardner in their discussion of how the building of a knowledge base from abilities depends upon the availability of relevant learning experiences in the environment (Chapter 7). Knowledge can either be declarative or procedural, and each kind of knowledge is used separately as well as in interactions. Obviously, expertise in any area requires a vast store of knowledge. It is for this reason that we teach children as well as adults, and have on-the-job training in order to perfect skills of people in various jobs. Oddly enough, though, it is possible to have too much of a good thing.

I suspected for some time that too much knowledge can lead to an entrenched perspective on problems. In other words, one becomes so used to seeing things in a certain way, it becomes difficult to see them in any other way. Thus, with increased crystallization can come a loss of flexibility. Peter Frensch and I conducted a study that illustrated this point (Frensch & Sternberg, 1989). We had bridge players who were either experts or novices play bridge against a computer. As would be expected, the experts did better than the novices. When we made superficial structural changes in the game, both experts and novices were hurt slightly. Both, however, quickly recovered. When we made deep structural changes in the game, however, the experts were hurt more than the novices. This finding makes sense, as novices don't have a deeply structured approach to accomplishing a task because of their lack of expertise. Thus, our results confirmed the notion that with knowledge can come entrenchment, and as people become experts, they need to find ways to maintain their flexibility in the domain of their expertise.

Thinking and learning styles

Styles of thinking and learning can also influence performance, both in training and on the job. Styles are not a major focus of this volume except for Snow's chapter. Because little was said in the earlier chapters, I will say a bit more here. My own work on styles is motivated by my theory of mental self-government (Sternberg, 1988). The basic idea is that the forms of government that we have in the world are not coincidental or arbitrary, but are external reflections of ways in which we can organize our minds. Just as countries or states or cities need to be governed, so do people, and there are different ways in which they can organize themselves.

A style is not a level or even a kind of ability, but rather a way of utilizing an ability or set of abilities. In other words, it is a proclivity, not a talent. Consider just a few examples of the styles in the theory of mental self-government.

Just as governments have three different functions – legislative, executive, and judicial – so do the minds of people. These three functions correspond to three different styles. A legislative person is someone who likes to come up with new ideas, new ways of doing things, and who basically has his or her own agenda and goals. An executive person may be just as intelligent, but is someone who prefers to be told what to do. Given directions, executive stylists can do a very good job in an intellectual task, but they do prefer to be given direction and to work within the framework that is provided for them. Judicial people tend to be critical, evaluating and judging most things and people.

Different styles are ideally suited to different occupations. For example, as I tend to be a legislative stylist, my job as a university professor is probably very well suited to me. I am paid to generate ideas and experiments, and within broad restrictions, can do whatever I want. At the same time, a contracts lawyer I know is clearly an executive stylist. He draws up contracts between investment bankers. The perfect contract, he says, is one that is so airtight the bankers can't get out of it without paying him additional legal fees. Another friend with a judicial style has found an ideal job as a psychotherapist. He spends his days evaluating the problems of other people and deciding how to treat them.

Do styles matter in learning? Data collected by Elena Grigorenko and myself suggest they do (Grigorenko & Sternberg, 1992 – submitted for publication). We measured styles of both students and teachers, testing the hypothesis that independent of student ability, the match between a student's and a teacher's profile of styles would be a predictor of the student's performance in the teacher's course. Put more bluntly, the hypothesis was that teachers prefer students whose styles match their own. Our hypothesis was confirmed.

Styles also matter on the job. Consider, for example, what styles one might seek in a lower-level business executive. One would probably want an individual who has an executive style – one who will do well when he or she is told what to do. One would probably also look for someone who is rather local in the kinds of problems that he or she prefers to deal with, as the problems confronted by lower-level executives tend to be more local than global. Finally, one might seek an individual who is "monarchic," meaning that the individual focuses his or her sights on a particular problem and then pursues that problem until a solution is reached, not allowing other things to interfere with the problem solving. Monarchic people are strongly oriented toward the attainment of a single goal, to the exclusion of all else.

But if you ask yourself what you would want in an upper-level executive, it would probably be quite different. You would probably want someone who is legislative or possibly judicial rather than executive, someone who is global rather than local in orientation, and someone who is hierarchical rather than monarchic. Styles sought at the lower levels of management may be quite different from the styles sought at the upper levels of management. The problem is that when one promotes lower-level managers who are successful, one may be promoting precisely those people whose styles do not match the needs of higher-level management. At the same time, one is derailing those people whose styles would be more appropriate for the higher levels of management. In other words, the system of promotion may promote exactly the wrong people!

This problem is not limited to management. If one asks what stylistic characteristics lead to success in science as it is taught in most schools, one would probably come to the conclusion that it pays off for a scientist to be executive and local. For example, in order to get good grades in school science, one needs to be able to memorize textbooks and solve problems at the back of chapters. But if one asks how many times scientists in the profession actually need to do these things, the answer is probably never. Rather, scientists need to be legislative and global in their work, trying to formulate large problems that are of scientific and practical significance. Once again, some of the students who potentially may make the best scientists may be derailed during their school careers. I am particularly sensitive to this fact because I received a grade of C in introductory psychology, a course that essentially involves memorizing a book. At that point, I decided to seek out another major, mathematics. After doing worse in mathematics than I did in psychology, I returned to psychology. But the point is that we may derail from a given scientific pursuit those who later would actually thrive in it, and we may encourage others to pursue a career when they might be ideally suited to something else.

Personality

People who focus on abilities often discount personality. Indeed, there is little in this volume that deals with personality directly. In our investment theory of creativity, Todd Lubart and I (Sternberg & Lubart, 1991) have emphasized attributes that seem to be crucial to creative endeavors: tolerance of ambiguity, persistence in overcoming obstacles, willingness to grow beyond where one is, willingness to take risks, and courage. One could have all the cognitive attributes of creativity but lack the personal ones and never do any creative work because of a fear of taking the risks that are necessary to buy low and sell high, or a lack of the courage needed when going against the grain. In general, then, one needs to match personality traits to the demands of the job, and select people who are a good fit.

Motivation

Perhaps no single personal attribute is more important to success or learning than is motivation. Snow has studied the role of motivation in learning, and motivation also plays a major role in the epigenetic theory of Valsiner and Leung, in that people construct experiences in line with their motivations to pursue certain directions but not others. It is interesting to note that the Japanese, who have been so successful both in the outcomes of their schooling and in the competitiveness of the world market-place, have little interest in or tolerance of our theories of intelligence. They believe that the difference between levels of success is dependent on how hard they work – in other words, their motivation (Stevenson & Stigler, 1992). I believe their theory is wrong, but at the same time I also believe it probably leads to more beneficial outcomes than do our own implicit theories of success. According to this theory, success can be attained if one just tries hard enough. Such a theory motivates people to work harder. Our own implicit theory – that some people can do the job that others can't, or that some people can learn and others can't – can lead many people into discouragement, frustration, and ultimately, failure to make the effort necessary for success. Thus, an implicit theory of success that emphasizes motivation may be more likely to lead to success than one that emphasizes immutable abilities.

There is a great deal of work that suggests people do their most creative work when they're highly intrinsically motivated for that work (Amabile, 1983). In other words, creative people almost always love what they do. In steering children toward careers, therefore, and in steering employees toward lines of work, we should take their interests into account at least as much as their abilities. Although there may be a correlation between what people like to do and how well they do it, it is far from perfect. Many people who lack the talent want to be professional athletes, for example, just as some people with tremendous athletic ability would prefer to do something other than sports. In assigning people to jobs, we sometimes forget that one of the best predictors of how well they'll do is how much they really want to do the job.

We need also to remember the now well-replicated finding that emphasizing extrinsic rewards can undermine intrinsic motivation (Lepper & Green, 1978). In the United States, for example, we tend to place a great deal of emphasis on extrinsic motivators – grades, money, tokens, trophies, and the like. The problem with this emphasis is that it leads those people who are intrinsically motivated to come to believe that they're working for the extrinsic rewards, rather than the intrinsic satisfactions. As we undermine intrinsic motivation, we undermine the creativity that accompanies it. Thus, we need to redirect our emphases in order to help people do their best on the job, and to maximize their creativity in their work.

Roles

In considering how to optimize human potential, one aspect of the Person × Situation interaction is to look at the kinds of roles in which a person feels comfortable. Some people prefer to be leaders; others, followers. The role of leadership is considered in the chapter by Fiedler and Link (Chapter 6), especially as it relates to intelligence. Some people enjoy entrepreneurial roles; others, managerial roles. Some people would rather be thinkers; others, doers. Some people prefer staff jobs; others, line jobs. Still others want to be perpetual students. We can expect far greater productivity and creativity in work when the kind of role a person plays matches the kind of role the person feels comfortable taking. The chapter by Fiedler and Link shows that how well people fulfill roles interacts with their abilities and the kinds of situations in which they find themselves.

Consider, for example, the scientist. One could give a set of ability tests, and even interest tests as well, and conclude that a person would make a good scientist. Some people would be happy to say that all they need is a high level of g. But such analyses are superficial. Different scientific jobs emphasize different roles. For instance, the demands on a person who enters a university setting as a scientist are quite different from those on a person who chooses to work in industry. Even within such jobs, there are different roles. Some scientists prefer the role of researcher to that of teacher, whereas others prefer the reverse; still others prefer a balance. Some scientists are comfortable in the role of adaptors to existing scientific paradigms; others prefer to shape such paradigms. Some scientists are intellectual entrepreneurs whereas others prefer to be team players. Some scientists enjoy performing research, whereas others prefer to be research managers, rarely involving themselves in the research except at the level of orchestrating and coordinating it. Thus, even within a single occupation, there are many role possibilities, some of which will work better for a given person than others.

The same would be true in other jobs. Consider, for example, the lawyer. Some lawyers might prefer the role of prosecutor; others that of defense attorney. Some lawyers prefer corporate law; others, trial law. Some prefer a specialty such as tax; others, criminal law. Some prefer public interest law while others prefer the private sector. Once again, satisfaction and productivity on the job are more likely to be related to the specific roles within the job than with the name of the job itself. We need to take into account what a person actually does, not what he or she is called.

Situations

People's satisfaction with and adjustment to jobs will depend not only upon their personal attributes and the roles they play, but upon the kinds of situations in which they find themselves. For example, some jobs involve high stress and others low stress. Fiedler and Link consider at some length the importance of stress in determining who will succeed as a leader and who will not. Ceci and Roazzi also show how a given person may be able to solve a problem in one kind of situation, but not another.

Jobs differ as well in terms of whether the goals that need to be met are short-term or long-term. Further, an employee may work in a situation that is physically comfortable, or one that is characterized by physical discomfort. A person's fit to a job, I would argue, would depend largely upon how well the situation in which the job is carried out fits that person's needs. For example, I had a secretary who might well have been perfect except for her tendency to crumble under conditions of high stress. Because there were always times that were in fact stressful – for example, right before the submission date for a grant proposal – she did not adjust well to the job. She had the abilities, and was comfortable with the role, but the particular situation in which she found herself was a poor fit to her needs.

The same issues apply to other jobs, such as the scientific and legal jobs considered above. For example, some scientists may find themselves happy only when they're working in an area of endeavor that is very competitive, and in which individual scientists or teams of scientists are competing to make the same discovery first. Other scientists may prefer to work out of the mainstream, or in paradigms that are not as "hot," precisely so that they may avoid competition. Similarly, the kinds of stresses involved on the job are different for university scientists who, for instance, do not have tenure. Some scientists who might have very productive careers if they had job security find that they are unable to function effectively when they don't.

Similarly, the situations are quite different for a lawyer in the courtroom versus the law office, as a partner versus as an associate, or defending criminals who have committed misdemeanors versus capital crimes (for, in the latter case, a guilty verdict may literally mean the death of a client). How well the lawyer adapts to his or her job may depend as much upon the kinds of situations faced as it does upon any abilities or roles that are relevant to the legal profession.

Values

The match between the values of a person and the organization in which he or she works or studies is another variable that I believe tends to be neglected. I have personally known any number of people who have had far more than the requisite amount of ability to succeed in their job, yet they either did not succeed, or decided to leave the job despite their success because of a mismatch between their own values and those of the organization for which they worked. The chapters by Berg and Calderone (Chapter 4) and by Wagner (Chapter 5) highlight values because what is a "good" answer in their tests depends on values one brings to the situations they describe.

Although values are not specifically a topic of discussion in this book, they underlie, at some level, all of the work that is reported. The reason is that what one calls intelligence, how one tests it, and how one develops it in children and adults, all depend on values. For example, the authors in this book generally do not place a high premium on the results of typical tests of intelligence, but many investigators do.

A number of different kinds of values enter into play in the world of work, as well as the world of the school. For example, some organizations emphasize productivity at the expense of people, whereas others focus upon the people that work for them. Some care only about the product and productivity achieved, others about the process by which the products are achieved. Some organizations value conformity, whereas others permit a degree of independence. In some organizations individualists thrive, whereas in others, the values lean toward a group orientation. In some organizations, the only key to advancement is the valuing of one's own self-interest, whereas in other organizations one can succeed and still be altruistic.

Once again, we can see the effects of values on specific occupations. For example, consider once again the scientist. Some organizations, such as university departments, highly value theory and are less concerned with the particular empirical operations used to validate theories. My own university department values theory highly, and presentations that are atheoretical do not tend to be well-received, regardless of how clever the experimental work may be. Other organizations and departments value empirical work much more highly, whether or not it is backed by a well-elaborated theory. Similarly, organizations differ with regard to their valuing quality versus quantity in research. Our own department, for example, is more concerned with quality and with the impact the work has upon the field. Other departments count publications when decisions are made about hiring or promotion. Similarly, departments differ in their relative valuing of teaching versus research. The professor, especially the nontenured professor, who puts a great deal of time into teaching may find that he or she is not valued by a department that is research-oriented, and may feel very frustrated. The same is true of the scientist who values research in a teaching-oriented department.

The same kinds of issues arise in business. For example, organizations vary in terms of the extent to which they value the quality of the products they make versus simply how the product sells, regardless of the quality that backs them. If someone who values quality works for a firm where quality is only a back-burner issue, he or she is bound to be frustrated. Organizations also differ in the extent to which they value stability versus innovation. An innovator in a firm that discourages innovation will once again be frustrated. Thus, the fit of values between the individual and the organization can be crucial to the extent to which the person succeeds in the organizational setting.

I have proposed a theory of contextual modifiability (Sternberg, 1992) that considers different organizational climates that result from different value systems within an organization. Two of the key variables in this theory are the desire for change on the part of the organization and the desire for the appearance of change. The two variables are not the same: Some organizations genuinely desire change, whereas others may desire the appearance of change without any change at all. If an employee who values growth and change finds him or herself in an organization that doesn't, he is likely to feel very frustrated.

Luck

We may not like to talk about it, but luck plays a role in whether a person is able to get a job and in how well the person does in a job. Status variables such as the socioeconomic status of the family of origin, gender, ethnic group, nationality, and handicaps, all play roles in whether one can be considered for or is likely to obtain a job. For example, a Catholic woman cannot be a Roman Catholic priest, no matter how much she may want to be. A woman is also at a disadvantage if her goal is to become a professional boxer. A resident of Bosnia is at a distinct disadvantage these days in being able to follow a satisfying professional career, given that the entire region has become a war zone. And as much as a given person might want to become King of England, he is not a likely candidate unless he happens to have been born into the right family at the right time. The chapter Granott and Gardner (Chapter 7) perhaps most directly points out the role of luck in intellectual development. Much of how the multiple intelligences develop will depend upon the environment into which one happens to be born and in which one happens to develop.

Event variables also enter into one's ability to adapt to a job. For example, various kinds of hazards can affect one's degree of success. These hazards can be earthquakes, fires, wars, violent outbursts of prejudice, and the like. Breaks in opportunities also affect one's ability to take a job. For example, in many European countries, there's just one professor per department. Other members of the faculty can wait years until the current professor dies in the hope that they will be chosen to replace him. Or, to take another example, Prince Charles is still waiting to be King of England, and is likely to wait a bit longer until his mother either dies or decides to abdicate. He's still waiting for that "lucky break."

Conclusion

In conclusion, several variables – person, roles, situations, values, and luck – need to be taken into account in considering what it is that determines a person's ability to interact successfully with his or her context. But it is clear that a view that only takes into account abilities, or worse, only general ability, is inadequate. We once thought that the earth was at the center of the universe. It's not: the geocentric theory was wrong. Some now think that g is the center of the universe. It's not: the new g-ocentric theory is wrong as well. The authors of this book without exception recognize this face. Abilities cannot be fully understood in terms of g, or even in terms just of what is "in the head." We need to consider as well the interaction of mind in context.

Note

Research for this article was supported under the Javits Act Program (grant No. R206R00001) as administered by the Office of Educational Research and Improvement, U.S. Department of Education. Grantees undertaking such projects are encouraged to freely express their professional judgment. This article, therefore, does not necessarily represent positions or policies of the Government, and no official endorsement should be inferred.

References

Amabile, T. M. (1983). *The social psychology of creativity.* New York: Springer-Verlag.

Frensch, P. A., & Sternberg, R. J. (1989). Expertise and intelligent thinking: When is it worse to know better? In R. J. Sternberg (Ed.), *Advances in the psychology of human intelligence* (Vol. 5, pp. 157–188). Hillsdale, NJ: Erlbaum.

Grigorenko, E., & Sternberg, R. J. (1992). Thinking styles in school settings. Manuscript submitted for publication.

Lepper, M. R., & Green, D. (1978). Turning play into work: Effects of adult surveillance and extrinsic reward on children's intrinsic motivation. In M. R. Lepper & D. Green (Eds.), *The hidden costs of reward* (pp. 109–148). Hillsdale, NJ: Erlbaum.

Sternberg, R. J. (1982). Nonentrenchment in the assessment of intellectual giftedness. *Gifted Child Quarterly, 26,* 63–67.

Sternberg, R. J. (1985). *Beyond IQ: A triarchic theory of human intelligence.* New York: Cambridge University Press.

Sternberg, R. J. (1988). Mental self-government: A theory of intellectual styles and their development. *Human Development, 31,* 197–224.

Sternberg, R. J. (1988). *The triarchic mind: A new theory of human intelligence.* New York: Viking.

Sternberg, R. J. (1992). *Reforming school reform.* Unpublished manuscript.

Sternberg, R. J., & Gastel, J. (1989). If dancers ate their shoes: Inductive reasoning with factual and counterfactual premises. *Memory and Cognition, 17,* 1–10.

Sternberg, R. J., & Lubart, T. I. (1991). An investment theory of creativity and its development. *Human Development, 34,* 1–31.

Sternberg, R. J., & Lubart, T. I. (1992). Buy low and sell high: An investment approach to creativity. *Current Directions in Psychological Science, 1*(1), 1–5.

Sternberg, R. J., Wagner, R. K., & Okagaki, L. (in press). Practical intelligence: The nature and role of tacit knowledge in work and at school. In H. Reese & J. Puckett (Eds.), *Advances in lifespan development.* Hillsdale, NJ: Erlbaum.

Stevenson, H. W., & Stigler, J. W. (1992). *The learning gap.* New York: Summit Books.

Wagner, R. K., & Sternberg, R. J. (1986). Tacit knowledge and intelligence in the everyday world. In R. J. Sternberg & R. K. Wagner (Eds.), *Practical intelligence: Nature and origins of competence in the everyday world* (pp. 51–83). New York: Cambridge University Press.

Name index

233

Subject index

ability
  learning task correlation of, 18, 19
  markers of, 9, 10
  treatment interactions of, 18–20
  variations of, 15
ability factor G, *see* general intelligence
ability-situation complex, 12
ability testing, *see* cognitive-ability testing
academic intelligence, 18–9, 145, 146–7
  versus practical intelligence, 65
academic task abilities, 3–37
  affordance concept of, 28–9, 31
  artifact concept of, 29, 31
academic tasks
  perception of, 16, 17
  types of, 12–4
accommodation, Piagetian theory of, 59–60
adaptation
  in cognitive-ability testing, 26
  Piagetian theory of, 59–60
  of practical-contextual abilities, 223
  in problem-solving, 110–2
adopted children, IQ test scores of, 195
adverse impact, 143–5
affordances, in person-situation interfaces, 28–9, 31
age factors
  in creativity, 222–3
  in fluid and crystallized intelligence, 62–3
  in practical versus academic intelligence, 146
aggregation, problems of, 15
ambiguity, of academic tasks, 14, 17
American College Test scores, 142–3
analogies
  as general intelligence measures, 41
  information-processing of, 47–8, 53–4
  as rule-induction items, 40, 41
apprenticeship, collaboration in, 183, 185
aptitude complex hypothesis, 9, 11
  of discovery learning, 21–3
aptitude-treatment interaction (ATI), 4
  ability-treatment interactions and, 18–20
  affordance concept of, 29
  with contextual effects, 21–3
  low-structure/high-structure of, 21–3, 30
  person-situation interaction process model of,
  24, 26
  task, treatment and context variables of, 12
  with task adaptation, 23–4
Armed Forces Qualification Test, 155, 157
Armed Services Vocational Aptitude Battery, 223
army squad leaders, performance under stress, 155, 157–8
artifact theory, of academic task ability, 29, 31
artificial intelligence, 47, 48
assembly process, of cognitive task performance, 26, 27–8, 29–30, 31, 32
assimilation, Piagetian theory of, 59–60
Australian aborigine children, spatial skills of, 171, 173, 177, 180, 193, 196–7, 198

BETTERAVEN computer program, 52, 53
bias, in testing, 143
bioecological theory, of intelligence, 64–6
bodily-kinesthetic intelligence, 174
Body Adjustment Test, 45–6
Brazilian children, learning transfer studies of, 85–99
  class-inclusion problem-solving, 89, 90–3
  conservation-task performance, 93–8
  mathematical skills, 87–9

California Psychological Inventory, 147, 148
California Test of Mental Maturity, 56
classification problems, 40, 41
  information-processing of, 49–51, 53–4
class-inclusion problems, 89, 90–3
cognition, situated, 5
cognitive abilities
  hierarchical organization of, 8–12
  interactionist theory of, 4
cognitive-ability testing
  academic task analysis and, 17
  adaptation in, 26
  for college admissions, 40, 135, 142–3
  general intelligence measures of, 40–1
  for job selection, 133–51
    causal model of, 137–8
    correlations adjustments of, 138–40
    economic costs of, 133–4, 140, 141–2, 149
    g-eocentric view of, 137, 138

239